Beyond the Ivory Tower

Beyond the Ivory Tower

International Relations Theory and the Issue of Policy Relevance

Joseph Lepgold and Miroslav Nincic

COLUMBIA UNIVERSITY PRESS NEW YORK

COLUMBIA UNIVERSITY PRESS
Publishers Since 1893
New York, Chichester, West Sussex

Copyright © 2001 Columbia University Press

Library of Congress Cataloging-in-Publication Data

Lepgold, Joseph.
    Beyond the ivory tower : international relations theory and the
issue of policy relevance / Joseph Lepgold and Miroslav Nincic.
        p. cm.
    Includes bibliographical references and index.
    ISBN 0-231-11658-6 (cloth : alk. paper) — ISBN 0-231-11659-4 (pbk.
: alk. paper)
    1. International relations. 2. Diplomacy. 3. International
relations—Philosophy.   I. Nincic, Miroslav. II. Title.
    JZ1305 .L36 2002
    327.1′01—dc21
                                2001047011

Columbia University Press books are printed on permanent and durable
acid-free paper.
Printed in the United States of America

c 10 9 8 7 6 5 4 3 2 1
p 10 9 8 7 6 5 4 3 2 1

To Alexander L. George, with admiration and fondness

Contents

Preface

This book stems from a sense of unease with the current state of theory and research in international relations. It is rooted in a conviction that knowledge in this area must be judged by two criteria: its scholarly soundness and its policy relevance. The conviction stems not so much from a sense of social obligation as from a feeling that the study of international relations and foreign policy implies, by its nature, relevant knowledge, and that scholarship explicitly seeking to be relevant is likely to be good (perhaps better) scholarship. This is not a fashionable position, but it is entirely defensible. A failure to see this, we believe, is grounded in an unacceptably emaciated conception of relevance, in an overly simplistic view of how relevant knowledge is produced and conveyed, and in a misconceived notion of the scholarly merits of relevant knowledge. We hope that this volume may lead to the revision of some flawed assumptions and encourage greater academic receptivity to work that is both useful and sound.

The project took shape in a panel at an annual meeting of the American Political Science Association. Since then, it has occupied much of our time and thinking. As is always the case with such projects, we have benefited from the interest and advice of a number of colleagues. We would like, in particular, to thank Alexander George, who recently rekindled the profession's interest in the issue of relevant scholarship. Bruce Jentleson, a fine example of professor-practitioner, has been a friend and source of advice to both of us. Larry Berman, Emily Goldman, Donna Nincic, and George Shambaugh read and commented on several draft chapters.

Joseph Lepgold
Miroslav Nincic
May 2001

Beyond the Ivory Tower

1 The Theory-Practice Gap in International Relations

> It is by action—in my terms, by the practice of politics—that theory . . . can be kept in touch with reality. . . . The two are inseparable; theory and practice being complementary, they constitute harmonic aspects of one whole.[1]
>
> —Paul H. Nitze

> It is natural to assume that, of all the institutions focusing on public policy, the free realm of the universities would have the most to offer in knowledge and insight. Challenges to conventional wisdom and provocative explorations of international issues not possible in the political world should be and are part of the domain of the scholar and teacher. . . . [Yet] much of today's scholarship is either irrelevant or inaccessible to policy makers. . . . much remains locked within the circle of esoteric scholarly discussion.[2]
>
> —David D. Newsom

> . . . the more [scholars] strain for policy relevance, even if only to justify our existence in the eyes of society at large, the more difficult it becomes to maintain intellectual integrity.[3]
>
> —Christopher Hill

The first two observations, both from distinguished former U.S. officials, typify many policymakers' views about contemporary scholarship in international relations: while it *ought* to be useful to practitioners, little of it is. Much, they believe, is useless and arcane. These particular statements are striking because they do not reflect ignorance about the mission and culture of university scholars. The individual quoted in the first passage has written widely on foreign policy and helped to found the Johns

Hopkins School of Advanced International Studies, one of America's premier professional schools of international affairs. The author of the second passage held a faculty position at the University of Virginia and was Acting Dean of Georgetown University's School of Foreign Service. The book in which the second passage appeared was published by a university press and was addressed to a largely academic audience. Indeed, much of the chapter from which the second passage was taken betrays keen disappointment that scholarly writing on international affairs *does not* speak more clearly to the many uncertainties and daunting analytic tasks practitioners face. The author of the third passage, a professor at the London School of Economics, offers a view common among international relations scholars—that they will lose professional independence and credibility by trying to speak about practical issues.

Such sentiments, however, have become common only in the last few decades. As readers of Machiavelli, Hobbes, and Hobson appreciate, theory in the study of politics, including world politics, has traditionally been intended to guide practice. Diplomats of earlier generations would have found quite odd the notion that university scholars who studied international relations had little of interest to say to them. Important examples of such influence are not hard to find. Several generations of post-World War II U.S. officials had much of their general worldview formed or reinforced by exposure to Hans Morgenthau's stark Realpolitik in *Politics Among Nations*. During the 1970s, models that focused on the catalysts and implications of transnational economic forces had a comparable, if more limited, impact on official thinking. From the late 1950s onward, the important conceptual literature on arms control—work derived from theories focused on unintended conflict spirals—had an impact on key aspects of U.S. nuclear weapons deployments, investments in the command-and-control apparatus, and operational nuclear doctrines. Since this work focused on the interplay between military postures and the likelihood of inadvertent war, it gave policymakers a coherent way to diagnose an important problem as well as manipulable levers—tacit and formal measures to promote invulnerable nuclear forces—through which they could try to deal with it.[4]

For many reasons, connections between scholarly ideas and policymakers' thinking in international relations are less common today, and the gap may grow unless we rethink carefully our approach to policy relevance. Deep, often ritualized rivalry among theoretical schools makes it unlikely that future officials will leave their university training in this subject with a clear, well-formed worldview. Such intellectual competition, of course, *could* be stimulating and useful, especially if it led officials to question their basic causal assumptions or consider rival explanations of the cases they face. More commonly, officials seem to remember the repetitive, often strident theoretical debates as unproductive and tiresome. Not only is much international relations scholarship tedious, in their view; it is often technically quite difficult. Partly for this reason, much of it is so substantively arid that even many scholarly specialists avoid trying to penetrate it. From a practitioner's perspective, it often seems as if university scholars are increasingly "withdrawing . . . behind a curtain of theory and models" that only insiders can penetrate.[5]

In addition, for many observers, the end of the cold war has made it harder to find models providing a compelling link between the international environment and manipulable policy instruments. One exception to this growing split between scholars of international relations and policymakers is the work on the inter-democratic peace, which we discuss in chapter 5. This work, as we will show, has deeply influenced many contemporary policymakers. But, for the most part, it remains the exception; the professional gap between academics and practitioners has widened in recent years. Many scholars no longer try to reach beyond the Ivory Tower, and officials seem increasingly content to ignore it.

According to much conventional wisdom, this situation is unsurprising. International relations scholars and practitioners have different professional priorities and reflect different cultures. Not only is it often assumed that good theory must sacrifice policy relevance; but also those seeking guidance in diagnosing policy situations and making policy choices, it is often thought, must look for help in places other than contemporary social science research.

This book challenges much of the conventional wisdom on these issues. It argues that IR theorists and foreign policy practitioners have important needs in common as well as needs that are different. Social science theory seeks to identify and explain the significant regularities in human affairs. Because people's ability to process information is limited, they must perceive the world selectively in order to operate effectively in it; constructing and using theories in a self-conscious way helps to inject some rigor into these processes.[6] For these reasons, both theorists and practitioners seek a clear and powerful understanding of cause and effect about policy issues, in order to help them diagnose situations, define the range of possibilities they confront, and evaluate the likely consequences of given courses of action. At the same time, a deep and continuing concern for the substance and stakes involved in real-world issues can help prevent theorists' research agendas from becoming arid or trivial. This book therefore has two objectives: to elaborate and justify the reasoning that leads to these conclusions, and to illustrate how scholarship on international relations and foreign policy can be useful beyond the Ivory Tower.

Three issues should be clarified at the outset. One concerns the primary audience for this book. It is not a handbook for the conduct of foreign policy. We lack the detailed substantive and process knowledge needed to write such a book, not to mention the practical, accumulated experience that would make it credible. Our comparative advantage is in framing issues for our fellow academics to think about, and it is primarily to them that this work is directed. In arguing that IR scholars should embrace policy-relevant work, we clearly cannot guarantee that it *would* resonate widely outside the Ivory Tower. For that to happen the potential audience outside the scholarly community must be willing to listen, a matter over which academics have relatively little control. What they do control is their own agenda—one that we argue has become progressively and needlessly narrowed to issues that resonate *only within* the academy. This book argues that this agenda can be broadened in ways that would benefit both scholars and foreign-policymakers. In support of this position, the chapters that follow describe the various types of policy-relevant knowledge, how such knowledge is acquired and could be used, and illustrate these arguments with a variety of real-world examples. In doing this, we emphasize that relevant scholarship implies no necessary compromise of professional scholarly standards.

A second issue concerns the way in which the terms "international relations" and "international relations theory" are used in this book. International relations consist of the political, economic, military, social, and cultural exchanges that occur across the boundaries of sovereign states, in institutionalized as well as ad hoc contexts.[7] Likewise, the study of international relations has always enlisted participation from historians, lawyers, theologians, philosophers, psychologists, and economists in addition to political scientists. We thus need to distinguish between international relations as a set of real-world processes and the scholarship that analyzes these processes. We will designate the former as IR and the latter—academic scholarship in international relations—as SIR. Finally, despite the many dimensions of IR activity in the real world, the *theory* of IR in its modern guise is largely, though certainly not entirely, the work of academic political scientists. For that reason, we take IR *theory* in its modern sense to mean efforts by social scientists, especially political scientists, to account for inter-state and trans-state processes, issues, and outcomes in general causal terms.

A third issue concerns an important type of policy relevance we do not discuss. In addition to the substantive knowledge that might help officials identify better options or better understand their environments, "process knowledge" might help them better organize their decisionmaking proce-dures. The assumption behind this claim is that improving the policy ma-chinery, all else equal, will lead to better policy choices.[8] Sound decision processes are certainly preferable to poor ones, but those processes, no matter how well designed, can work only as well as their inputs—that is, the sub-stantive questions, assumptions, and empirical generalizations that are brought to bear on the conduct of foreign policy. Much SIR addresses issues of *substance* rather than process, and we discuss why and how it could im-prove the substance of thinking on foreign policy.

The balance of this chapter serves four purposes. The first two sections explain why international relations has important, practical implications. Whatever their precise professional duties and roles, most observers of the subject care about these practical issues; for many, these interests bring them into the field in the first place. While traditional SIR was often narrowly focused on the concerns of a small handful of states and policy constituen-cies, much of it was solidly rooted in the real-world problems that preoc-cupied those actors. It spoke to thoughtful practitioners, much as the influ-ential periodicals *Foreign Affairs* and *Foreign Policy* do today. In their efforts to create a rigorous science of politics, many of the scholars who champi-oned the behavioral revolution in political science moved away from any-thing smacking of policy commentary. In so doing, they fostered a style of academic work that inevitably—in some cases deliberately—created the cur-rent theory-practice gap. Section three discusses these developments, high-lighting the way in which notions of appropriate scholarly inquiry in inter-national relations changed some four decades ago. The shift toward a more technically intricate style of research meant that whatever analytic guidance SIR could provide policymakers was increasingly placed out of the latter's reach. Section four discusses those needs of policymakers that should be satisfied by scholarly guidance, laying the basis for a closer examination in chapters 3 and 4 of how explicitly relevant research and theorizing could improve both policymaking and scholarship. Section five discusses the organization of the book and spells out a bit more about the content of the subsequent chapters.

Scholarship's Practical Implications

Unlike literature, pure mathematics, or formal logic, the study of international relations may be valued largely for its practical implications and insights. SIR, like the major social-science disciplines, initially gained a firm foundation in academia on the assumption that it contributes to improved policy.[9] It is part of what August Comte believed would constitute a new, "positive" science of society, one that would supersede the older tradition of metaphysical speculation about humanity and the social world. Progress toward this end has been incomplete as well as uneven across the social sciences. But, in virtually all of these fields, it has been driven by more than just curiosity as an end in itself. Tightening our grip on key social processes via improved understanding has always been a major incentive for new knowledge in the social sciences, especially in the study of international relations.[10]

This broad purpose covers a lot of specific ground. Policymakers want to know what range of effective choice they have, the likely international and domestic consequences of various policy decisions, and perhaps whether, in terms of more general interests and values, contemplated policy objectives are really desirable, should they be achievable. But the practical implications of international issues hardly end there. How wars start and end, the causes and implications of economic interdependence, and what leverage individual states might have on trans-state problems greatly affects ordinary citizens' physical safety, prosperity, and collective identity. Today, it is hard to think of any major public-policy issue that is *not* affected by a state's or society's relationships with other international actors.

Because the United States looms so large within the international system, its citizens are sometimes unaware of the range and impact of international events and processes on their condition. It may take an experience such as the long gas lines in the 1970s or the foreign-inspired terrorist bombings in the 1990s to remind them how powerfully the outside world now impinges upon them. As Karl Deutsch observed, even the smallest states can no longer effectively isolate themselves, and even the largest ones face limits on their ability to change others' behavior or values.[11] In a broad sense, globalization means that events in many places will affect people's investment opportunities, the value of their money, whether they feel that their values are safe or under attack, and perhaps whether they will be safe from attack by weapons of mass destruction or terrorism.

These points can be illustrated by observing university undergraduates, who constitute one of the broadest categories of people who are potentially curious about IR. Unlike doctoral students, they care much less about political science than about the substance of politics. What they seem to understand is that the subject matter of SIR, regardless of the level of theoretical abstraction at which it is discussed, inherently has practical implications.

One might argue that whatever our purpose in analyzing IR might be, we can have little confidence in our knowledge absent tightly developed theory and rigorous research. One might then infer that a concern with the practical implications of our knowledge is premature until the field of SIR is better developed on its own terms. But if one assumes that SIR inherently has significant real-world implications, one could also conclude that the balance in contemporary scholarship has veered too far from substance and too close to scholasticism.

As in other fields driven by a concern with real-world developments, SIR research has been motivated by both internally- and externally-driven concerns. The former are conceptual, epistemological, and methodological matters that scholars believe they need to confront to do their intellectual work: Which research programs are most apt to resolve the field's core puzzles? What is the meaning of contested concepts? Which empirical evidence or methods are especially useful, convincing, or weak in this field? The latter consist of issues relevant to policy practitioners and citizens: How can people prepare to deal with an uncertain future? More specifically, how can they anticipate future international developments to which they might need to adapt, assess the likely consequences of measures to deal with that future, or at least think about such matters intelligently?[12] While the best scholarly work tends to have important ramifications for both types of concerns, the academic emphasis has shifted too far toward work with little relevance outside academia. This balance must be redressed if SIR is to resonate outside the Ivory Tower.

Beyond this, shifting scholars' attention toward the claims about the world they seek to account for would help improve their work by the standards of academic scholarship itself. If SIR were, at least partly, justified by the light that it sheds on practical foreign policy issues, this would help academics identify significant substantive questions, and, we feel, provide answers that clearly pass the "so what" question. Curiosity about practical problems and how they can be manipulated is what gives scientists many ideas about what areas of basic research need to be explored, what is generalizable within those areas, which empirical patterns can be explained by existing theory, and which puzzles require further attention.[13] Just as important, a grasp of practical issues helps ground theory in the facts for which it seeks to account.

In making the case that the balance between internally- and externally-driven concerns could be readjusted *without* diluting the intellectual value of SIR, it is worth noting that the large emphasis on the former is quite recent. Accordingly, it is worth examining the field's traditional preoccupation with externally-driven concerns, as a way to see where we have been and why that intellectual stance toward policy-relevance was taken for so long.

The Focus and Purpose of Traditional Scholarship

If "traditional" SIR implies work that preceded efforts to build a cumulative social science of international relations, such work goes back to Thucydides, if not Homer and Herodotus.[14] It was dominated by external concerns.[15] Most of the major ideas were developed in Europe during the early modern period, prompted by a desire to understand and address the problems of state building, the gradual acceptance of a norm of sovereign autonomy, and efforts to rationalize the use of force among states. Over time, a fairly coherent picture of world politics emerged. Relations among states were conducted through diplomacy, though the threat and use of force provided a continuing backdrop. Diplomacy was further shaped by a minimal international legal code that laid down the essential rights and duties of states. While the intellectual heirs of Machiavelli shaded this framework in one direction, emphasizing that sovereignty had to be continually defended, and those who wrote in the Grotian tradition shaded the picture differently, emphasizing the pull of common norms, there was broad agreement that the separate states had to find mutually advantageous ways to coexist.[16] In terms of method, historical, practical, legal and philosophical reflection helped to stimulate these insights.

This intellectual framework has been remarkably durable. According to Michael Banks, it produced "a conceptual toolbox which continues to this day to dominate both the practice of world politics and much of its interpretation."[17] The key concepts and terminology that went with it—national interest, sovereign rights, just war, and so on—continue to provide a *lingua franca* for much of the field, among practitioners and scholars alike.

What was missing until well into the twentieth century was a discrete, coherent area of inquiry. Until then, SIR consisted of rather disconnected observations scattered across political philosophy, political economy, international law, and diplomatic history. As a distinct field in its own right, SIR was catalyzed by the shock of the First World War. Before the War, a certain complacency afflicted European thinking on international affairs—a sense that the key problems could be managed effectively, given existing practices and knowledge. That smugness was destroyed by a sense that the unprecedented destruction might have been prevented by more effective crisis management, a different approach to Germany before the crisis, or a less power-centered approach to diplomacy more generally. Galvanized by these might-have-beens, a broad elite consensus concluded that existing knowledge was inadequate; inter-state relations were sufficiently important and complex that a greater understanding was required. John Hobson summarized this view soon after the War began: " . . . at the present stage it is of paramount importance to try to get the largest number of thoughtful people to form clear, general ideas of better international relations, and to desire their attainment."[18]

The result was "a burst of activity in the universities," producing a rudimentary scholarly field of international affairs. Professorships were created, new curricula developed, and academic conferences abounded.[19] Alongside the new academic institutions, other organizations were created to educate professional elites about the importance of international affairs: the British Royal Institute of International Affairs and the U.S. Council on Foreign Relations were inaugurated in the early 1920s. The impetus for this activity, both inside and outside the universities, was externally-driven. The world statesmen had known for centuries had broken down along with deeply rooted assumptions, and some way had to be found to repair it. The title of the book in which Hobson's plea appeared—*Towards International Government*—captured the orthodoxy as well as the sense or urgency within the new field during the 1920s and 1930s in much of Anglo-America.

Whether inside or outside universities, most of the people who created this new field were "public intellectuals" whose purpose was to communicate ideas to a broad audience. Until quite recently, political and social intellectuals have been those who by virtue of their interests have been deeply engaged in public discussion and debate. The term "intellectual" was coined to describe the writers who came to the defense of Captain Alfred Dreyfus when he was charged with treason in France in 1898. During the twentieth century a "public intellectual" was typically a writer, often driven by moral or political convictions, who addressed a general, albeit literate audience about public issues.[20] This description fit many key figures in the new field of SIR in the early post–World War I years: E. H. Carr, David Mitrany, Pitman Potter, and Alfred Zimmern. Somewhat later, Hans Morgenthau also fit the pattern. Trained as a lawyer in Europe, he was animated by the way Max Weber simultaneously pursued scholarship and social activism.[21] Morgenthau's political "realism" was shaped by his deep disappointment with the appeasement of the 1930s, and even though he was best known among academics for his theoretical work, he became a very public critic of U.S. policy in Vietnam during the 1960s.

As public intellectuals, these thinkers saw no sharp division between theory and practice in international relations. At various points in their careers, many combined writing and reflection with policy practice or advice to other practitioners. Before wartime service in the British Foreign Office gave Mitrany an opportunity to help design the functional agencies of the UN, he had honed his outlook on economic and social progress in a practical way as a director of the Unilever Corporation. Walter Lippmann was much better known for his newspaper columns, lectures on contemporary issues, and advice to senior political figures than for forays into academic scholarship. Because their observations about more general issues often grew out of contemporary policy concerns, the professors within this group drew little distinction between the language and content suited to the four major audiences for international relations thinking: university students, fellow academic professionals, foreign policy officials, and the wider public. Consequently, they published in the leading journals of opinion as well as in more specialized academic outlets.

Thoughtful traditionalists articulated a distinct logic of inquiry, one characterized as a "wisdom-centered" or holistic view of knowledge. From this perspective, social and political knowledge is gained by long experience with and deep immersion in substantive policy issues, historical periods, or specific actors. Rather than invoking general causal laws, holists believe that action can be explained by understanding it from the actor's own frame of reference, located within a rich historical or ideational context.[22] In an influential essay, Hedley Bull made a strong case for the broad relevance of this approach. He argued that efforts to formulate and test general hypotheses about IR—that is, efforts aimed at establishing a scientifically cumulative base of knowledge—could not succeed. Social science, he claimed, could not be used to come to grips with the inherent "substance" of international relations; it inevitably would miss or trivialize questions about social meaning, purpose, and causation in the international realm, or would seek uniformities and generalizations where they do not exist.[23]

By 1966, when Bull's essay appeared, methodological traditionalists were already losing ground to scientific behaviorists in many U.S. universities. Since foreign-policymakers found that they could go on with their work without paying attention to most of the new SIR literature, a significant gap between theory and practice began to develop. If SIR had remained methodologically where Bull wanted to keep it in the early 1960s, practitioners and theorists would have retained more of a shared language and there would be less of a theory-practice gap today. Still, these methodological developments did not make a widening gap inevitable. The gap grew out of changing scholarly fashions *combined with* the incentive structure within the academic profession, one that increasingly rewards internal and self-referential scholarly communication at the expense of concerns originating outside the Ivory Tower.

The Development of a Theory-Practice Gap in International Relations

In some areas, foreign-policymakers *have* been deeply influenced by the theoretical literature in International Relations. Aside from the work the work on the interdemocratic peace discussed in chapter 5, and, to a lesser extent, some of the literature on international institutions examined in chapter 6, strategic studies has been most important in this respect. Such concepts as "escalation dominance" as well as the more general notion of the prisoners' dilemma were conceived by academics but have become part of the daily vocabulary of many practitioners. Work on deterrence, nuclear proliferation, arms control, and the use of coercive force has influenced a host of U.S. weapons-acquisition and force-management issues.[24] At one time, such an impact on official thinking was not unusual. Concerns about effective public policy have traditionally been part of the academic study of politics;

the American Political Science Association (APSA), for example, was founded in part to "bring political science to a position of authority as regards practical politics."[25] By moving professional scholars away from externally-driven issues, the professionalization of political science has molded the kind of work by which they earn professional prestige, making them less able or willing to communicate with policymakers. From the perspective of many officials, SIR scholars are comfortable on their side of the gap, free of any obligation to address practical issues.[26] As a result, the public intellectuals who address current foreign policy issues now tend to have few or weak connections to universities, while the prominent scholars in this field tend to write almost exclusively for their own colleagues.

The Scientific Revolution in Political Science and International Relations

Scholarly focus on policy issues in international relations declined in the 1960s, as the social-scientific movement gained momentum. We use the term "scientific" rather than "behavioral" to characterize this shift, since traditionalist scholars were also interested in the sources and consequences of policymakers' behavior. What differentiated the scientists from those in the older tradition was their view that politics should be studied through the presentation and testing of explicit, falsifiable hypotheses, and that methods of testing should emulate those employed by the natural sciences. Consequently SIR's language, method, and focus drifted away from the "practical" matters that had animated APSA's founders.

As the "scientists" saw it, traditional scholarly literature about politics was a hopeless conflation of factual and evaluative propositions. To separate these elements, systematize the empirical side of the discipline, and deemphasize anything approaching policy prescription, the scientists articulated a strongly positivist conception of science. Their objective was a system of theoretical propositions from which testable implications about concrete observables could be derived, and where, in the absence of possibilities for strict experimentation, tests would employ as rigorously systematic methods as possible. Science was viewed as a methodological unity across the empirical disciplines; in principle, students of politics could aspire to the same logic of discovery and verification as those who studied physics.[27] As one prominent member of this movement put it, this view entailed "the idea that methods of investigation, in all their aspects, are problematic and, accordingly, merit special concentrated attention."[28]

Two implications for research and teaching were quickly evident. Once "methods of investigation" are seen to merit privileged attention, internally-driven concerns tend to become much more important relative to externally-driven ones. And "if it is no longer necessary to test the relevance of research findings by their significance as possible solutions to practical problems,"[29] as this same scholar argued, the professional culture no longer even values the externally-driven concerns much at all. By the mid-1960s, the scientific revolution had encompassed SIR, especially at the major public universities in the U.S. Midwest. Scientifically oriented scholars disparaged the traditional IR literature, arguing that the field essentially had to be reinvented from the ground up. Ultimately, it was argued, to every empirical proposition a precise measure of confidence should be assigned: " 'knowledge' which is unconfirmed, incomplete, or based on the prestige of the source rather than the credibility of the evidence" should be rejected.[30] By these criteria, little existing work comprised acceptable knowledge.

This attitude impugned the traditional wisdom that had accumulated over the centuries *before* anything comparable had been developed to re-place it. In place of propositions that had, however imperfectly, provided some guidance to thoughtful statesmen, much more attention was now paid in university courses to aggregate data analysis, research design, mathematical modeling, and philosophy-of-science issues. However much this self-conscious attention to rigorous strategies of inquiry paid off in actual knowledge acquired—and that remains a controversial issue among many scholars even today—it profoundly changed the ethos of the scholarly field. Rather than trying to help thoughtful practitioners interpret the world in which they operate, SIR scholars increasingly talked among themselves about the means rather than the ends of their enterprise.

More recently, many SIR scholars have gravitated toward self-contained groups of like-minded scholars who share epistemologies and research agendas. In many (though certainly not all) of these groups, the driving intellectual issues are of a technical, not substantive, nature. Thus, for reasons to be laid out shortly, most of SIR has not moved back closer to an immersion in real world problems, nor in many cases even to work that could be plausibly connected to such problems.

The extent of the gap between scholarship and policy can be appreciated by noting that an academic background in SIR is not a requirement for policy positions. Senior foreign-policymakers are just as likely to come from law, business, or other fields as they are from a university background in SIR. This pattern can be compared to the usual situation in economics, where formal training is generally considered a prerequisite for policymaking responsibilities in international as well as domestic economic policy. Economic theorists and policymakers thus have little trouble understanding each other's intellectual frames of reference, making it likely that they will at least appreciate each other's concerns. Lacking such a basis for communication, scholars and practitioners of international relations learn from each other much less often, in part because professional mobility between the two groups is very limited.[31] While candidates for the U.S. presidency now routinely rely on scholars to provide them with position papers and material for speeches, the people who play this role today for foreign policy issues tend not to contribute to cutting-edge IR theory. In effect, those IR experts who "speak to the Prince" in the tradition of Machiavelli are now almost wholly distinct as a group from those who speak mainly to the academic field. This distance between the two groups reduces officials' incentives to seek academic guidance and theorists' incentives to produce policy-relevant knowledge.

The Effects of the Academic Incentive System

The chasm separating scholarship and policy in IR is not inevitable, especially when compared to the situation in other fields with applied and theoretical facets. Although scientists typically do not earn scholarly recognition in their own fields by sharing knowledge with those in applied areas or the general public, they often derive other professional rewards from doing so.[32] Just as medical researchers see physicians as their primary audience, IR scholars *could* measure their professional prestige at least partly in terms of how seriously their ideas are applied outside the academy. The modern academic incentive system, however, operates to frustrate any such goal. At least since Max Weber discussed the differences between the vocations of politics and science, a large literature has developed that probes the sociology of modern academic life, especially within disciplines that are scientific or aspire to that status.[33] From that work, and an insightful critique of the political science profession written from a sociology-of-knowledge perspective, three features of academic life stand out as particular culprits in the growing practical irrelevance of much SIR. First, scholars are increasingly inclined to tackle smaller, often trivial, research problems, rather than questions of a more fundamental nature and broader reach. Second, technique has in many cases triumphed over substance in IR research programs. Third, the professional status of academics depends mainly on how their work is received by fellow scholars, rather than by those outside the Ivory Tower.

Narrowed Concerns: Within scholarly communities, a recognition for originality signifies professional accomplishment. Since originality comes at more of a premium the older a field becomes, scholars tend to define original to mean "novel." In practice, they often look for research projects and intellectual niches that are novel precisely because others have ignored them. Academic fields thus tend to shrink into ever-smaller areas of specialization and expertise, "so that some scholars can quickly stand forth as patently competent with regard to subjects that other scholars have somehow overlooked."[34]

These patterns are clearly evident in contemporary scholarship. SIR academics do relatively little creative work, if that is taken to mean the charting of new intellectual paths. Instead, they tend to be professionally risk-averse, and thus tend to remain well inside the boundaries of inquiries in which most of their colleagues operate. These behaviors seem to be driven by several related assumptions. Like other scholars, IR scholars tend to assume that issues occupying a sufficient number of others must indeed merit a substantial investment of scholarly resources. They also appear to believe that possibilities for intellectual support and useful feedback are better in well-trampled areas. Finally, professional visibility and advancement require that one's work be frequently cited by other academics, and this generally occurs when one works within an area that claims the attention of many scholars. As a result, novelty is achieved by looking for new, usually smaller questions within broadly traveled approaches and areas. The result is an expanding but increasingly hyperspecialized and often arid body of knowledge.

A good indicator of these patterns is the growing number of academic journals in the field. The most recent edition of a guide to publishing in political science journals lists twenty-two English-language journals devoted exclusively or largely to international relations, aside from the general politics and policy journals that also publish IR articles. (There are more than one hundred such English-language politics and policy journals.[35]) These journals comprise qualitative and more quantitative outlets, as well as those that specialize by subject matter within the IR field. While much of the work published in these journals is valuable, one trend is clear: as the overall readership within the field has segmented along substantive and methodological lines, scholarly authors have less reason to communicate to a broad audience about fundamentally important arguments or research results. For example, when an article titled "Alliance Formation and National Security" uses an expected-utility model to discover that "the pattern of alliance formation through time is related to the opportunity to enhance security" and that "*realpolitik* considerations of security are crucial to alliance formation decisions,[36]" practitioners might reasonably wonder what IR theory can tell them that do not already know.

The triumph of technique: The related tendency for research techniques to triumph over substance constrains our ability to derive real meaning from our subject matter. As Max Weber noted:

> Science . . . presupposes that what is yielded by scientific work is important in the sense that it is "worth being known." In this, obviously, are contained all our problems. For this presupposition cannot be proved by scientific means. It can only be *interpreted* with reference to its ultimate meaning, which we must reject or accept according to our ultimate position towards life.[37]

Weber was reacting to the professionalization of scientific research in German universities during the late nineteenth century, a development that spawned imitation elsewhere but was viewed with suspicion by those with a more humanistic outlook. As science came to require highly technical procedures, it ceased to be an amateur activity; to be able to do scientific work, one had to become an accomplished craftsman in those techniques.[38] This ethos has served important functional purposes for the growth of scientific disciplines. But it has also allowed techniques to define the essence of some disciplines and research traditions, aside from any independent assessments of their substantive results. For example, according to a respected game theorist, so many formal models have been developed that political scientists cannot meaningfully compare their empirical performance. Failing such a test, "the discipline of political science bases its evaluation of them on their mathematical elegance, the complexity of their notation, the journals in which they appear, or simply the reputations of those who design them."[39]

A more extreme example of this syndrome is found in economics, where tool-driven training has come to dominate graduate education. In 1999, the

MacArthur Foundation sponsored a conference at which PhD students in economics were shown how they might do applied research. The sponsors believed that first-year graduate training in economics has become so relentlessly mathematical that students in those programs do not know how to formulate an applied research project. Aside from the sponsors, a number of prominent economists fear that this kind of disconnect with the real world might drive bright undergraduates from the field. One of them, while reluctant to criticize the field's graduate training as "too theoretical," was quick to label it "increasingly aloof and self-referential."[40] A significant part of political science seems to be moving in the same direction. Many social scientists in other fields have long envied economists for their seeming ability to capture a complex reality through elegant models. Because political science deals with a more confined area of human activity than anthropology and sociology, the questions it asks have seemed more susceptible to formal approaches. Ordeshook is again cautiously skeptical about this trend, arguing that debates over such real-world topics as lags in investment and unanticipated inflation have been a more important catalyst of theoretical insights than statistical tests of formal models.[41]

These arguments should not be interpreted as a blanket critique of statistics or formal models, both of which have been quite valuable in IR work. Statistical methods are necessary to find or verify many empirical generalizations. Formal models can be used to clarify key concepts; they also serve to establish the logical preconditions of more as well as less obvious research results, thereby increasing our confidence in both. SIR work that uses these methods can be just as policy relevant as work that uses qualitative approaches. Nevertheless, the scholarly work that uses formal and statistical techniques often hides behind them and fails to yield results that appear interesting or important outside a very small, self-referential audience. Ultimately, the quality of such scholarship is too often assessed by how esoteric its techniques are. Preferred techniques tend to be those employed by disciplines at least one rung higher on the ladder of academic prestige: in the case of political science and SIR, the techniques emulated tend to be those of tool-rich contemporary economics.

A *Restricted Audience*: All of these problems are reinforced by academic faddishness, a pattern that reflects scholars' tendency to take their cues from one another rather than any external standard. Especially in the United States, a scholar's standing within her discipline, or within a still narrower subset of that discipline, is the key to professional prestige.[42] Scholarly standards must, of course, be applied when that kind of expertise is necessary to judge the value and quality of scholarly work. But those standards also tend to become a professional benchmark for narrower, more instrumental reasons—reasons that often have negative effects on the direction of scholarly agendas. By deciding what is published in which outlets, who gets which grants, and how other scholarly rewards are distributed, one's scholarly colleagues and especially the leaders of one's field have a large impact on a scholar's professional reputation and visibility. Accordingly, "most academics are only concerned about the good opinion of about a dozen other academic specialists in their particular sub-sub-field."[43] The result is to make scholarly fashions, including those that discourage policy-relevant work, strongly self-reinforcing.

The cost has been a growing gap between the field's applied and theoretical sides. Insofar as the field's language and methods have moved toward those of the hard sciences, few foreign policy practitioners understand its literature. Insofar as its content has become narrow and self-referential, they have little incentive to try. Unlike the situation in economics, where practitioners must retain their scholarly fluency to communicate with other practitioners, foreign-policymakers can ignore the theoretical literature in that field if they wish. Foreign policy practitioners tend to think eclectically and holistically, drawing on their knowledge of particular states, regions, or people when they confront a problem. They do not draw the disciplinary lines that scholars, especially contemporary ones, typically draw. It is no accident that the most broadly influential recent scholars of international relations— Francis Fukuyama, Samuel Huntington, and Paul Kennedy—are big-picture thinkers who address a wide audience. Though each is a respected scholar, all in recent years have functioned more as public intellectuals of the older type than as technique-intensive academics.

This is not to suggest that one cannot be a significant theorist *and* an effective public intellectual, as a number of scholars of international security (such as, for example, John Mearsheimer) have demonstrated. As we will argue in chapter 4, there is no *necessary* incompatibility between scientific excellence and policy relevance in international relations. But any effort to pursue these agendas simultaneously raises basic questions about what knowledge is for and how it is packaged. As one British observer asked,

> What is the relative importance of the three different audiences for which we write and speak: our colleagues, our students, and the wider public? Does the intellectual have a duty to all three audiences—to

educate a wider group than her own students, even to contribute to raising the quality of debate in society as a whole?[44]

If the answer to these questions is affirmative, it has implications for the kinds of problems SIR scholars examine, the publication outlets they choose, and the style in which they package the arguments and evidence. If we take seriously what policymakers themselves say about these issues, they will continue to ignore the Ivory Tower until it focuses more seriously on policy-relevant matters.

Policymakers and the Theory-Practice Gap

An obvious question at this point is whether decisionmakers would *ever* be likely to find SIR useful; everyday observation suggests that practitioners tend to ignore it. To push the point a bit further, wouldn't this book, written by two professors, be more compelling if it were written by policymakers who decided after a lot of trial and error that they could use more scholarly guidance after all? These are important questions. It may be that the theory-practice gulf in IR is too wide to be crossed with any regularity. We believe, however, that such a judgment is premature. If one examines what thoughtful IR practitioners say about this problem, it is evident that they want useful guidance from SIR, including theorists, and that they might actually use it if theorists were to meet them half-way.

To do that, academics must appreciate the constraints and incentives under which decisionmakers operate. Officials have very little time to read and reflect. Joseph Nye, one of the few people who has flourished as both a scholar and a policymaker, was surprised at how "oral" the culture of top-level government service has become. As he put it,

The pace did not permit wide reading or detailed contemplation. I was often bemused by colleagues who sent me thirty- or forty-page articles they thought would be helpful. It was all I could do to get through the parts of the intelligence briefings and government papers that my various special assistants underlined for the hour or two of reading possible on a good day.[45]

Nye also emphasized, as has Henry Kissinger, that one typically operates in office on the basis of whatever intellectual capital had been accumulated beforehand. So unless an official tries to stay in touch with academic developments while in office—and Nye's comments suggest that this is unlikely—getting her (or even those busy special assistants) to pay attention to what scholars say will be difficult.

One might deal with this problem by assuming that even though officials will *not* read the scholarly article, let alone the book, they might read an op-ed piece or a *Foreign Affairs* article that digests it and highlights the policy-relevant implications. Along with his work in scholarly journals, Mearsheimer produced a steady stream of opinion pieces during the 1990s in *The New York Times*, mainly on such front-page topics as the Balkans conflict. Along with an intriguing but distinctively "academic" version of an argument linking the probability of war to the process of democratization, Edward Mansfield and Jack Snyder produced a shorter, more accessible version of the same material for *Foreign Affairs*.[46] Even if busy officials cannot read the more user-friendly versions, their staffs might do so, and *future* officials will be more likely to absorb the ideas if they are presented in accessible forms and outlets.

When asked, policymakers tend to be forthright about what they find useful from SIR. "The simple, well-founded empirical proposition"[47] is one such contribution. For example, the link between democratization and the incidence of conflict has been influential because it is intuitive: it accords with common sense and can be explained easily to almost any audience. Of course, few SIR generalizations are as straightforward and well-supported as this one. Still, decades of empirical work have yielded more of them than is often realized. We now understand reasonably well how cooperative and more coercive strategies can be used to maximize the likelihood of cooperation, when deterrence is likeliest to fail, the conditions under which economic sanctions seem to work, and the causes and effects of nuclear proliferation. If it were presented in digestible forms, such research might be more useful to policymakers than it now seems to be.

Another such contribution consists of "models of strategy"[48]—propositions that link various tools of statecraft to foreign policy objectives. Alexander George's influential book *Bridging the Gap* argues that such models, along with the case studies that show how the various strategic options have performed, constitute the IR theorist's most effective contribution to better policymaking.[49] George's suggestion is buttressed by the organization of the

IR field, especially in the United States. Most scholarly work in IR either consists either of "issue-specific" puzzles that examine empirical or theoretical problems in generic causal terms or more detailed, less generalizable case studies, often dealing with these same issues. Some of the most enduring, important IR puzzles include those mentioned or implied in the previous paragraph: Are economic sanctions useful? If so, when and for what? When is accommodating an adversary likely to avert war, and when is such a strategy likely to induce it? These are precisely the kinds of issues policymakers must deal with and the questions they want answered. IR scholars have produced a wide body of empirical literature that might, if appropriately packaged, provide them with guidance.

Foreign-policymakers are equally clear about the elements of academic work and culture they dislike. Not surprisingly, these sound a lot like the worst products of the contemporary academic incentive system. They have little use for research that does not address important, real-world problems. As the belief takes hold that SIR scholars no longer care about these issues, even officials with academic backgrounds pay less attention to scholarly conferences and publications.[50] They dislike excessive jargon, especially when it seems employed in the service of trite findings. And they have no use for work that seems overly self-referential; it seems designed *not* to appeal to a wider audience.[51]

These sentiments reflect the fact that foreign-policymakers come to such work from a variety of backgrounds and lack a common professional language. Unlike, for example, lawyers, economists, or political scientists, they share neither a specific professional vocabulary nor any specific type of methodological training. The knowledge they need to do their jobs is mainly acquired in other ways, typically on or just prior to taking the job. In the United States, junior foreign service officers are recruited from a wide range of educational backgrounds and pick up the languages and substantive knowledge they need in intensive, government-run programs. Senior officials learn the detailed substance of their positions on the job as well. Policy specialists earn that status by immersing themselves in the substance and process of their work and by being recognized as such by fellow practitioners; there is no standardized intellectual socialization or certification.

From the point of view of scholars who want to produce relevant research and to communicate it outside the Ivory Tower, these patterns present a double-edged sword. The absence of a common language connecting foreign policy specialists makes it difficult for scholars to speak to them. To be credible within *their* professional circle—that is, among fellow scholars—academics typically must use and assume their primary audience's familiarity with certain concepts, lines of argument, and research tools. Any or all of these may be "foreign" to segments of the policy community. For this reason, even substantively important, relevant SIR may not travel equally well to all constituencies of policy specialists.

At the same time, of course, a greater reliance on the common vocabulary employed by social scientists could improve the clarity and reliability with which concepts are communicated *within* the policymaking community. Moreover, policymakers can often benefit from the more detached perspective and greater rigor that scholars can provide. Because working officials learn by doing, they often become very skilled in analyzing today's problems. What they often miss, because they lack the time or detachment to consider it, is how the present might reflect important features evident from the past, or how comparable cases in different issue-areas might shed light on their own immediate problems. In this sense, academics may be able to help decision makers see patterns evident at the level of the forest that are obscured when one stands in the shadow of a single tree.

So far, we have treated "policymakers" and "theorists" as if each were a highly homogenous group. While useful heuristically, this simplification also obscures some key distinctions within the groups. Some policymakers resist the notion that there are significant regularities in IR about which one can generalize, while others accept that premise. Correspondingly, some IR theorists are interested in patterns that are *not* issue-specific, though most tend to generalize at a somewhat lower, issue-specific level of abstraction. For the foreseeable future, the most obvious bridge across the theory-practice divide will probably connect "mid-range" theorists to those policymakers who have some familiarity with the literature, often produced in think tanks, that *uses* generic knowledge to explain certain types of real-world problems. Given the way the overlapping but distinct IR groups are organized, at least in the United States, these professional connections are already the best developed and seem likeliest to flourish in the future.[52]

Why Revisit the Scholar-Practitioner Problem?

Even if there is a reason for scholars and practitioners of international relations to communicate better than they now do, the thrust of the previous pages must surely indicate that the gulf is wide. Why then bother to revisit this issue again? The answer is twofold. The world has changed in ways that make officials less confident about what they know or believe they can project about the future, and many of them frankly admit it. If ever there was a time when pertinent scholarly expertise might really help them, this is it. In addition, the existing literature on policy relevance in international relations has, in our view, interpreted the notion and benefits of "relevance" too narrowly. As policymakers increasingly need to understand a complex, unfamiliar word, they may come to see academic knowledge as useful in new ways.

The last several decades of SIR have been dominated by concerns with the superpower conflict, but the end of the cold war and newly emerging international concerns have decreased the relevance of traditional issues. During the cold war, bipolarity seemed so stable that little effort was made to explore other aspects of conflict and community in world politics, such as the genesis and evolution of values across states, the consequences of intense ethnic loyalties, or the impact of an increasingly globalized market-place. But these issues now occupy center stage in the real world, and both practitioners and scholars have incentives to understand them better.

Since the fall of Communism in Eastern Europe, the sources of security threats, the composition and cohesion of alliances, and the shape of regional orders have been in flux. The further enlargement and responsibilities of NATO, not to mention the broader possibilities and limits of multilateral security cooperation, hang in the balance. In this new century, ethno-religious conflicts are likely to dominate the security landscape in much of the Third World, even as a zone of peace seems to be taking hold over much of the Northern Hemisphere. Policymakers have a clear interest in anticipating and understanding possible conflicts across these two broad regions. The effects on Japan and on Eurasian stability more generally of a rising China and an imploding Russia are likely to be profound, and officials will want to understand them. Controlling the proliferation of weapons of mass destruction is likely to become harder as it becomes more urgent. Since these problems are developing against a strategic backdrop quite different from that of the cold war, decisionmakers may require and desire help in sorting them out. Security-focused SIR that brings in considerations of ethnicity and community and work on identity that has implications for security might shed light on key policy issues.

Outside the realm of security as traditionally defined, the picture has become even more complex. Deepening but often destabilizing economic linkages, massive refugee flows and other humanitarian emergencies, and unprecedented global ecological problems have created a new set of issues that also vie for official attention—issues that challenge old ways of thinking about national interests and appropriate policy tools. None of this renders the traditional Westphalian analytic paradigm obsolete or unhelpful. It still provides analytic leverage on concerns related to inter-state conflict and conflict prevention. But many issues on the contemporary foreign policy agenda arise from internal societal pressures and thus fall outside its purview. Policymakers may thus benefit from consulting those areas of SIR that strive to connect general insights about international relations to country and region-specific knowledge about community and identity. As scholars are coming to appreciate, that kind of academic work has much to recommend it on intellectual grounds.[53] As a significant byproduct, it could also become highly policy-relevant.

Interestingly, decisionmakers recognize these intellectual challenges and seem to desire help in dealing with them. As the late Joseph Kruzel—a senior Defense Department official at the time of his death and a one-time professor at Ohio State—put it,

> with the collapse of the Soviet Union, there has been a profound breakpoint in the policy process. The bureaucratic predilection to do tomorrow what you did yesterday does not work when the whole world has changed. When the Berlin Wall came down, bureaucrats looked at each other and asked "what do we do now?" They did not know, and they looked to the academy for ideas about how to deal with this new world.[54]

Kruzel inferred that "the academy," meaning the theoretical side of the IR profession, had not responded to this opportunity. We should not be surprised: as suggested earlier, powerful incentives within university life have pushed much of political science toward practical irrelevance.

Not all scholars are content with this state of affairs. Often enough, SIR works end with thoughts on policy implications, even if they look like afterthoughts and receive little notice from reviewers and other readers. The unwillingness to neglect policy implications entirely suggests a residual desire on the part of some SIR scholars to be useful. Every issue of applied IR periodicals such as *Foreign Affairs, Foreign Policy, The Washington Quarterly*, and *Survival* is full of articles dealing with the policy-relevant implications of the new security environment, the consequences and effects of globalization, and so on. Yet precisely because their methodology and analytic approaches are similar to those employed by many policymakers, this literature may not tell officials much that they do not already know. What many of these works supply in relevance they often lack in a studied distance from issues in the headlines, not to mention scholarly rigor. Articles in *World Politics*, *International Organization*, and *International Security* at times deal with these same topics, albeit from a professional social-science standpoint. Even if the scholarly agendas that produce these pieces reflect mainly internally-driven concerns, their authors *could* highlight and elaborate upon their practical implications.

Doing so would add relevance to the rigor contributed by social science. The combination could conceivably lead to the emergence of a new breed of public intellectuals who speak about foreign policy. These intellectuals would combine a concern for real-world issues, a desire to communicate to a broad audience, and a systematic set of analytic procedures.

Well-designed scholarly research could provide a key analytic check on officials' reasoning. Whether implicit or explicit, theoretical frameworks affect what one sees and how it is interpreted. No phenomenon can be perceived meaningfully without prior conceptions of it; knowledge is therefore embedded in theoretical understanding. Like other ideas, international relations concepts such as "engagement," "containment," "power," and so on are intelligible and acquire meanings only in the context of some explanation. Since people have a strong tendency to fit incoming information into their existing assumptions, images, and beliefs, it is important that they understand how such ideas affect search, evaluation, and decision procedures.[55] Explicit encounters with appropriate scholarly work can serve as a check on the content and suitability of policymakers' assumptions, images, and beliefs—embedded as they will be in ideas that may need to be unpacked, analyzed, and modified in light of new evidence or better scholarly understandings of the subject. One could even argue that *unless* policymakers are self-conscious about their assumptions, they will be likely to act on the basis of oversimplified, outdated, or otherwise inappropriate premises. Theoretical self-consciousness in this sense cannot eliminate perceptual and analytical errors, but it should help in reducing their scope and impact.

Just as IR academics can do more than they are now doing to be relevant outside the Ivory Tower, their work would often be enriched by more frequent and meaningful encounters with practice. As we discuss in more detail in chapter 3, the relationship between theory and practice is a two-way street.

Not only can good theory influence practice by shaping the questions people ask and the hypotheses they consider; a careful study of past experience is often helpful, even necessary, in developing good theories. In our everyday lives as well as our professional lives, it is the unexplained but persistent behavioral pattern we often want to make sense of, or the deviant case that we strive to "make fit," given what we think we know. In these senses, past practice provides many of the questions academics want to explain. Even scholars who do deductive work benefit when their substantive assumptions are shaped by a perceptive reading of past experience. To take just one example, it was long assumed that when deterrence failed, it was by a process that occurred all at once or not at all. By carefully examining a number of important cases of deterrence failure, Alexander George and Richard Smoke showed that deterrence can also fail in stages, as an initiator gradually nibbles away at the status quo.[56] The kinds of questions this opened up for scholars were matched by their policy relevance: if deterrence fails in stages, the initiator's *and* the defender's resolve is continually challenged, heightening the need to better understand how costly miscommunication can be avoided.

The Outline of the Book

This book discusses the possibilities and limitations of policy-relevant knowledge, its forms, its range, and the paths by which it may be brought to the attention of policymakers. Chapter 2 argues that knowledge is relevant under two conditions: if it establishes the range of possibilities for policy, and if it identifies the consequences of various courses of action. Within this framework, we discuss the forms of knowledge and reasoning upon which policymakers base their decisions, and we explain how this knowledge and reasoning can (and cannot) be complemented or supplemented by the contributions of social science. In the process, we focus on the properties of explanation, and show how good explanations of important phenomena lie at the foundation of the academic contribution to better policy. Chapter 3 discusses the various paths by which academic knowledge can enter the policymaking process: either in response to a specific demand for scholarly assistance expressed by government, or as a result of improved understanding generated autonomously within the academic community. Here, we also examine the various professional contexts within which such knowledge is produced, and the manner in which they may operate as links in the transmission mechanism by which understanding travels from the Ivory Tower to policymaking institutions.

We believe that the value of policy-relevant IR theory should be assessed not simply from the decisionmaker's vantage point, but also from the perspective of the scholarly enterprise itself. Many scholars fear that knowledge tethered to practical purposes may cause them to lose their independence or impair their uncommitted speculative curiosity. Chapter 4 argues that both beliefs are mistaken. The first part of the chapter identifies two attributes of good theories—soundness and attention to meaningful questions. The second part examines whether there is a tradeoff between good theory and practical relevance. We argue that policy-relevant knowledge stands to be as good, or better, from a purely scholarly perspective than knowledge produced with no regard to its utility.

Chapters 5 and 6 discuss specific instances of scholarship that seem relevant to the conduct of contemporary U.S. foreign policy. Chapter 5 examines contemporary literature on the interdemocratic peace, discussing its assertion that democracies, unlike other types of political systems, do not fight one another. If this claim is to serve as a foundation for the architecture and conduct of U.S. foreign policy, its empirical truth must be closely evaluated. Beyond this, questions must be raised about the ceteris paribus conditions that qualify the relationship between democracy and peace, and about the indirect consequences of acting on this assumed relationship. This chapter does that. Chapter 6 discusses scholarship on institutionalized cooperation in world politics. Policymakers who want to pursue coordinated policies within the framework of international institutions must ask several questions: Is the distribution of state preferences conducive to cooperation at all? Even if cooperation is possible, what kinds of costs and benefits would a regime carry? The school referred to as *political realism*, and that designated by the term *liberal institutionalism*, offer very different advice: their claims and counterclaims are evaluated here.

Chapter 7 concludes by emphasizing the common interests of international relations scholars and practitioners in knowledge that clarifies the range of the possible and the consequences of various courses of action. It also suggests ways in which firmer bridges between the two communities may be built.

2 Types of Knowledge and Their Practical Uses

As chapter 1 emphasized, it is ironic that there should be a chasm separating theorists and practitioners in a field explicitly designed to be policy-relevant little more than three generations ago. Since this gap is best explained *sociologically*, in terms of professional habits and reward structures, there may be no inherently *intellectual* reason why SIR should not address policy issues while maintaining or even enhancing the quality of scholarship. At the same time, since scholars may legitimately be interested in issues with few practical implications, not all scholarship can be directly relevant. Moreover, the forms of thinking appropriate to academic analysis and to policy guidance are not identical. Thus it is important to examine the intellectual foundations of relevant knowledge, asking what forms it may assume, what distinguishes that produced within academia from that typically employed by policymakers, and what comparative advantages the two communities have when it comes to policy-relevant thinking.

Types of Policy-Relevant Knowledge[1]

Typically, relevant knowledge is thought of as knowledge that sheds light on the means by which policy objectives can be attained, i.e., "if the end is y, the policy instrument should be x." Although this is the most obvious function of relevant knowledge, scholarship's purpose must be viewed more broadly. Knowledge is also relevant when it establishes the range of choices and the consequences of action. For one thing, not all desirable policy objectives are equally feasible, and it may be difficult to find the means that will promote their attainment most effectively within certain ranges of possible conditions. Scholarship can help identify these means and the conditions within which they might best be employed. This requires, first of all, statements about the link between a policy instrument and a desired outcome, subject to certain qualifying conditions (specified in the form of control variables). All of the above may be subsumed under the rubric of *instrumental* relevance. But an appreciation of the range of the possible and the consequences of various policies also requires a grasp of the circumstances under which the policy instruments are available and malleable, and of the values that the pertinent control variables may assume. Knowledge of this sort will come under the heading of *contextual* relevance.

Instrumental[2] Relevance

The meaning of instrumental relevance may be illustrated with reference to the link between a specific type of foreign policy instrument and a specific category of foreign policy ends. The use of economic coercion as a tool of statecraft illustrates how sound instrumental knowledge could benefit policymakers. Sanctions, in Richard Haass's words, "are fast becoming the United States' [foreign] policy tool of choice."[3] Between 1993 and 1996 alone, 35 countries were targeted by U.S. sanctions.[4] Sanctions include such policy levers as foreign assistance reductions and cutoffs, export embargoes and import boycotts, the freezing of target actors' assets, increases in tariffs, reductions in import quotas, and revocation of most favored nation (MFN) trade status.

Sanctions have become popular because they allow governments to seek to enforce certain standards of behavior in a more measured and controlled manner than some other policy instruments seem to allow. On moral as well as political grounds, the prospect of applying coercion while avoiding the use of military force may be attractive. As a statement issued by the U.S. National Conference of Catholic Bishops put it, "Sanctions can offer a nonmilitary alternative to the terrible options of war or indifference when confronted with aggression or injustice."[5]

This observation leads naturally to the question of what sanctions can do, and the further question of when they work. The circumstances under which sanctions are likely to work have been extensively debated within academia.[6] There is broad agreement that to change a target state's behavior, that target should not be able to absorb the costs of the disrupted relationship more easily, or for a longer period of time, than the initiator. This will depend in part on the objective magnitude of the economic benefits foregone on the two sides. It will depend on the domestic vulnerability of the respective governments, as this may determine their ability to absorb the domestic economic and political impact of such losses. Accordingly, the basic instrumental relationship could be expressed as follows: the ability to change a target's policies depends on the type and magnitude of the economic costs imposed on the target, controlling for the extent of the initiator's and target's respective economic dependence on each other and the comparative political vulnerability of the two governments.

Scholars have recently begun to further unpack the ceteris paribus clause in this model. One of them argues that a target's dependence on the initiator reflects not just its immediate vulnerability, but also, assuming incentives to resist a initiator's demands, its ability to find alternative suppliers and markets over time as well. Such an ability to adjust, he contends, is as fundamental an aspect of dependence as the initial distribution of economic resources in the target's economic relationship with the initiator.[7]

As the example suggests, scholarship can be instrumentally relevant by explaining why certain links should exist between contemplated policies and desired outcomes, and how these links are mediated by certain ceteris-paribus conditions. Nevertheless, even this knowledge may be an insufficient basis for sound policy, for it cannot be assumed that the right policy levers will be available and sufficiently malleable when needed, or that the ceteris paribus conditions will assume certain values in the short run. To determine whether such assumptions are tenable, policymakers must also understand the broader *context* within which instrumental relationships operate.

Contextual Relevance

Contextual knowledge tells us what conditions shape the availability or malleability of a policy instrument. It further alerts us to the circumstances that determine what values the ceteris paribus conditions assume.

The missions of instrumental and contextual knowledge are depicted in figure 1. Y (the dependent variable) represents the anticipated policy out-

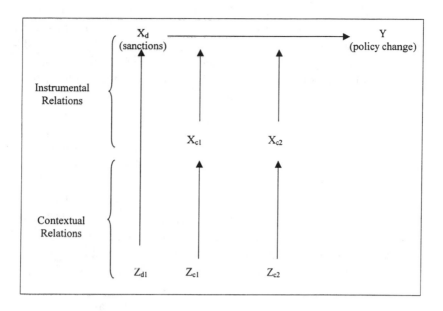

FIGURE 1 Instrumental and Contextual Knowledge

come (here illustrated by a change in the external behavior of a foreign government). The X's are the variables involved in the instrumental relation. X_d is the policy designed to produce the altered behavior of the target government (here illustrated by the application of economic sanctions). X_{c1} and X_{c2} are control variables that qualify the policy's impact. They are illustrated here, respectively, by the relative political stability of initiator and target governments and by their relative economic dependence on each other. The Z's are contextual variables. Z_d influences the availability or malleability of X_d, (illustrated here by the legal regime which determines what economic measures the initiator can legally take). Z_{c1} and Z_{c2} are variables affecting the values of X_{c1} and X_{c2}, respectively (for example, in the first case, the two governments' relative success in addressing key issues of domestic policy; in the second case, the factors determining the ratio of the value of the goods and services foregone by the two countries because of the disruption to their respective GNPs).

Policymakers may want to understand contextual relationships for a variety of reasons. If a particular policy instrument is unavailable or very costly to use, perhaps due to international or domestic norms that sharply circumscribe its use, its theoretical suitability for the purpose at hand may be irrelevant practically. If so, some other policy option would have to be considered. For example, even if sanctions were in principle feasible, the initiator government's domestic political vulnerability may make it difficult to absorb the anticipated costs of the sanctions to the domestic economy.

Relevant contextual knowledge may also assume a predictive form. One can imagine propositions about the future status of policy instruments employed to pursue currently accepted policy objectives, or about the ceteris paribus conditions. Even if based only on an extrapolation of current trends, such analyses might be useful heuristically for long-term planning purposes. Edward Luttwak, for example, has argued that Americans' refusal to accept any significant military casualties likely precludes for the foreseeable future any large-scale use of American ground forces in combat.[8] The implication is that unless it could be applied in situations where technology can effectively substitute for manpower, large-scale force would be unavailable.

An understanding of the circumstances under which multilateral institutions can be used to impose economic sanctions illustrates the practical benefits of contextual knowledge. Aside from favorable domestic conditions within the initiating state, three factors affect this instrumental relationship.[9] One involves the nature of the international institutions through which multilateral sanctions are coordinated. Their substantive mandates, internal structures, or voting procedures often affect the kind of intra-coalitional bargaining, including issue-linkages, that allow a group of sanction-initiators to work together effectively. Second, the extent to which actors can cooperate often reflects the type of sanction imposed. Reduction of foreign aid is typically the least costly to sanctioners, unless it has been tied to purchases from donors; import or export restrictions tend to be costliest. Third, the distribution of power among sanctioning states may affect their ability to cooperate. The experience of the Gulf War suggests that a hegemonic state can coerce or bribe others to support sanctions it favors, especially if it commits itself early and irrevocably to costly actions in support of those policies.[10] On the other hand, such a state may be unable to prevent smaller states from riding free on its efforts, which could undermine domestic support for sanctions in the large state or render them so leaky as to be ineffective when applied.

Policymakers might also benefit from an ability to anticipate the values of the key control variables in a statement about instrumental relations. In the case of sanctions, a target government's base of domestic political support might fall into this category. Initiators of sanctions rarely have much direct leverage over this factor, making it a reasonable candidate for them to set aside as part of relatively invariant ceteris paribus clause. But if sanctions that harm the general population in a target state have the effect of actually strengthening its government, as a population rallies "round the flag," officials in the sanctioning state would presumably want to know that in time to head off the worst effects.

In two different ways, policymakers may find contextual knowledge especially useful when the international environment is in a state of flux. First, expected instrumental relationships may no longer apply, and revising them would require an appreciation of the new context. The post-cold war period illustrates this point. Long-held assumptions about the purpose and cohesion of alliances, the strategic importance of nuclear weapons, and the uses of military power more generally—assumptions on which many policies rested—were thrown into question when the Soviet Union collapsed. Re-evaluating how such foreign policy tools might now be used requires analysts to understand the central tendencies of the present era, a task that now occupies much work in SIR. A recent article about unipolarity, for example, contends that the U.S. lead in material resources over other states is now so large that key changes in the international power structure are unlikely in the "the policy-relevant future."[11] That claim attempts to rebut a number of influential scholarly arguments to the effect that unipolarity is likely to be ephemeral.[12] Policymakers will want to know which position is correct, since the answer could affect their willingness to invest in developing certain policy instruments rather than others.

Second, key changes in the international environment can affect the goals that are considered feasible or desirable. That, in turn, can spur fresh thinking about instrumental relationships. For example, even though Western calls for democratization in the Communist bloc during the cold war may have been sincere, the goal was then so infeasible that they often assumed a ritualistic, if not propagandistic, air. Once the Berlin Wall fell and the promotion of democracy became a top policy priority in many capitals, discussions on how to achieve that goal occupied foreign policy journals and captured the interest of many social scientists.

The need for adequate forecasts notwithstanding, scholars should be cautious about their ability to predict outcomes very far into the future, even if their basic explanatory model is largely correct. Because causal propositions extrapolate what has been seen to hold true in the past into the future, they assume that known causal relationships will remain approximately constant over time. Unless this assumption is correct—and in many cases it is not—forecasts will fail when important thresholds that change the basic nature of the causal relationship are crossed. Many forecasts ultimately fail because it is often impossible to predict beforehand when such a threshold will be crossed.[13]

Anticipating Costs and Consequences

Policymakers are rarely content to grasp the objectives they can achieve via certain policy instruments. Typically, they want to know what impact their actions might have beyond those that are directly intended. Lyndon Johnson gave up the option of winning the Vietnam War through a general military mobilization and a major tax increase, even though these might have substantially increased the chances for a U.S. victory, because he feared the consequences for his domestic programs. Social scientists have likewise deemed it important to understand the direct and indirect consequences of action. As one of them put it, "the practical utility of social research consists not only of finding means to achieve stated goals, but also of discovering unanticipated consequences and ramifications of policies and other social actions."[14]

One kind of consequence involves the costs associated with policy choices. Almost all policies impose *direct* costs, of which the resources expended often are the most visible. The budget outlays associated with military preparedness or foreign assistance are obvious examples. But not all direct costs are paid in tangible resources: a leader who twists an ally's arm for a particular concession may be using up goodwill that will then be unavailable later for other purposes. Most policy choices also entail *indirect*, or secondary, costs: these result from the policy, though they are not linked to that instrument. One important kind of indirect cost is the opportunities foregone by some choice. Any use of economic sanctions, for instance, deprives the sanctioner of the benefits it derives or might derive in the future from commercial or financial ties with the target. More specifically, secondary sanctions—those the initiator of the sanctions applies to third parties who continue dealing with the target of the original sanctions—may damage relationships with those other states. Not only do the others tend to retaliate, further eroding economic relationships, but attempts to coerce unwilling states to join in punishing some target may set back efforts to liberalize the overall international trade regime, a key U.S. objective.[15] Indirect costs may also result from the objective's attainment. Because the United States allowed its Western European allies and Japan to discriminate against American exports during the early cold war era as a way to rebuild these countries' economies after the devastation of World War II, domestic support for open trade with these same states eroded over time, as Americans in less competitive economic sectors came to increasingly resent the effects of the one-sided concessions.

Indirect consequences can imply benefits as well as costs. At times, military investment can have positive effects on the domestic economy. The United States' tremendous lead in metallurgy and commercial internet technology grew out of work done initially for the Pentagon. Economic sanctions designed to weaken an adversary's economy may also strengthen the initiator's broader diplomatic position, assuming that a major portion of the international community agrees with the need to confront the target of the sanctions.

To summarize: knowledge is policy-relevant if it addresses the instruments, context, and/or consequences of policy. Inasmuch as these are categories of issues dealt with by SIR, it can benefit policymakers in ways that reach well beyond establishing direct relationships between policy instruments and expected outcomes. Nevertheless, the reluctance of policymakers to rely on the products of academia results not only from the sociologically based impediments to communication between the two worlds of endeavor, but also from the fact that those entrusted with the conduct of foreign policy do not normally seem to consider the ways in which noninstrumental knowledge can help them. One reason for this pattern is that policymakers may simply not realize that a well-supported generalization on an issue they care about may be very helpful to them.

Despite these problems, professional scholars can produce work that could (and should) have an impact on foreign policy decisionmaking. Relevant knowledge can be applied to two, conceptually distinct, but in practice overlapping, purposes that are central to policymaking: diagnosis and prescription. Diagnosis consists of defining the sources and parameters of a challenge. Prescription is the business of determining the best apparent response to the challenge, given the diagnosis. Each of the three forms of relevant knowledge can inform both tasks, but the purpose and emphases differ in the two cases.

When *diagnosing* the origins of a challenge, generally one must know whether and how it can be attributed to the actions of other nations and to the preferences behind those actions. It may also be necessary to appreciate to what extent this situation may have been produced by one's own actions. In either case, the instrumental link (the direct link and the ceteris paribus conditions) between the behavior and policy challenge must be understood. Diagnosing a situation does not reduce to determining how it came about; it is also, and significantly, a matter of assessing how it affects a government's ability to realize its aims. The link behind these aims and elements of the situation must be established. For example, it is an aim of U.S. policy to ensure secure and affordable sources of oil from abroad, a goal partially pursued via a policy of firm and secure relations with Arab nations in the Gulf area. Regional stability and peace are ceteris paribus conditions qualifying the U.S. ability to pursue its aims via this policy. A grasp of how local conflict and instability can jeopardize U.S. ability to meet its objectives follows from a good diagnosis of the regional situation. An appreciation of other, perhaps indirect, costs and consequences of local turmoil is also part of what a comprehensive diagnosis would produce. As an illustration, unrest in the Arab world may make it harder for the U.S. simultaneously to pursue its traditional policy of staunch support for Israel.

When *prescribing* policy responses to external challenges, the likely impact of any contemplated course of action must, of course, be assessed and the qualifying circumstances affecting its impact must be considered. In the preceding example, having decided that local turmoil is a threat to oil supplies, the U.S. might contemplate military action to impose order and stability in the Gulf. The goal is stability, the tool is armed force. One might ask whether military power is, in principle, instrumentally related to the sort of local problem involved. A circumstance qualifying the promise of this policy might be the diplomatic support the United States would receive from its major allies, leading one to ask whether such support would be offered. The policy instrument's availability must also be considered (a matter of contextual relevance). Will public and/or congressional opposition preclude dispatching U.S. forces to the area? Moreover, would the policy have certain secondary costs, e.g., harming relations with Russia or China?

If diagnosis and prescription employ similar intellectual ingredients, their purposes and analytical emphases differ. Diagnosis tends to focus on the calculations of others and on their consequences. Prescription emphasizes one's own calculations and their likely consequences. Diagnosis seeks to characterize an existing situation; prescription emphasizes ways of changing it. Effective prescription assumes sound diagnosis; both require a sound foundation of relevant knowledge.

Explanation, Scientific Method and Ordinary Knowledge

The credibility of policy-relevant knowledge rests, in the final analysis, on its ability to explain why particular policies stand to produce certain effects, why some contextual circumstances may affect their likelihood of doing so, and why certain costs and consequences, either direct or indirect, are implied by these policies. It may be thought that an ability to predict is all that is required—that no explanation is needed as long as a statement of what can be anticipated is provided. But this is not so. As we will explain in chapter 4, prediction, per se, is not a very impressive intellectual achievement in the absence of explanation. It is, moreover, hard to convince anyone that a prediction would be borne out if no credible reason can be provided. Whether the policy-relevant proposition deals with instrumental or contextual statements, or with costs and consequences, it will be valuable in direct proportion to the quality of the explanation it provides.

The Nature of Explanation

Although the notion of explanation can be interpreted in various ways, the dominant interpretation among philosophers of science is the *nomological-deductive* view. The root of the first term in this phrase, nomos, is the Greek word for law. In this sense, "to explain [i.e., deduce] something is to exhibit it as a special case of what is known in general." One shows that some phenomenon or outcome is to be expected, given some general proposition (typically in the form of an "if → then" statement) and a particular set of circumstances, known as initial conditions.[16] The specific form an explanation takes depends on whether the phenomenon to be accounted for is singular in nature (e.g. "why don't Britain and France wage war against each other") or an empirical generalization (e.g. "why don't democracies ever fight one another?").

Explaining a singular statement requires that it be identified as a specific instance of a more general proposition. To do that, an argument would have to include among its premises at least one generalization (G) or "covering law," and at least one singular statement that specifies an initial condition (I). From these premises, it is possible to infer the singular statement (C) that we seek to explain. Consider the following example:

(1) Democracies never fight each other (G)
     Britain and France are democracies (I)

_____

     Britain and France never fight each other (C)

In this sense, we might also say that the *cause* of the fact that Britain and France do not fight is that both are democracies, since democracies do not fight each other.

There is a strain within the philosophy of science, associated with "scientific realism," that denies that particular events can be explained by subsuming them under a general proposition. In this view, to explain an event is to describe the mechanism—the structured set of processes—leading to its occurrence. Thus, Mario Bunge feels that "In all cases, we explain facts by invoking some mechanism or other, perceptible or hidden, known or suspected."[17] Similarly, John Elster argues that, "Usually, and always ultimately, [explaining an event] takes the form of citing an earlier event as the cause of the event that we want to explain, together with some account of the causal mechanism connecting the two events."[18]

We do not dispute the explanatory value of mechanisms. Quite the contrary, it is often helpful to know, particularly if the goal is policy-relevant knowledge, *how* the outcome was generated, whatever its trigger. We nonetheless believe that the ability to explain in this manner assumes that we have in mind some general and lawlike statement relating the mechanism in question to the occurrence of some event. Plainly, we cannot assume that the mechanisms leading from cause to effect operate in an ad-hoc manner. It is the regularity with which the mechanism produces the effect (given certain antecedent conditions) that allows us to invoke it as a basis for explanation. Thus, while we are alert to the value of describing causal mechanisms, we believe that for this to lead to useful knowledge, generalizations of the covering-law variety are required.

General propositions can be produced in three basic ways. In some cases, a general proposition, such as the first premise in argument (1), can be derived from a covering law of an even higher level of generality, in addition to at least one antecedent condition at the same level of generality as the first premise in (1). In this case, the explanatory argument is simply an extension of argument (1). For example,

(2) Governments responsive to public opinion never fight others so
       responsive (G)
     Democratic governments are responsive to public opinion (I)

     Democracies do not fight each other (C)

In other cases, a general proposition is produced without recourse to a statement involving an initial condition. In this type of explanation, two or more equally general propositions constitute the premises of an argument, producing a generalization as a conclusion. For example,

(3) Public opinion in democracies disapproves of war against other
       democracies (G1)
     Democratic governments act in accordance with public opinion
       (G2)

     Democracies do not fight each other (C)

No initial condition needed to be specified here, since the phenomenon to be explained was general rather than singular. As such, the reasoning that forces the conclusion is logical in nature, provided by the conjunction of the two general premises.

Generalizations can also be produced in a purely inductive fashion, by noting a correlation between changes in the values of different variables. Provided that reasonable care is taken to rule out the possibility that the association is spurious, such generalizations may be useful as premises in an explanatory argument, even if they cannot be derived deductively in one of the ways just discussed.

It is typically assumed that one of the main contributions scholars can offer policymakers is *generalizations* that shed light on instrumental and contextual relationships, or on the secondary consequences of action. Scholars can, of course, also provide information of a factual nature—in other words, the "initial conditions" in the nomological-deductive model of explanation. However, since theory is their primary stock in trade, it seems that their comparative advantage is more pronounced with regard to empirical generalizations, while that of policymakers rests in access to specialized factual knowledge.[19] However, this does not imply that government officials do not rely on generalizations; just like anyone else, they would find it impossible to reason without them. Even a prototypical "historical" explanation—one that is rich in context and relies little on overt generalizations—implicitly invokes generalizations "of some sort" to explain specific behavior.[20]

Thus, while scholars appear more suited to producing generalizations than policymakers, the latter do so to a significant extent as well. If so, we must ask whether the explanations produced by social scientists should be considered superior to that possessed independently by the government decisionmakers?

If many academics consider self-evident the superiority of scholarly knowledge, its value is much less apparent to many policymakers. For example, Paul Nitze, one of the most experienced of the nation's foreign policy statesmen tells us that

> It is my view that most of what has been written and taught under the heading of "political science" by Americans since World War II has been contrary to experience and common sense. It has also been of limited value, if not counterproductive, as a guide to the conduct of actual policy.[21]

Plainly, scholars would disagree, at least with the first of these assertions. Whichever of these views is correct, the costs to policymakers of ignoring scholarship would depend on the respective qualities of the explanations, principally the generalizations, that academics and policymakers are in a position to produce. In turn, this quality depends on the modes of analysis they bring to bear to the analytic task: scholars are, in principle, guided by an ideal of scientific method, policymakers by what may be described as specialized ordinary knowledge.

Scientific Method and Ordinary Knowledge

The Ideal of Scientific Method   Unlike the humanities, science (social or natural) concerns itself with verifiable knowledge about the empirical world, aiming to establish the factual bases of truth.[22] This truth may be descriptive, or it may be analytical. If descriptive, its purpose is to characterize the state of affairs with regard to one or several variables viewed independently of each other (for example, the frequency of armed conflicts in the post–cold war era, the attitudes of men and women toward the United Nations). If analytical, the aim is to account for the manner in which the values of some variables are influenced by the values of others (for instance, how the frequency of international conflicts is affected by the state of the global economy). Whichever type of knowledge one is concerned with, for it to be scientific it must rest on certain principles of inquiry that are deemed to define the scientific community.[23] Admittedly, we lack a perfect consensus on these rules at the margins, and not all social scientists adhere to them uniformly. Nevertheless, these principles represent an ideal toward which scholarly endeavors tend and one that distinguishes scientific inquiry from ordinary knowledge.

Adherence to several principles of inquiry qualifies the resulting knowledge as scientific.[24] It must be based on rules of inferential thinking that apply to any scientific endeavor, and that encompass rules for collecting and assessing evidence and for making inferences. These rules must follow recognized principles of deduction or induction. Concepts must be unambiguously defined and empirically meaningful. Data on which scientific conclusions rest must, in principle, be available to other investigators. Measurement must adhere to recognized rules of reliability and validity. The common theme of scientific principles is *inter-subjectivity*: idiosyncratic judgment must play a minimal part in the argument behind the conclusion, since objective principles of inquiry are more likely to yield empirical truth than the vagaries of individual judgment.

In short, by relying on explicit and professionally accepted rules of inquiry, scientific knowledge reduces the analyst's subjective judgment to a minimum. Ordinary knowledge, by contrast, does not do this. Consequently, even though differences with respect to the truth of claims rooted in ordinary knowledge cannot be resolved within the terms of reference of this knowledge, those associated with scientific knowledge usually can be resolved within its own terms of reference.

Ordinary Knowledge: Its Value and Pitfalls   The ordinary knowledge of policymakers is not the same as that of "ordinary people." While it is based on a very considerable foundation of specialized factual knowledge, policymakers' grasp of the issues is also influenced by a variety of professional incentives and perceptual frameworks that shape the way they interpret and draw inferences from the facts. Accordingly, it is not to the ordinary knowledge of the person in the street to which SIR should be compared, but to the ordinary knowledge of policymakers. In particular, attention should be drawn to some of the aids to reasoning that policymakers may rely on, and some of the organizational constraints on their analysis.

Cognitive Dispositions and Analytical Shortcuts: An absence of explicitly accepted rules of inference and research within ordinary knowledge implies, by default, a substantial role for rules rooted in cognitive processes and beliefs. Some of these involve responses to recognized psychological needs. For example, the need for consistency among one's various cognitions (beliefs and opinions) often leads people to redefine some subset of their cognitions so as to bring them into balance with others. In the process, some violence can be done to the truth of the cognitive element that has been modified, imparting a perceptible bias to the attitudes that spring from the cognitive equilibrium thus established.[25] Consider, for instance, Ole Holsti's analysis of the thinking of John Foster Dulles. Holsti sought to identify the various components of the negative image that Dulles held of the Soviet Union and to examine how that image correlated to actual evidence regarding Moscow's behavior.[26] Through a careful quantitative analysis of Dulles' speeches and writings, Holsti managed to map out the structure of a belief system that, as far as the Soviet Union was concerned, consisted of one core element and three related perceptions. The core element was the Secretary of State's intense dislike for the Soviet system; the three related perceptions were (1) his view of the degree of Kremlin *hostility* toward the United States, (2) the extent of Soviet foreign policy *success*, and, (3) an assessment of Soviet *capabilities* for pursuing its external objectives.

Shifts in each of these component perceptions were monitored to evaluate their stability and the extent to which they covaried. The study revealed that Dulles' appraisal of the Soviet Union was remarkably resistant to change. When Soviet hostility seemed to decrease, Dulles would either infer that Moscow's prior policy had been less successful (temporarily causing the Soviets to reassess their behavior), or that Soviet power capabilities had decreased (leaving the Kremlin no choice but to act in a more cooperative manner). In no case did he seriously consider that Soviet objectives might have changed in any significant way. The implication drawn by Dulles was that there was never any reason to behave in a conciliatory fashion toward the Soviets.[27]

While dissonance theory examines the way in which people resolve cognitive clashes and how they adapt their attitudes accordingly, it says little about how they go about analytical problem solving, i.e., how intellectually they establish connections between a challenge and the manner of dealing with it. Because policymaking often involves attempts to influence the behavior of others, it is often important to know to what the decisions and activities of others should be attributed. Attribution Theory, a subfield of social psychology,[28] seeks to explain by what logic people establish such attributions. One of its tenets is that, lacking the guidance of scientific epistemology and acting as "naïve scientists," people tend to account for undesirable conduct of their own, or of those with whom they identify, in terms of external duress. By contrast, the misbehavior of others—especially those to whom they feel ill-disposed—is more apt to be explained by the latters' inherent negative traits. Thus, the military growth of an adversary would be interpreted in terms of naturally expansionist designs, while one's own would be explained in terms of the externally-imposed demands of security. A careful examination of early U.S. cold war policy concluded that U.S. policymakers' made attributions about Soviet intentions and actions in a way that coincided with psychologists' expectations.[29]

Another of attribution theory's findings is that people neglect the importance of nonoccurrences in explaining situations or behavior. This inference pattern violates a core logical and scientific principle: if an outcome (y) is to be linked to a cause (x), it must be shown: (1) that occurrence of x coincides with occurrence of y and (2) that the absence of x coincides with the absence of y. Causality cannot be established unless both associations are demonstrated. Thus, if the occurrence of lung cancer were proven equally likely when the assumed cause (smoking) was present as when it was absent, no link between smoking and cancer could scientifically be claimed. However, attribution theory indicates that ordinary knowledge often involves disregarding the causal meaning of a nonoccurrence of x, leading to dubious attributions. For example, during the coldest years of the cold war, examples of Soviet attempts to act on an expansionary advantage made a deep impression on leading U.S. policymakers; by contrast, instances where Moscow refrained from pursuing such advantages did not significantly undermine the official view on Soviet expansionism.

Quite apart from psychological mechanisms that encourage fallacious inferences from available data, faulty conclusions may also be rooted in the way inferences are drawn from inadequate substantive understanding, within the context of ordinary knowledge. While decisionmakers typically have access to much factual information about policy problems, that knowledge may be partial and specialized, linked to a policymaker's particular functions, responsibilities, and organizational identity. If so, there may be a surfeit of partial data and a correspondingly impaired grasp of the policy challenge. Even apart from a possible inadequacy of factual data, decisionmakers may not possess authoritative *general* propositions through which to make analytic sense of that information. Under the circumstances, a variety of aids to reasoning, in the form of "cognitive heuristics" or substantive "schemas," typically attend the interpretation of information. Such aids may involve an excessive reliance on simple rules of thumb, such as benchmarks or analogies, a tendency to think of the policy challenge in terms of a single value although several are affected, or an inclination to think in terms of simple bivariate cause-effect relations although causality is multiple and complex.[30]

The use of analogical reasoning by decisionmakers (the Munich Analogy, the Vietnam Analogy) has been extensively documented, and the analytical mistakes that this use produces have also been examined.[31] The problem is that analogies often provide only a shaky foundation for understanding, while the use of other cognitive heuristics often compounds the problem. Kahneman and Tversky have stressed the importance of two such heuristics: the "availability heuristic" and the "representativeness heuristic."[32] The former implies that, in seeking to predict the consequences of a situation or the behavior of an individual, people tend to predict the outcome that is most easily drawn from memory. The latter implies that the outcome most likely to be predicted is that which seems to represent the most salient features of the situation or behavior in question. An implication of the availability heuristic is that recent events are more likely to affect prediction than more distant events, whether or not there is any logical or substantive foundation for this choice. An implication of the representativeness heuristic is that policymakers are most likely to form their predictions around definitions of the situation related to their own particular responsibilities. Both heuristics also imply a tendency to place greater emphasis on specific examples than on systematic empirical generalizations when seeking to predict outcomes.[33] To the extent that generalizations provide the foundation for adequate explanations, explanatory ability is correspondingly undermined.

So far we have discussed only biases stemming from habitual cognitive shortcuts, not those resulting from emotion or vested interest, which may distort may analysis just as badly. While the latter's impact can also be minimized by properly applied procedures of empirical inquiry, we note that cognitive biases, i.e., those not rooted in emotion or interest, may be more insidious because they are less easily recognized.

While we have focused on some of the typical forms of naïve epistemology that guide decisionmakers' thinking about foreign policy challenges, more sophisticated analytical categories are also sometimes encountered under the general heading of ordinary knowledge—especially when policymakers themselves have an academic background. Even when this is the case, however, it appears that the thinking involved, and thus the associated policy, would have benefited from a more thorough or rigorous evalutation of the issues involved.

Henry Kissinger, for example, had relatively developed thoughts on the logic of linkage policies in international relations, and these provided a basis for they way he dealt with the Soviet Union. In order to elicit Soviet cooperation on arms control, and in facilitating a face-saving extrication from Vietnam, Kissinger dangled the promise of improved economic relations with the United States, and he brandished the threats implicit in U.S. rapprochement with China. He explained that

> One of the principal tasks of statesmanship is to understand which subjects are truly related and can be used to reinforce each other . . . in other words to create a network of incentives and penalties to produce the most favorable outcome.[34]

And he observed that, "Nixon and his advisers did succeed in making the various strands of policy support each other."[35] However, when George Shultz became President Reagan's Secretary of State, he stated equally firmly that,

> we needed to get away from the old concept of "linkage," of thinking that by exerting pressure or offering rewards in one area, particularly trade, we could induce a change in Soviet behavior in a regional conflict or in some other area. . . . we were taking the position that regional conflicts had to be confronted on their merits . . . just as arms control agreements had to be worked out on their merits.[36]

Both statesmen considered regularities of international politics, they reasoned in terms of a similar conceptual framework, yet they reached opposite conclusions.

Problems of this sort do not spring from cognitive shortcuts. Their source may lie in the way logical inferences are drawn from certain common postulates, or from the different (and necessarily subjective manner) in which relevant evidence is evaluated. Such subjective differences cannot and should not be entirely eliminated, since democratic societies may prefer different policy values at different times. But systematic scholarship can make the differing policy conclusions reached less arbitrary. For example, neither Kissinger nor Shultz operated from a clearly reasoned model of the logic of linkage policies, of the assumptions on which it might based, and on the implications for the situations in which these policies were or were not likely to be effective. Political scientists, on the other hand, have developed much of the logic involved in linkage situations. For example, one useful analysis of linkage policies starts with a statement of the assumptions that can be made about the interests of the parties across various issue areas, their ability to communicate this information to each other, and the implications for the outcomes that may be reached.[37] On this basis, the analysis distinguished between the likely outcomes of situations where, on the one hand, only one of the two parties seeks to apply a linkage across issue domains, and, on the other hand, where both parties practice linkage politics vis-à-vis the other. With regard to the former, the study distinguishes situations where the first side threatens to make the other side worse off in the related issue area, from situations where the former promises not to make the latter any worse off, and it derives the likely outcomes for each context. Armed with such deductively rigorous reasoning, both Kissinger and Shultz might have had clearer and more realistic expectations concerning policies of linkage toward the Soviet Union.[38]

If a comparison of social science and ordinary knowledge reveals some of the latter's shortcomings, it does not fully encompass the constraints on the reasoning of policymakers, which may also be rooted in the specific organizational setting within which they operate.

Organizational Constraints on Analysis: The way challenges are perceived and solutions are considered by policymakers often depend on the place each occupies within the decisionmaking machinery. Habits of thought, including the salient aspects of foreign policy issues, the links of causation involved, and so forth are likely to emerge from thinking related to the structure and missions of the organization with which the policymaker is affiliated, and this too may become part of the policymaker's ordinary knowledge, resulting in a constrained ability to interpret foreign policy challenges and to propose appropriate solutions. This point is summarized in the pithy observation, "Where you stand depends on where you sit."[39] By this reasoning, salient facets perceived of any situation vary depending on the purpose of the specific institution involved—each individual focusing on the aspects most relevant to his unit's responsibilities. Policy preferences are often molded accordingly. The Secretary of Commerce and the Secretary of Defense are likely to direct their analytical lenses at the features of a problem (for example, India's or Pakistan's decision to test nuclear weapons) most relevant to the responsibilities with which they are charged. Similarly, the responses they advocate are most likely to follow from the sorts of responses their institution is in a position to make.

In this regard, it is interesting to note the sources of the views held by Joseph Kennedy, a former banker and head of the Securities and Exchange Commission, of Hitler's Germany at the time when Kennedy was ambassador to Great Britain:

> His primary interest lay in economic matters. . . . The revolutionary character of the Nazi regime was not a phenomenon that he could grasp. . . . It was far simpler, and more in accord with his own premises, to explain German aggressiveness in economic terms. The Third Reich was dissatisfied, authoritarian, and expansive largely because her economy was unsound.[40]

Thinking constrained by bureaucratic blinders may be a common characteristic of the policymaking process. For instance, an analysis of decisions preceding the April 1979 attempt to rescue U.S. hostages in Iran found that altogether nine individuals participated in the meetings and that in the "key meetings that led to the decision to undertake the rescue mission, the evidence . . . suggests that the participants adopted positions that reflected their location in the bureaucratic structure."[41]

When policymakers move from one institutional setting to another, their thinking on how policy should be structured is likely to shift as well. Thus, when Winston Churchill was First Lord of the Admiralty (1911–1915), one of his early actions was to press for increased levels of naval expenditure. However, when he became Chancellor of the Exchequer (1921–1929) he urged substantial reductions of naval spending. Similarly, Casper Weinberger favored hefty increases in military outlays when he was Secretary of Defense. By contrast, while Director of the Office of Management and

Budget, he was known for his eagerness to slash government budgets (he was then referred to as "Cap the Knife").[42]

Although reasoning colored by institutional positions often is important in shaping substantive policy preferences, it also affects thinking in more general ways. Henry Kissinger, with experience both in the White House and The State Department, observed that:

> Institutionally, the Foreign Service generates caution rather than risk-taking; it is more comfortable with the mechanics of diplomacy than with its design, the tactics of a particular negotiation rather than an overall direction, the near term problem rather than the longer-term consequences.[43]

Not only does institutional context impose perceptual constraints on policymakers; but also their decisions often are guided by their organization's substantive interests. Officials must compromise between the institutional needs of the various units for which they are responsible, and they often feel compelled to promote the interest of their own organization as a whole (the latter generally defined as a quest for expanded missions and budgets). For all these reasons, foreign-policy problems may be perceived through organizational filters and responses to them may reflect relatively parochial organizational filters, and responses to them may reflect relatively parochial organizational concerns. Either way, "objective" knowledge brought in from the outside may have relatively little bearing on policy choices.

This caveat aside, no matter how it fits into the structure of foreign-policymaking, scholarship's ultimate value flows from the scientific episte-mology that, as an ideal, reduces subjectivity to a minimum, maximizing the likelihood that both descriptive and analytical knowledge would be empirically correct. In this regard, it is generally more reliable than psychologically-driven cognitions and "naïve epistemologies," or the occasional reliance on quasi-scholarly scholarly concepts, that furnish the foundation for much foreign policy decisionmaking. It also makes it possible to cut through reasoning that is bent around institutional blinders and interests. It would be equally naïve, of course, to argue that use of social scientific work will necessarily produce better policy. But the process by which decisions are made should improve insofar as officials make their assumptions, beliefs, and inferences as explicit as possible. Careful use of social-scientific SIR should help achieve this goal. To the extent that this is the case, the quality of policymaking stands to benefit from reliance on scholarly knowledge.

The Limitations to Policy Relevant Scholarship

While policy relevant knowledge may benefit the policymaking process in a number of ways, a realistic assessment of the role it can play must also include an appreciation of its limitations. Even if the partial superiority of scientific method over ordinary knowledge is recognized, and even if the need for rigorous generalizations is understood, it remains that there are tight limits to the extent to which policymakers are likely to rely on the insights of scholarship. Such limitations have two general sources. The first involves the motivations of *policymakers*; the second concerns the limitations of *social science*.

Limitations Rooted In the Incentives of Policymakers

The attainment of policy objectives depends more than on the awareness that even the best scholarship can produce, because policy decisions are only partly driven by the objective that is their professed purpose. *Political* problem solving, for needs ranging from electoral advantage to interorganizational jockeying, is often as important a part of policy choices as the international stakes involved. Firm action in a crisis can be meant to boost presidential popularity, the decision to procure some military system may be a partial response to the pressures of domestic lobbies, the choice of one policy instrument over another (e.g., economic over diplomatic) may reflect the relative power of their respective bureaucratic constituencies, and so forth. Plainly, the impact of analytical knowledge that seeks to link policy to its professed objective is reduced if that objective is not its true purpose.

Even where the attainment of the apparent policy objective *is* government's main purpose, success depends on more than just the understanding directly relevant to the challenge: it depends as much on the power and commitment of the interests with which policymakers must contend. Attaining policy goals depends not just on understanding the likely outcomes of policy, but also on dealing with interests that might not be well served by the policy. Interest-based opposition to the policy may originate within the political system, or it may be found abroad, and strategies involving compromise, inducements, or pressure, may be more effective in dealing with these interests than the force of arguments rooted in even a very good scholarly understanding of the problem. In this way, the requirements of political problem solving may trump those of good policymaking.

It is also necessary to understand that policymakers, or their political opponents, do not always seek scholarly analyses for the purpose of improving understanding. For example, such analyses may be sought simply as political ammunition. Although the use of scholarship as political ammunition may appear to preclude its ability to inform policy, it could be argued that this need not invalidate its usefulness. Even if knowledge is used mainly for political purposes, it may nevertheless improve the quality of policy through the clash of competing explanations and perspectives marshaled in the context of political confrontation. If each of the opposing scholarly arguments has merits, the result of such competition may be a synthesis that yields improved understanding. Alternatively if the confrontation proves that one point of view is clearly superior to the other, then rejecting the inferior argument advances understanding. Thus, even where scholarship is invoked initially for political ends, it can still encourage the growth of knowledge, and the quality of policy may benefit accordingly.

This reasoning may seem plausible in the abstract; in fact, this is not how knowledge is likely to advance. The reasoning assumes that the clash of perspectives would be resolved on the quality of the opposing intellectual arguments, using acknowledged standards of evidence and logic. In practice, and except perhaps in the very long term, the way such differences are settled within the context of political confrontation depends far more on the parties' relative political power than on the intellectual merits of their arguments. Thus, when the products of scholarship are used as political ammunition, not with the primary end of informing effective policy, neither the quality of knowledge nor the effectiveness of policy is likely to benefit. Only if senior policymakers insist on resolving disagreements based on the cogency of arguments and quality of the evidence—and they may have a high enough stake in effective policy outcomes to do this—SIR may be able to contribute a good deal.

Limitations Stemming from the Character of Scholarship

So far, we have implicitly assumed that policymakers would probably be able to find SIR work pertinent to their needs if they chose to use it. That may not be so. One limitation on social science's impact on policymaking comes from an insufficient volume of potentially relevant scholarship, which falls far short of the amount needed to guide the conduct of foreign affairs. Correspondingly, the ordinary knowledge of policymakers will continue to dominate decisions, if only by default. To some extent, the quantitative short-fall in relevant academic work arises because policy-relevant scholarship is not sufficiently highly regarded within universities, where the "disinterested" quest for pure science generally benefits academic careers more than does the pursuit of policy-relevant knowledge. Academics' willingness to devote much effort to being useful declines accordingly. Even if the pattern of academic incentives were altered to favor relevant work, the costs and time required to produce authoritative and usable knowledge might very often cause it to fall short of the need.

The problem with pertinent SIR is not limited to quantity. Policy-relevant scholarship often is simply not authoritative enough to provide a reliable basis for policymaking.[44] Plainly, social science is not of uniformly good quality, and its epistemological canons are unevenly applied. As important, while scientific methods may ensure that many of the mistakes associated with ordinary knowledge will be avoided, it does not guarantee conclusive propositions about the phenomena it studies. Its purpose is to debunk as much as to provide positive conclusions, and even the conclusions provided, being of a very contingent nature, may furnish no affirmative guide to action. Caveats can be enormously useful, but the pressure to "do something" often leads policymakers to want immediate and positive guidance, not advice that does not reach beyond counsels of prudence.

Related to this is the fact that one purpose of research is to *raise* questions, even if immediate answers are not available. Both the natural and social sciences engage in exploration and discovery, a result of which is to identify an expanding number of phenomena, as well as an increasing number of facets of a given phenomenon, requiring description and explanation. As Thorstein Veblen accurately observed, "the outcome of any serious research can only be to make two questions grow where one question grew before."[45] Raising good questions can help thoughtful policymakers over the long run, even this provides no assistance when some action must be taken quickly.

A further constraint on the authoritativeness of social science is that schol-ars often disagree among themselves. The lack of credible axiomatic pos-tulates in the social sciences, the indirect nature of measurement, and the probabilistic and contingent quality of many of the conclusions drawn, en-sure that consensus on the credibility of various knowledge-claims is often lacking. Challenges to extant scholarship are a necessary stimulus to its growth, and to the development of academic careers, but the character of the social sciences ensures even greater room for disagreement than in the natural sciences. Obviously, the rigor of inference and accuracy of evidence are greater in the latter than in the former, but even where research techniques appear most advanced, knowledge is not automatically authoritative. In any case, ongoing and unresolved scholarly debates may cause policymakers to tire of academic discourse, and to feel that it reflects academic gamesmanship with no clear bearing on their practical concerns.

Sophisticated exercises in mathematical deduction often produce conclusions that, where not self-evident (as often they are), are nevertheless based on a foundation of axioms and theorems that are, in fact, largely conjectural, raising the possibility of disagreement about the *truth* of associated conclusions. The problem is different with *inductive* social science, especially that which relies on advanced statistical tools, since the structure of statistical reasoning often diverges from that of even the most sophisticated ordinary knowledge. Accordingly, what may be authoritative from the perspective of conventions adopted within the social sciences may appear too meaningless to the decisionmaker to serve as a credible basis for decision.[46]

Rules of reasoning applied in SIR (especially its technically more esoteric variants) are often so different from the rules proper to ordinary knowledge that policymakers often find the former incomprehensible or meaningless within their own frame of intellectual reference. Regression analysis, probably the most widely used statistical tool in the social sciences, illustrates the problem. Regression's principal purpose is to allow us to assess the impact upon the values of an outcome variable (e.g., public support for presidential foreign policy) of one or more explanatory variables (e.g., presidential popularity, the perceived costs of the foreign policy, the perceived stakes of the policy). In the social sciences, this is usually done by estimating: (1) the coefficient values (usually by the least squares method) associated with each explanatory variable, (2) their respective standard errors, and, (3) the t-statistics expressing the ratio of the former to the latter. On the basis of the t-statistic, the researcher decides whether or not to reject the "null" hypothesis that the actual (not estimated) value of the coefficient is zero (i.e., that the independent variable has no impact on the outcome variable), a decision made subject to some accepted probability of a "type I" error (falsely rejecting a true hypothesis).

Even if the statistical procedures themselves were explained clearly, this frame of reference may not be meaningful to a policymaker. When trying to decide what weight to assign to some causal influence, few people (policymakers or otherwise) think in terms of comparing that weight to zero, then deciding whether to accept or reject the possibility that the two values may be statistically different. In any case, it makes little sense by many standards to think of the credibility of a statistical hypothesis in binary terms (accept or reject). Most policymakers, indeed most people, naturally think of their hypotheses in terms of a continuum of credibility determined by the strength of the evidence. Thus, on the basis of the available evidence, they may be moderately confident that a policy (e.g., economic sanctions) would produce its desired policy effect. As the character of the evidence changes (say, new information about the target government's domestic vulnerability), the extent of their confidence may increase. But, they rarely decide to think that either the policy will succeed or fail, subject to a 95 percent probability of falsely rejecting a true hypothesis!

Thus, there is substantial gap between statistical thinking and the thinking that guides most real activity. Substituting for the binary form of statistical tests concepts that reflect this sort of continuum—for example, confidence intervals bracketing coefficient estimates or Bayesian probability models—could mitigate the problem. Nevertheless, some part of statistical reasoning may have come to diverge too much from thinking associated with ordinary knowledge to provide meaningful criteria for determining, from a policymaker's perspective, how authoritative the knowledge claim really is.

Even when authoritative enough, the knowledge furnished by academia may shed little or no valuable light on policy issues. The problem sometimes flows from the self-evident nature of the scientific propositions involved—providing no increment to what policymakers already know. The banality of many claims and findings within the social sciences is often recognized,[47] and, as we discussed in chapter 1, it is frequently attributed to the fact that the reward structure of many universities places far greater weight on the techniques employed than in the substantive importance of scholarly findings.[48]

If scholarship confined to the restatement of the trivially obvious contributes little to policy-relevant knowledge, a number of nonobvious general propositions simply do not encompass policy problems. They may deal with matters of no interest to anyone but some subset of the academic community. They may be too abstract to reflect the challenges we encounter, or they may diverge too much from what policymakers have come to believe. As one practitioner-scholar observes: "The major obstacle to imparting abstract conceptualizing ability so needed by practitioners is that the vast majority of what passes for IR and comparative theory appears to such individuals to be so abstract or distorting of the real situation that it is useless."[49]

As we will argue in the following chapter, academic work need not address policy-relevant matters in order to be meaningful or interesting, since many things are worth knowing even if no practical utility follows from that knowledge. Of course, the lack of practical utility does not guarantee that the work will be meaningful or interesting, but it does justify efforts guided by no thought of application, and it further accounts for our restrained estimate of the likely scope of policy-relevant scholarship.

Conclusions

Contrary to the typically held conceptions of it, policy-relevant knowledge reaches well beyond establishing direct relations between policies and their desired outcomes. It also sheds light on the ceteris paribus conditions that qualify such relations, and it establishes the circumstances under which the policy instruments will be available and malleable, as well as the considerations that govern the values of the ceteris paribus circumstances. Finally, it alerts policymakers to the various consequences of their actions beyond those that the policy is directly intended to produce.

When policy-relevant knowledge is rooted in scholarly activity, its primary purpose is to establish explanatory propositions bearing on the above kinds of issues. Doing this involves both pertinent generalizations and apposite initial conditions. Both can benefit from academic rigor, but the scholarly community's greatest comparative advantage lies in the provision of generalizations rooted in the canons of scientific method. Although the ordinary knowledge of policymakers will always provide much of the foundation for the thinking behind their decisions, the flaws inherent in casual empiricism and the analytical habits shaped by professional incentives and perceptions imply that policy would often benefit from greater reliance on relevant scholarship. These benefits notwithstanding, it is important to appreciate the limitations on the ability of policy-relevant scholarship to inform the conduct of foreign policy-limitations that stem both from the character of the academic enterprise and from the incentives of government leaders.

3 How Knowledge Is Acquired and Used

Having discussed the forms that relevant knowledge may assume, and the comparative advantages that academia may have in its production, we ask *how* such knowledge can shape the conduct of foreign policy. Two broad issues will be addressed in this chapter. The first concerns the processes and institutions that govern the relationship between scholarship and policymaking, for this largely determines how the knowledge is used. This relationship is structured around the manner in which knowledge, typically in the form of general propositions, enters the policy process, and the shape it assumes when it does so. The second issue involves four distinct organizational settings within which policy relevant knowledge is generated, the forms of relevant knowledge each is likely to yield, and the relationships between these contexts.

Policy-Relevant Knowledge and the Policymaking Process

The structure of the link between scholarly knowledge and foreign-policymaking can be examined from two perspectives. The first involves the *sequence* (logical or chronological) in which the policy challenge and the knowledge relevant to addressing it enter the policy process. The second is defined by the nature of the *path(s)* by which scholarly knowledge is conveyed to policymakers responsible for meeting the challenge.

The sequence can be of two types. In the first, the policy challenge precedes the quest for relevant understanding, determining what sort of knowledge is called for. Here, a problem is defined, a gap in the understanding required to deal with it is identified, and knowledge needed to fill the gap is sought from the academic community. In the second, acquired knowledge appears before a policy challenge is acknowledged, and it then proceeds to shape that challenge. In this case, the knowledge helps to characterize the problem as well as to contribute to its solution. Sequence, then, determines the purpose of the relevant scholarship: in the first case, to solve an existing and specific problem; in the second case, to define and characterize the problems that foreign policy must address. Other consequences also follow from sequence, including the form that the knowledge is likely to assume (how specific and focused it tends to be), and how closely it may reflect the values and objectives of the incumbent policymakers.

Paths, in turn, can be direct and singular (e.g., a straight path from scholar to decisionmaker), or else they can be multiple and indirect (operating, for example, via interest groups, or the media). The applicable type of path determines how direct and unmediated an impact the social-scientific knowledge produces, and, by implication, how clearly defined is the link between the two. Not only does awareness of the type of path involved illuminate the connection between scholarship and statesmanship; it also clarifies important but often implicit assumptions about the appropriate way of conceiving of the manner in which national policy decisions are made.

Theoretically, then, four possibilities suggest themselves, but the two underlying dimensions are not independent, since the nature of the path is often determined by the sequence involved (see figure 2).

When an issue on the foreign policy agenda cannot be dealt with effectively because of a gap in the required knowledge base, policymakers may try to remedy the problem by turning to the academic community. Alternatively, and in response to an implicit demand, scholars may seek to fill the knowledge-gap on their own initiative, conveying the fruits of their efforts to decisionmakers as best they can. In either case, the path by which knowledge is led from scholar to statesman is likely to be singular and direct. By contrast, where potentially relevant knowledge precedes the appearance or recognition of a challenge, or its placement on the policy agenda, it is more likely to travel from its source to decisionmakers by multiple and circuitous paths. Consequently, although none of the four cells in figure 2 is necessarily empty, the bulk of social science's contribution to policy is found in the two off-diagonal cells—one describes what we call the *demand-driven* model of policy relevance, while the other describes the *supply-driven* model[1].

		Sequential Priority	
		Issue	*Knowledge*
Paths	*Singular*	Demand-driven model	
	Varied		Supply-driven model

FIGURE 2 Structure of Knowledge-Policy Relation

The Demand-Driven Model

This is the most common model of how policy-relevant knowledge makes its way to decisionmakers. Here, at the time the issue is placed on the general policy agenda, relevant knowledge falls short of what an effective policy requires. Either of several scenarios might then ensue. In one, policymakers explicitly commission studies intended to furnish the missing intellectual links: from individual scholars or, perhaps, from think tanks (e.g., RAND). In another scenario, government officials appoint to positions within the foreign-policymaking establishment academics whose expertise is thought likely to furnish the needed knowledge, once the scholar is placed in the appropriate policymaking setting. Relevant knowledge produced in response to a pre-existing policy challenge may also spring directly from the scholarly community, independently of any explicit governmental effort to acquire it, but in response to an *implied* demand. In fact, it is hard to think of many major U.S. foreign policy challenges during and since the cold war that have not evoked spontaneous scholarly efforts to improve the basis for policy-making.

Thus, policy-relevant knowledge may take the form of scholarly responses to a national need elicited without financial incentives in the form of government grants, contracts, and so forth, or because of any explicit official attempt to acquire the needed knowledge from the academic community. Since here the quest for knowledge begins when an issue is placed on the policy agenda, the type of knowledge most often sought is instrumental, indicating how policy instruments are linked to desired policy outcomes, including the various influences (control variables) that qualify this link. Once the instrumental knowledge is acquired, it may additionally be thought useful to carry understanding further, by specifying the contextual conditions that stand behind the instrumental relation. For example, it may be pointless to explain how some policy instrument could produce a desired objective if the instrument itself were unavailable, or barely malleable from the policymakers' perspective.

With the demand-driven model, the line connecting knowledge to the decision process generally is straight and singular. Plainly, this is so where government takes the initiative by soliciting scholarly knowledge bearing on issues prominently on the agenda. But even where the knowledge is directed upward in response to academia's self-generated desire to inform policy, the road from scholarly contribution to policymaking structure may lead quite directly from the source of the knowledge, to those within government who monitor knowledge in that area, to those (perhaps the same people) who are responsible for decisions.

The Supply-Driven Model

With the supply-driven model, the sequence in which the relevant knowledge and the policy challenge appears is reversed: the presence of potentially relevant knowledge is logically or temporally antecedent to the placement of a given challenge on the policy agenda. This can occur in three ways. The first begins with a disinterested type of knowledge, while the second and third directly involve applied scholarship.

In the first of the three cases (pure science), potentially relevant knowledge appears before *any* significant challenge to which it is apposite is recognized, within or outside of government. Acting on incentives unrelated to policy concerns, scholars discover law-like propositions about international relations and foreign affairs that, at the time or in the context of their discovery, have no apparent policy applications. Eventually, however, problems or opportunities may develop that are in some way covered by the previously acquired knowledge. Once the link between knowledge and challenge is recognized, the former may contribute to the latter's solution. For example, game-theoretic models of strategic interaction were developed considerably before they came to be applied to such problems as nuclear deterrence between the superpowers or to crisis management in the Middle East.

The sequential order may be chronological but it may also be of a *logical* nature. This typically occurs when a potentially policy-relevant argument is framed at a high level of abstraction, before specific cases to which it could be applied have been identified. Thus, for example, recent work on the conception of "fair" negotiated solutions to disputes has been tackled at a rather abstract level by Brams and Taylor.[2] Developing criteria of fairness focusing on either *proportionality* or on *envy-free* division (where each party believes it has received the most valuable portion of the goods in dispute), the authors propose what they call the Adjusted Winner (AW) solution as a generalizable resolution that ensures both proportionality and envy-freedom. This is an instance potentially very relevant to scholarship, with wide applications to dispute resolution. In a subsequent piece of research, the authors demonstrated what an AW solution applied to the Camp David Accord might have been—demonstrating how the general principle could be applied in a specific instance.[3]

In the second case, the challenge, while recognized as such within certain segments of society, had not actually been placed on the policy agenda in the sense that, at the time the quest for understanding was undertaken, government had not identified it as an issue engaging its responsibility. This could be because no organized interest had pressed for action; but it could also be because the likelihood of successful action seemed very low, given the inadequate knowledge-base.[4] If the latter, then the attainment of improved understanding, by adumbrating the outlines of a possible solution, could lead the government to assume responsibility for a solution. In this sense, knowledge precedes placement on the agenda, although the existence of an issue had already been recognized. The knowledge is not elicited in response to the policy challenge—it is already available once the challenge is defined as one engaging foreign policy. Recent scholarship on preventive diplomacy illustrates this case.[5]

The third, and final, item on our list of possibilities recognizes that the very realization that a challenge exists may stem from scholarly work. Here, the identification of a challenge results from the discovery of a problem or opportunity (e.g., the shrinking ozone layer, crisis instability in a nuclear rivalry) that requires policy action once the causal forces behind it (and its likely consequences) are identified. Calls for a policy response could also follow the discovery of a direct causal sequence whereby a recognized condition (e.g., Third World poverty) might produce a politically undesirable outcome (e.g., political or religious radicalism leading, in turn, to intense anti-American sentiment). In a slightly different vein, identification of a previously unexpected problem could result from an empirically supported suggestion to the effect that contemplated policies, while likely to attain their proximate objective, may carry far heavier costs than initially expected, or produce unanticipated secondary consequences. In all of these instances, scholarship encourages the realization that a challenge exists, a realization that may cause its placement on the policy agenda.

Where antecedent knowledge is brought to bear on an emerging challenge, as in the first of our two cases, this is most likely to involve instrumental, and in some cases contextual, knowledge. However, where scholarship contributes to problem identification (the third case), it often does so in the form of contextual understanding (including predictive knowledge), or as knowledge bearing on the consequences of policy. For example, in the late 1970s, predictions that the Soviet Union would soon become a net importer of oil caused U.S. foreign policy to take added steps to discourage Soviet attempts to gain a foothold in the Persian Gulf.[6] If the problems concern the unexpected costs of actual or proposed policies, the relevant knowledge involved would obviously be that which focuses on the consequences of various courses of action. For example, at the time of the 1991 Gulf War, scholars pointed out to government officials that public support for the intervention could not be sustained in the face of any significant number of U.S. casualties and a realization that, in addition to other considerations, may have deterred the Administration from taking the war to Baghdad in an attempt to remove Saddam Hussein from power.[7]

By contrast with the demand-driven model, and with the partial exception of first of our three illustrations, the supply-driven perspective does not imply a straight and singular path from knowledge to policy. Since policymakers, unaware that there is an issue to be addressed, have taken no steps to elicit the relevant understanding, it comes to their attention indirectly, from a variety of sources and in various ways. It may indeed have entered the policy process because decisionmakers, once alerted to the issue, begin casting around for existing and helpful knowledge. But it may also have been brought to their attention through a variety of other channels, including the media, journals of opinion, interest groups, congressional caucuses, foreign governments, and so forth. Even within this list of possible sources, the knowledge may have been transmitted from one to another as it made its way to decisionmakers' attention, and the path may have been far from straight.

Applicability and Desirability

The supply-and-demand–driven models represent stylized conceptions of a reality more complex than here portrayed. In many cases, the path by which SIR reaches decisionmakers reflects some elements of demand *and* some prior supply of ideas, arguments, or evidence. For example, a governmentally commissioned study may produce an impact upon policy, causing, in turn, a reconfiguration of domestic interests concerned with the policy, encouraging scholars to redefine certain research priorities, discovering in the process a new challenge, and so forth. It is also possible that scholars may be producing knowledge at their own initiative, while policymakers are seeking *additional* academic input within the same area of relevant knowledge. Coexistence and interaction notwithstanding, the two models do point to qualitatively different relationships between knowledge and policymaking, and we may inquire whether either is the dominant, or indeed preferable, relationship between the two.

The demand-driven model is sometimes dismissed as barely applicable to the world of actual democratic policymaking. It implies, in some eyes, a top-down rationalist society, in which decisions are made synoptically, by a unified decisionmaking machinery acting on the basis of a thoughtful consideration of alternatives in a situation of relative value consensus. Consequently, it is said to reveal an inaccurate conception of how knowledge is actually incorporated into policy.[8]

This criticism is overstated: while the demand-driven model does not dominate policymaking, it is a more meaningful part of the process than is often recognized. It may be especially pervasive in the foreign policy realm, where, in contrast to domestic policy, decisionmakers tend to agree on how problems should be defined and have some autonomy from legislative and interest-group pressures. In any event, there is no lack of examples of foreign policy challenges proceeding in search of applicable scholarship, either by consulting directly with knowledgeable scholars, by commissioning needed studies, or by incorporating scholars with appropriate expertise into the policymaking process.

For example, during the cold war, academia was called upon to provide analyses of Soviet politics and policy, of its capabilities and intentions, to explain to a barely comprehending government the motivations of the Soviet leadership and the roots of the regime,[9] and to help it understand how to avoid the dual pitfalls of superpower conflict and appeasement. Scholarship on Vietnam, and on counterinsurgency warfare, ranging from the work of Paul Mus to that of Ithiel de Sola Pool, was scrutinized as the Kennedy and Johnson Administrations sought a solution to their entanglement in Southeast Asia. Middle-Eastern experts, such as William Quandt and John Waterbury, have been called upon to help formulate effective policies concerning the Arab-Israeli conflict. The work of economists and political economists is consulted for clues on such problems as IMF reform and currency speculation.

Perhaps the most sustained and visible example of governmental reliance on scholarship has involved matters of military doctrine and its relation to foreign policy objectives. Scholars have been asked to explain how armed force could be used for political ends, in a situation where the imperative of nuclear war-avoidance competed with the desire to promote U.S. geopolitical cold war aims. How nuclear weapons could actually be put to political use was an issue that bedeviled many military and civilian policymakers, and the advice of academics was sought—possibly because generals had no more experience than social scientists in this area, and also because military experts were less skilled at the largely theoretical reasoning on which, in the absence of practical experience, nuclear strategy had to rely. Thus, RAND was intially established as a research unit for the Air Force. Scholars such as Bernard Brodie, William Kaufmann, Albert Wohlstetter, Colin Gray, and others, in a consulting capacity to the Department of Defense, made a significant contribution to early doctrines on the uses to which the nuclear arsenal could be put. In fact, much of the nation's declared nuclear doctrine in the early phases of the superpower competition was based on reasoning developed by scholars.[10]

When faced with the dilemma of how conventional force could support policy ends in the context of the balance of nuclear terror, academic advice was again solicited. The work of such political scientists as Henry Kissinger and Robert Osgood came to inform much official thinking in this area. Academic advice has since been sought on many related issues, ranging from

Mutual Assured Destruction, counterforce doctrines, the pursuit of crisis stability, to the implications of ballistic-missile defense systems.

Moreover, and to a greater extent than in most other nations, scholars have been brought directly into government service to help deal with issues on the foreign policy agenda. The list has not been limited to the likes of McGeorge Bundy, Walt Rostow, Henry Kissinger, Zbigniew Brzezinski, or Jeane Kirkpatrick, and others intimately linked to the history of America's postwar diplomacy. The staff of the National Security Council generally counts among its members a significant number of professional scholars, as do the upper reaches of the State and Defense Departments. Thus, in a variety of ways, but within the general confines of the demand-driven model, an enduring link between social science and policymaking has been established.

Its significance notwithstanding, the dominant relation between knowledge and policy may not be reflected in the demand-driven model's assumptions. Most social science does not enter the policy process in response to an identified challenge, or by a singular and direct path, while policymaking can only exceptionally be conceived in terms of a defined decisional unit (perhaps an individual) that makes decisions according to its understanding of the optimal course of action.

Problems usually do not precede the scholarly work that may aid its solution. Because it tends to be rooted in professional incentives that do not include practical applications, scholarly knowledge generally does not take the form of a response to a practical problem. Social scientists usually select their research tasks on the basis of simple intellectual curiosity, a sense of what is most challenging, disciplinary agendas, career calculations, and a variety of idiosyncratic circumstances. Typically, these choices have little to do with the policy consequences their findings may produce. A substantial portion of the knowledge social scientists generate may eventually find policy applications, but most often that is not the initial purpose. Accordingly, much of what scholarship has offered policymakers by way of improved understanding of the challenges they face has not been in explicit response to an issue on the government's agenda regarding which the counsel of social scientists has been sought. For example, much academic thinking on the viability of the Soviet Union antedated the junctures at which these questions were seriously addressed in Washington DC. Similarly, work on the origin and behavior of "rogue states" has appeared before government placed this issue high on its foreign policy concerns.[11] The consequences of a discrepancy between rates of social mobilization in developing nations and the ability of their political institutions to respond were recognized by academics before they were acknowledged by policymakers.[12] Even within the nuclear area, questions of crisis stability often were raised by scholars before they were addressed by national decisionmakers.[13]

The most obvious virtue of the demand-driven process is that it involves a direct response to established needs. Its limitation is that it provides no service beyond that which those in power currently seek. By contrast, the supply-driven model assumes a willingness and ability to anticipate and shape the agenda—to guide policy goals as well as means—by contributing to the democratic dialogue a fund of knowledge that otherwise would not be considered. By implication, the demand-driven model assumes a considerable degree of value congruence between scholars and statesmen, while the supply-driven model is constrained by no such assumptions.

In addition, the supply-driven model does not imply a straight path from the Ivory Tower to the corridors of power, since the information and analyses used in policymaking rarely flow in a linear fashion. In any political system, but most obviously in a democracy, policy reflects a complex process of bargaining among a wide variety of groups and institutions, one that involves intricate and overlapping channels of information and influence. Preferences and power flow from many directions, in a series of sometimes intersecting paths, while policy choices represent an amalgam of partial decisions and commitments made at various points.[14] Accordingly, a model reflecting this complexity implies a different role for social scientific knowledge than one focusing on vertical flows of information and influence along unique paths, under the assumption that decisions are taken at the system's pinnacle in response to an idealized, highly rationalistic consideration of options and their implications. In the more complex model, knowledge originates in various parts of the polity, it traces multiple, indirect, and sometimes discontinuous trajectories, and its impact on decisions may have little to do with the reasons for which it was produced. As one scholar has pointed out:

> If the decision-making process is perceived as a looser coupling among problems, solutions, choice opportunities and participants, we should not expect research results to be disseminated and used as the integrated totality they are in research reports. Instead, knowledge, including scientifically-produced knowledge, flows into the decision-making process through obscure channels from many different sources, and this results in a more general awareness of the way the world appears and is structured.[15]

Even within the context of the focused purpose and hierarchical structure of government bureaucracies, the most appropriate model of how the process works may be the "garbage can" model.[16] Here, the policy process within the organization presents itself as a series of "choice opportunities," into which participants may throw problems and proposed solutions by expending a certain amount of energy. Inputs into the final policy decision are many, their sequence may be impossible to trace, and the final decision may not exactly resemble any of the individual inputs that shaped it. Every individual input may stem from a fairly rational decision, but none may be identifiable in the final policy.

Consequently, the path by which some subset of that knowledge is led to decisionmakers is unlikely to be singular or linear. It may, if published in a sufficiently accessible form, affect the process by way of its impact on public opinion—especially elite opinion. Potentially relevant knowledge may reach specialized congressional staff (e.g., the staff of the House International Relations Committee or the Senate Foreign Affairs Committee); or that knowledge may be consulted within a variety of federal agencies, perhaps finding its way, along with other inputs, to the upper reaches of the administrative hierarchy. Academic knowledge may be also injected into the policy process via the influence of the media—which, having acquainted itself with potentially relevant scholarly findings, brings them to the attention of other actors in the political process. For example, Thomas Homer-Dixon's research on the impact of population growth and environmental degradation on international conflict was referred to in an *Atlantic Monthly* article by journalist Robert Kaplan. The article, in turn, was read by Vice President Gore, who invited Homer-Dixon to brief him on the problem; soon, President Clinton's Undersecretary of State for Global Affairs described this research as "immensely valuable and important," as "giving some intellectual content to a crucial debate."[17]

The various paths from scholarship to decisionmakers may be traveled simultaneously, and they may meet and even overlap in a complex pattern. A careful examination of the manner in which social science has affected U.S. foreign policy would certainly find that it has been far more subtle and complex than the demand-driven model alone could suggest. The flow of influence on matters of superpower relations involved various layers of both the executive and the legislative branch of government, but it also included public opinion, the media, and a number of very active interest groups. Scholarly thinking on matters regarding East-West relations, the uses of force, and the prospects for arms control often reached educated strata of the public, as well as the media. And even interest groups such as the hawk-ish Committee on the Present Danger and the dovish Committee on East-West Accord often relied on scholarly analyses in support of their positions. Even on specific political-military questions, such as, for example, the desirability of a Ballistic Missile Defense (BMD) system, the national debate often engaged informed academics.[18] To the extent that this participation affected ultimate policy choices, the precise manner and path may be impossible to trace, since the impact was felt at too many separate junctures in an intricate, and sometimes opaque, structure of political influence. Nevertheless, the impact was certainly felt. As a leading student of the relationship between social science and policy explains it:

> the policymaker is often unaware of the source of his ideas. He "keeps up with the literature," or is briefed by aides, or reads state-of-the-art reviews of research in intellectual magazines or social science stories in the *New York Times*, *Washington Post*, or *Wall Street Journal*. Bits of information seep into his mind, uncatalogued, without citation. He finds it very difficult to retrieve the reference to any single bit of knowledge. If we ask him about the effect of social research on his decisions, he usually will not be able to given an accurate account—or even be aware that he derived his ideas from the social sciences.[19]

Thus, while the demand-driven model is appropriate in particular instances, the supply-driven model's applications are broader. Were this not the case, the relevance of scholarly knowledge would be limited to challenges already on the agenda. In fact, policy-relevant SIR has a broader role and more ambitious role, by shaping the definition of policy problems and priorities and by suggesting new ways of perceiving the world.

A caveat is useful here. The differences between the demand- and supply-driven models should not be equated with the distinction between applied and pure research that characterizes much of the hard sciences. In the social sciences, a smooth and frequent transition from pure to applied is not as often encountered, and we cannot assume that disinterested scholarship would often become policy relevant. In part, this is simply because the lines demarcating the two levels of knowledge are not etched in nearly as clear-cut a way. In the natural sciences, the movement from pure to applied knowledge generally implies one (or both) of two things. As a rule, it means that an empirical relationship discovered in one general context must be examined in some narrower subset of the same context, or in a slightly different context. For example, it may be necessary to find out whether a cure that is found to work on laboratory mice does as satisfactory a job when applied to humans. Often this will involve bringing additional control variables (ceteris paribus conditions) into the causal relation linking treatment and cure. Sometimes too, the transition from pure to applied knowledge involves finding ways to manipulate the causal variable discovered in a relationship, so that it can be used to produce the desired effect in a context other than the research setting.

In the social sciences, however, the research setting is no different from the world encountered by policymakers. For that reason, the barrier between pure and policy-relevant knowledge is determined mainly by *purpose*.[20] (In other words, the social sciences encounter the problem of external validity in their research much less frequently than do the natural and other experimental sciences.[21]) Knowledge may become relevant when that is its *intent*, i.e., when the questions asked are informed by a desire to produce policy consequences, or, at least by a realization that important practical consequences could follow. Where this is not the case, knowledge that has no potential for policy relevance does not usually become relevant by a further specification of the context to which the discovered relationships apply. As Lindblom and Cohen observe with respect to the social sciences: "what is ordinarily called 'applied research' is an effort of distinctive character in its own right, developing its own generalizations, when needed, through its own efforts. In short, when social engineers need authoritative knowledge, they must develop it for themselves."[22]

The Four Settings of Policy-Relevant Knowledge[23]

Whether relevant knowledge enters the policy process via a demand- or supply-driven mode, it is produced within a certain professional setting, which in turn determines the character of the knowledge that is offered. Four such settings seem to encompass most scholarly work on foreign policy. One way of distinguishing them is in terms of their proximity to the policy process; another is by the ratio of generalizations to specific, factual statements (initial conditions) they are likely to make. Obviously, the two criteria overlap: the most general and abstract work is likely to be produced by scholars farthest from the policy process, and vice versa. Thus, although

direct links between scholars and policymakers may exist at the level of each
setting, together the four tend to act as transmission mechanisms—leading
from the general to the specific, from the groves of academia to government
offices. As one moves through the four settings, generalizations get fleshed
out with increasingly specific initial conditions, becoming most directly useful to policymakers. Although each setting produces its own literature and
a defined group of scholars, they are more interconnected than might seem
at first glance.

The underlying continuum on which these groups are arrayed can be
visualized as a horizontal "ladder of abstraction" consisting of various categories of knowledge, arrayed in order of decreasing degrees of specific empirical content.[24] One might stop at a given rung of the ladder when satisfied
with the kind of understanding available at that level of generality.[25] But one
can also imagine moving back and forth across the levels, or borrowing from
one to enhance insights available at another, depending on the analytic
problem at hand. In practical terms, since there is less professional distance
between any two adjacent types of activities than across the entire spectrum,
a series of partial bridges is already in place across much of it.

These IR activities can be arrayed as indicated in Figure 3.[26]

Group I: General Theory

Scholars at this level seek to produce general propositions linking broad
classes of empirical phenomena. As such, their work is not typically attached

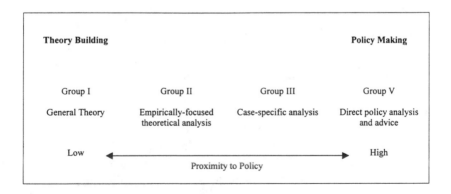

FIGURE 3 The Four Settings of Policy-Relevant Scholarship

to specific categories of issues, actors, time periods, or geographic regions. It focuses on truly general propositions rather than statements about initial conditions (in the terms used in chapter 2, all G's and no I's). Highly general work, these scholars contend, is preferable since it explains a greater range of specific cases than less general work.[27] Because general theories seek to transcend substantive contexts, they often (but not always) take a deductive form. The best developed Group I approach in International Relations is Rational Choice. It focuses on the processes and outcomes of strategic interaction, involving deductions about people's behavior from broad and simple assumptions about human incentives. In the United States, general theoretical work of this and other kinds is typically published in such journals as *International Organization, World Politics, International Studies Quarterly,* and *The American Political Science Review.*

Group I scholars ask such questions as: When do actors cooperate in world politics?[28] To what extent are actors' preferences a function of the strategic situations they are in, and to what extent are they exogenous to those situations?[29] How are domestic and international arenas connected?[30] More than other analysts, Group I scholars focus on the broader context in which foreign policy is made and carried out. One such issue of importance to IR analysts is the degree to which international anarchy necessarily creates a competitive context for action in world politics, a position long associated with the Realist tradition.[31] As these questions illustrate, while Group I scholars may suggest ways to produce particular policy outcomes, this is rarely their main concern. Their typical contributions to policy-relevant knowledge come in two other areas. Some of their work, such as that on the nature and limits of international anarchy and the conditions necessary for cooperation, focuses on the range of possibilities for effective international action. In addition, generic theories of strategic choice and interaction, by providing a way to understand other actors' reactions to certain choices, can help illuminate some indirect costs of policy options.

Group II: Empirically Focused Theoretical Analysis

Here, specific categories of empirical questions are analyzed—questions tied to particular categories of substantive issues, temporal, and spatial domains. Whereas General Theory deals with the most generic and perennial attributes of foreign-policy choices and outcomes, Empirically Focused

Analysis concerns itself with narrower sets of issues, and in addressing them pays closer attention to specific sets of empirical conditions. As such, the range within which explanatory variables vary is typically more restricted than in work done by Group I scholars, though this is often left implicit rather than explicit in Group analyses.

Group II work produces two kinds of SIR literatures. One consists of regional or area studies. This work assumes that certain mixes or ranges of variables distinguish regions from one another. Regional specialists often have some training or interest in general theory, but their expertise centers on an in-depth knowledge of the culture, politics, and historical context within which particular regional patterns are assumed to operate. A second kind of Group II literature explores theory-driven empirical puzzles. Puzzles are nonobvious phenomena for which there is no adequate (or at least widely accepted) explanation.[32] While this work implicitly shares the area-specialists' assumptions that certain mixes or ranges of variables distinguish one set of problems from others, the models in this type of literature tend to be grounded more explicitly in theories that purport to apply across actors and regions. Cognitive models, for example, allow scholars to specify how psychological variables can lead to biases in the choice process and, by extension, to suggest ways in which individuals or organizations can reduce such unwanted sources of error.[33] Similarly, some work on economic sanctions is grounded in more general notions of strategic coercion, vulnerability, and dependence. Group II scholars thus deal with initial conditions as well as generalizations (Is as well as Gs), though the emphasis is on generalizations.

Journals specializing in Group II work include, among others, *Latin American Research Review, Asian Survey, International Security, Security Studies, Global Governance,* and *Political Science Quarterly.* Group II publication outlets overlap with those of Group I: *World Politics* and *International Organization* examine some region-and issue-specific empirical puzzles, while *International Security* at times focuses on issues of more general scope. But what distinguishes Group II work is a focus on puzzles that originate in and apply to particular substantive referents, rather than arguments that seek to transcend such referents.

Group II work contributes to policy-relevant knowledge in each of the ways we have discussed so far. Its contribution to instrumental knowledge comes largely from work that explores how various policy tools can produce desired results. Alexander George's "abstract conceptual models of strategies"[34] fall in this category; there are now large literatures on the logic and track records of deterrence, coercive diplomacy, and economic coercion. What George calls "generic knowledge of conditions favoring a strategy"[35] is one way of providing what we call contextual knowledge: under what environmental conditions is success likeliest, or least likely, for the use of such instruments? And by illuminating the effects of psychological biases on people's perceptions of the tradeoffs they face, Group II work on cognition provides insight on a key kind of indirect cost associated with choice— the evaluation of opportunities foregone by choices.

Group III: Case-Specific Analysis

Work in this group directly addresses certain categories of foreign policy issues. For this reason, its empirical referents are more narrowly specified than those of Group II work, and the questions posed involve more narrowly defined outcomes. They thus deal in more depth with I's than Group II analyses, though the purpose is to understand G's as well. Group III scholars recognize that the logic underlying policy may need to be fleshed out in generalizable terms, so that lessons beyond specific cases can be drawn and decisionmakers might be spared needless trial and error.[36] Still, within this group of analysts, general knowledge is desired mainly for the insights it offers on specific policy problems. For example, a U.S. official who has directed the Foreign Policy Studies Program at the Brookings Institution wrote a book on how military power can be effectively used in the post–cold war period. He borrowed ideas about force and diplomacy from such classic Group I and II scholars as Thomas Schelling and Alexander George,[37] but focused on issues interesting a policy audience. Group III publication outlets include journals such as *Survival*, *Orbis*, as well as many products of think tanks.

Case-Specific Analysis is produced largely in think tanks, at least in the United States. For reasons discussed in chapter 1, Group I and II work dominates the study of IR within most U.S. university faculties. But Group III work can also be found in universities with international-affairs or public-policy programs, as these focus on professional training rather than generic knowledge for its own sake. Think tanks operate at the boundary between government and the part of the academic community that has a sustained interest in public policy.[38] They draw into dialogue people who "cross the conventional boundaries between types of expertise and experiences. University professors sit [a]round the table with military officers and diplomats, with journalists from the quality press, businessmen and bankers, politicians and their research assistants."[39] As a result, think tanks and policy programs are the major places where people move back and forth between more theoretical and more applied activities and roles, bringing the mental habits of one to bear on the concerns of the other.

A substantial amount of direct policy analysis is conducted in major think tanks, and they come in many varieties. Some cover much of domestic and foreign policy, while others specialize in military security issues, international trade policy, or region-specific issues. Research associates at these institutions typically examine the concepts that underlie policy, using approaches drawn from a variety of professional and academic fields. They remain involved with policymakers through seminars or through publications disseminated to working officials. At the same time, they try to remain detached from day-to-day operational issues. Their distinctive intellectual product is a longer-term perspective on foreign-policy issues than most day-to-day policy literature can afford.

Group III analysts might focus on either form of policy relevance we have identified, though their work on instrumental relations tends to pay closer attention to *ceteris paribus* conditions than work done at higher levels of generality. Because case-focused scholarship can be used to derive the kinds of singular statements (I's) that are needed to draw conclusions about specific actors and issues, it can often be directly helpful to policymakers in obvious ways. For example, practitioners and scholars agree that it can be useful to understand an actor's values and mind-set in dealing with him. Such "actor-specific behavioral models"[40] can help officials understand the key initial conditions relevant to the situation and actor they face, and perhaps some of the broader context as well.

Group IV: Direct Policy Analysis and Advice

Work at this level is different in purpose than in Groups I, II, or III. Rather than seeking to understand the world as it is, these analyses prescribe specific solutions to problems or particular approaches to international issues. In other words, the aim here is "engineering" rather than "basic science."[41] Work in this group is therefore concerned with issues even more specific than those addressed by Group III analysts, since Group IV studies are confined to a particular point in time and space. Consequently, the explicit focus is almost entirely on I's, while G's remain largely implicit.

This kind of work is written chiefly by current or former practitioners for other practitioners. It typically appears in *Foreign Affairs, Foreign Policy*, and the op-ed pieces of major newspapers. Those in the target audience typically see practical experience and the specific context in which a policy problem arises as the key factors that must be brought to bear in analyzing it. To the extent that they make explicit use of generalizations, it is the end product rather than the logical structure of the theoretical arguments that concerns them.[42] This segment of the IR profession is rarely found in universities, except in small numbers at international-affairs or public-policy schools. More commonly, those who do Group IV analysis hold positions in think tanks, international-affairs consulting firms, NGOs, and IGOs, as well as within government. Their main concern is with instrumental relationships and the direct costs of policy, and they focus more on identifying quite specific initial conditions of interest to top officials than on producing general propositions. What is found here is work closest to the ordinary knowledge of policymakers. The general propositions they do employ tend to be borrowed from Groups II and III, although the borrowed product is often poorly digested.

As this categorization suggests, policy-relevant work occurs at each tier of professional activity within the overall IR field. Contrary to the frequently expressed view, "policy relevance" does not require work at a low level of explanatory abstraction. To identify the possibilities for choice and the likely consequences of policy choices, knowledge of all four types is needed. To a greater or lesser degree, each relies on generalizations about how the world works and on statements about pertinent initial conditions. Even Direct Policy Analysis and Advice—a type of work that emphasizes how certain results might be achieved or avoided under very particular conditions— requires a general causal understanding of the linkages between independent and dependent variables.[43] This point suggests the fundamental practical value of sound and substantively meaningful research. Since policymakers will, in any case, use general propositions to do their jobs (even if these proposition remain implicit), they might as well be of high quality.

This conclusion would seem to invite SIR scholars to produce thoughtful, well-crafted work that speaks to the possibilities for action and its expected consequences. But for reasons discussed in chapter 1, IR theorists and policy specialists have tended to go their separate ways; conversations within these two broadly defined communities are much more numerous than conversations across them. How then can it make sense to argue that academic work in this field can be useful beyond the Ivory Tower only when they borrow *more* from each other? Solving this problem requires reversing well-entrenched professional incentives among both scholars and policymakers, possibly a Sisyphian task. Nevertheless, if we examine the way in which at least some people in these four groups actually share ideas and empirical findings, we find more pragmatic interaction than might be expected. Understanding these relationships and the synergies they produce will show *how* good academic work can become accessible and thereby at least potentially useful to policymakers, and how IR theories themselves might be improved as a result.

From the Ivory Tower to the Corridors of Power and Back Again[44]

When seen as adjacent to one another, these four groups of activity constitute transmission links between IR theorists and practitioners. Among the many possibilities for collaboration, Group I theories can be used to inform policy analysis directly, or they can help reframe Group II questions in ways that clarify various IR puzzles, making them more useful to decisionmakers. Group III analysts can borrow general propositions from Groups I and II and use them to derive theoretically informed yet timely analyses of particular types of issues that can help policymakers. Group II puzzles can similarly speak directly to policymakers or, to make them more accessible to officials, they can be interpreted through Group III work.

Let us examine some of these possibilities in greater detail. Consider, for example, the practical value of one particular Group I theoretical perspective, rational choice. Over the last few decades, rational choice has had a major impact on political science and economics. It is designed to predict policy preferences, given actors' objectives and their perception of the strategic situation they face. It does not constitute a general theory of politics, since it does not explain why people value particular outcomes, norms, or other objectives as ends in themselves. For these reasons and because of questions about the veracity of its fundamental assumptions, it has become highly controversial within the SIR community and the broader field of political science.[45] It can nonetheless provide policymakers with two kinds of useful knowledge. First, it can tell them how best to achieve their objectives, if they know the preferences and power positions of the relevant actors on some issue. In game-theoretic terms, this amounts to specifying any equilibria that exist in a strategic situation. By this criterion, rational choice has bridged at least part of the gap between IR theorists and some U.S. foreign-policy practitioners. In 1989, a CIA official said that spatial models, a type of rational-choice work, had generated correct predictions of outcomes in 90 percent of the instances with which he was familiar.[46] Depending on how and how often the consumers actually used these analyses, such a track record could amount to a direct, working connection between Groups I and IV.

A second way in which rational choice connects to policy practice in IR is less direct, yet no less important. By providing a general theory of strategic interaction, rational choice can situate within a common, intuitively plausible framework the Group II research that deal with particular types or conditions of strategic interaction. In this role, theory serves to organize existing knowledge of a particular type.[47] By understanding some key commonalities in strategic interaction across issues, actors, and time periods, Group III analysts might be better able to locate and frame for policymakers the specific empirical analyses officials need. For example, conflicting evidence about the usefulness of economic sanctions might be easier to sort out if actors' expectations of future conflict were built into the analysis. Surprisingly, the case-study literature seems to have ignored this possibility. A formal model shows that while initiators of sanctions are more eager to coerce adversaries than allies, since the policy rewards for success are greater, adversaries resist such pressure much harder, fearing a redistribution of material resources and reputation that could hurt them more than standing firm. As a result, while one gains more from coercing an adversary successfully than an ally, success is likelier with an ally.[48] The analytic payoff for policymakers here is greater clarity about the tradeoffs involved in using sanctions in these two types of situations.

It turns out that Case-Specific Analysts (Group III) play a key role in linking General Theory and Empirically Focused Theoretical Analysis to policymakers' concerns. Group III analyses benefit from Group II's efforts to put empirical meat on general theoretical propositions and, to a lesser extent, from Group I's interest in processes common to various substantive problems. In the same way, Group II analysts benefit from empirical studies, such as those done by Group III analysts, that explore substantively important real world cases in detail. But Group I and II analysts can focus on producing and fleshing out general propositions without *directly* exploring their practical implications. A distinct role for Case-Specific Analysts is to connect the work of theorists and policy specialists, which they do by deriving and disseminating statements about important sets of initial conditions in international relations. Insofar as these singular statements exemplify substantively important general patterns, practitioners have a generic frame within which to interpret specific cases.

Group III analysts are well-positioned for this role. While many of them have social-science training, they use it mainly to structure and inform policy choices rather than to extend purely academic knowledge.[49] Policymakers may find themselves in situations in which this kind of analysis can benefit them. Since they are rarely equipped to probe the logical underpinnings or evidentiary basis of theorists' analyses, they sometimes feel compelled to accept analyses that appear to be plausible more or less on faith. Because Group III analysts typically have enough scholarly training to understand the work of theorists and, at the same time, are familiar with policymakers' problems, they function well as go-betweens.[50]

Group III analysts may play an even more pivotal role in years to come. Since the end of the cold war, interest in foreign policy in the United States has dropped substantially outside the Executive Branch and the broader professional foreign-policy community. Despite the proliferation of global problems, many of which significantly affect U.S. interests, many members of Congress are reluctant to fund foreign projects, and the major foundations are less interested than before in funding foreign-policy studies. The challenge for international-affairs think tanks in this environment, as the head of the Brookings Institution put it, is to "shape the public agenda and [be] useful to policy makers." Brookings fellows are thus being asked to write shorter research summaries, or "policy briefs," for politicians and foreign-policy officials rather than the longer, denser monographs of years past.[51] To the degree that they reach their intended audience, they will have bridged the relatively short gap between Groups III and IV. The task may not be that difficult if the goal is to reach career foreign-policy professionals. While interested mainly in work that deals directly with issues on their desks, career professionals are likelier to use ideas from Group II and III work than political-level officials. This reflects severe limits on top officials' time, but also different training and intellectual habits, with career officials likelier to have been exposed to theoretical work at some point.[52]

One assumption behind such efforts to "sell" practical ideas to foreign-policymakers is that much of the conceptual work has already been done in SIR, especially in areas of high U.S. policy interest such as arms control and Middle Eastern conflict processes. The priority now, from this standpoint, is to get the ideas already available in front of officials, so that they might be used.[53] Such efforts deserve support in areas where the intellectual work is indeed ready to be applied. We have suggested a number of such examples thus far, and two more sets of examples are discussed at length in Chapters 5 and 6. Ironically, however, this view gives IR theorists more credit than they deserve. Most theory-driven work in IR falls into Group II, and much of that portion suffers from a fundamental problem. Many arguments found here are presented as if they are unconditional, when in fact they are highly conditional; the defining empirical conditions that affect relationships among the variables are often left unidentified. Moreover, the conditions that determine the status of these variables—i.e., the necessary ceteris paribus and contextual circumstances—often are left out.

In much of the contemporary Group II literature, disagreements often stem from very different empirical assumptions about the world. For example, Realists and Liberals implicitly agree that the compatibility of actors' preferences drives the strategic importance of power, and thus whether people care more about relative or absolute payoffs. What analysts in these two schools actually disagree about is how compatible preferences typically tend to be, with Realists assuming very little and Liberals typically assuming more so. Better specified arguments, incorporating the various sorts of relevant knowledge described in chapter 2, might attenuate these unproductive debates.

For example, a spiral model (one reflecting the lessons about inadvertent conflict generated by the 1914 crisis) claims that threats reinforce existing security dilemmas and are thus self-defeating. A Munich-syndrome model reflects the polar opposite kind of case and conclusion: threats establish or reinforce an initiator's credibility and induce adversaries to retreat. But neither indicates more generally when and why other cases fit these patterns.[54] If the issue of which argument is correct truly depends on the case(s) one is examining,[55] underspecification not only creates a false theoretical problem; it gives those that want to apply the model a misleading sense of which cases it really explains.

One way to improve the generalizations that dominate Group II arguments is by constructing and analyzing typologies. A "type" is a group of cases in which the values of the variables are strongly associated. A typology asserts the relevant variables tend to occur together in fairly few combinations.[56] For example, it is often claimed that war stems from misjudgments about another actor's capability or resolve. We may, however, be able to match more precisely certain kinds of perceptual errors and causal effects. Misperception of another's resolve may be common to actors within authoritarian systems, where the analysis or flow of information is politically circumscribed. Misperceptions about another's capabilities may be common where relative power positions are shifting rapidly. As these examples suggest, typologies present a systematic way to be precise about the mixes and values of variables.

Admittedly, relying too heavily on typologies could impede the development of more powerful Group II arguments. One can almost always specify contingent conditions that will yield a valid generalization, provided that a causal pattern appears in *some* cases.[57] To avoid the proliferation of very narrow empirical generalizations, Empirically Focused Theoretical Analysis must ultimately move beyond unconnected typologies and seek to explain how different mixes of ceteris paribus and contextual variables reflect more fundamental dimensions of variation in international relations.

From a Group I standpoint, better specified arguments would also be beneficial, by helping scholars see how various theory-driven empirical analyses are linked. If it is true that many supposedly generic SIR propositions actually reflect distinctive cases, no matter how distinctive these empirical patterns actually turn out to be, they ultimately presuppose a set of logically interdependent principles that would explain them.[58] A long-range theoretical task, then, is to situate typologies as instances of more truly generic arguments. Some policymakers—and not just committed holists—no doubt would bypass any such work on the grounds that it is too abstract to be useful. Others, though, might come to see that it can be intellectually efficient to explain specific cases through highly generic lenses. Group III analysts can be pivotal in making this kind of connection for those who want to use it.

Conclusions

The manner in which social science can improve foreign policy transcends the demand-driven model's vision in which decisionmakers, stymied by a gap in their knowledge, turn to scholars for the missing bit of understanding. Although policymakers frequently seek advice from academia on crucial matters of foreign policy, scholarship produces its impact in ways both broader and less direct. These paths are captured by the supply-driven model. One implication of this point is that social science can shape the policy agenda by providing an improved understanding of problems and of the context in which they are embedded. This can occur when ultimately-relevant knowledge is produced before any challenge to which it could be applied is identified. It can also happen when a recognized challenge not previously on the agenda is put there once plausible knowledge to deal with it has been generated. Social scientific scholarship also helps identify the challenges that must be addressed, alerting both society and policymakers to where their efforts should be directed.

Thus, the supply-driven model adds *agenda-shaping* to *problem-solving* on the list of scholarship's contributions to the conduct of U.S. foreign affairs. At the same time, the benefits suggested by the supply-driven model do not manifest themselves as a direct, unmediated, link between knowledge and policy, and the effect cannot always be identified.

Moreover, and whether the demand-or supply-drive model is applicable, the transmission links between the Ivory Tower and the corridors of power are best understood in terms of the roles of four major groups of international relations scholarship, and the links between them. They are primarily distinguished by the ratio of generalizations to initial conditions that is at the basis of their explanatory work, and of the scope of applicability of any recommendations they may formulate. Each plays a distinct role in the creation and transmission of relevant knowledge. Work at various levels would benefit from a specification of instrumental relations that was more attentive to ceteris paribus conditions and to the contextual circumstances that determine the status and values of the variables encompassed by the instrumental relationships.

In any case, the impact of rigorous scholarship is not limited to its ability to provide empirically correct understanding. Because of the reduction in subjectivity it assumes, it may also facilitate communication within the policymaking process. As Carol Weiss observes: "social science provides thinking people, in government and out, with a common grammar. . . . The common terms, data, models, and orientations bring coherence to the discussion of public policy making."[59] If assumptions are stated as clearly as academia's epistemological canons demand, if the inferential process underpinning scholarly thinking follows accepted rules of deduction and induction, if concepts are clearly defined and explicitly translated into empirical terms, then the likelihood that the actors in the process will talk past each other decreases.

For all the reasons discussed in this chapter, and within the limitations on the supply and authoritativeness of relevant scholarly work, there is room for relevant knowledge and for improved interaction between its producers and its consumers. However, all of this leaves one important question un-answered: if scholarship can benefit policy, should it seek to do so? The question is especially pertinent because of the frequent assumption that the quality of disinterested knowledge is bound to suffer from attempts at having it address policymakers' concerns. We take up this issue in the next chapter.

4 Scholarship and Relevance: Is There a Tradeoff?

Even if scholarship can help guide the conduct of international affairs, it does not necessarily follow that it should be used for that purpose. From a scholarly perspective the costs may be too great. Prima facie, it surely is better to be useful than not to, *unless*, perhaps, the costs in terms of international relations scholarship are too great. Academics have a responsibility to their own calling as well as to national policy goals—if the claims of the two should collide, it is not obvious that the latter's should prevail. The issue, then, is whether the production of knowledge with concrete bearing on practical problems may undermine the intellectual foundations on which that knowledge rests. Two broad and occasionally intersecting categories of concerns have been expressed in this regard: the first involves the proper relation of scholar to the society of which he or she is a part; the second concerns the consequences of a quest for policy relevance on the quality of scholarship—in particular, development of good theory. We will assess the two concerns in turn.

Relevance, Scholars and Society

The particular nature of the social scientist's position flows from the requirement of objectivity, which assumes that the scholar must examine his or her society from the position of a detached observer. Such a stance requires aloofness from societal values and interests that might interfere with

an objective approach to analysis and data-gathering.[1] In turn, this requirement is said to (a) constrain the scholar's professional ability to engage in
controversies about the fundamental values that should drive policy, and,
(b) require a commitment to preserving the epistemological integrity of his
work from standards of evaluation external to the academic community. It
is sometimes feared that the constraints may be violated and the commitment abandoned where knowledge seeks to guide the conduct of policy.

Ends, means, and the Problem of Value-Neutrality

The worry is that policy-relevant work may violate an ideal of education
and scholarship implied by the liberal, value-neutral, conception of the democratic state. As philosopher Michael Root has argued, the preference for a
value-neutral state, committed to procedures of democratic decisionmaking
but not to the promotion of one view of the public good over another, is a
core component of the liberal creed.[2] Often, within this creed, commitment
to value-neutrality is extended to the pursuit of knowledge. Thus, it is felt
that scholarship should encourage epistemologically proper methods of inquiry, without, at the same time, seeking to promote a particular set of social
values via this inquiry.[3] The latter are grounded in moral feelings and cor-
porate interests, with no scientific truth-value, whereas only a concern with
statements possessing truth-value is the business of the social sciences. "The
liberal state is forbidden to use the law; the liberal schools are forbidden to
use the classroom or curriculum; and the liberal social sciences are forbidden to use teaching or research to endorse one conception of the good over
another.[4]"

An implication sometimes drawn from the liberal ethos is that, while
political science may concern itself with the analysis of means, any discussion of ends lies outside its province. In George Herbert Mead's words,
"Science does not attempt to formulate the end which social and moral
conduct should pursue."[5] Decisions about ends flow from democratic procedures of aggregating societal preferences, not from the arguments of scholars. The business of the academic enterprise involves Questions of Path, not
Questions of Covenant.[6]

If Mead's dictum were accepted, there might be reason to worry that
policy-relevance could jeopardize scholarly independence. Because science
should be concerned only with means, those who advise on the pursuit of

ends would not be value-neutral. By proposing explicit courses of action, they cannot avoid urging certain ends over others and thus certain values over others. Such partisanship might then undermine their intellectual independence. The solution is sometimes thought to lie in an explicitly restricted definition of the analyst's role, in injunctions to the effect that such a person must act as an agent, not as a principal. In this vein, Alexander George and Richard Smoke have maintained that:

> Policy science, as we would define it, is itself value free, although in a different sense from the value-freedom of empirical theory. The policy theorist, acting as such, accepts the values of the constitutionally authorized decision-makers of his nation and offers contingent advice: "if you want to accomplish x, do y in your policy."[7]

This solution to the ends-means problem may seem simple and workable; actually it is elusive. It assumes that a meaningful distinction can be drawn between the ends and means of political action—that science can help society select the latter without affecting its positions toward the former. This can rarely be done. The distinction between ends and means is tenable only with regard to "pure" ends: those that can be defined as objectives in and of themselves, not as a means for attaining any other, more general or more elevated, goal. Although a set of "pure" ends surely exists, it remains that: (a) this set has very few members, and, (b) these are axiomatically desirable. Objectives of this sort may include "justice," "welfare," "felicity," i.e., goals that virtually everyone would embrace and whose meaning is definable only in the most abstract terms. Similarly, the ultimate goals of U.S. foreign policy—involving peace, prosperity, and the promotion of democracy—are never seriously questioned.[8] Lacking a firm empirical content, they are of very limited analytical use. By the same token, social scientists have no incentive to either urge or discourage their pursuit, and, in the abstract sense given to such objectives, no one would argue that we need to understand how they should be attained.

But once one moves even slightly away from what amounts to trivial statements of "pure" ends, almost every goal is, at some remove, subordinate to them by an assumed instrumental relationship, either direct or indirect. In other words, virtually every nontrivial societal goal is ultimately an instrumental goal, so that virtually all political arguments and policy debates, even within a relatively broad common frame of political values, really involve means. Democrats and Republicans, liberals and conservatives, hardly ever argue about pure, or "ultimate," ends; instead they typically argue only about the proper methods of proceeding toward them. For example, no one disputes the need to reduce poverty, but the desirability of doing so via government or market forces may be sharply debated. There is rarely disagreement on the need to improve American schools, but not everyone concurs on the sort of knowledge that should be conveyed to the nation's youth, or whether this best done via private or public schools, or perhaps by a system of school vouchers. Everyone agrees that peace is desirable, but not everyone agrees on the proper mix of force and diplomacy that its pursuit requires.

In this sense, it is emphatically not the case that ends are value-laden and sharply debated while means are value-free and uncontroversial. As a rule, it is precisely the other way around: virtually everyone seems to subscribe to the same restricted set of noninstrumental aims. There are, however, many possible ways by which one might try to achieve these ends, and much value judgment and consequent debate surrounds these means. Because quarrels almost always involve ways of attaining ends, the injunction that policy-relevant work must be value-free is quite inconsistent with a recommendation that it concern itself with means alone. It is also vacuous, because no one wishes to debate ultimate ends, but short of these the distinction between ends and instruments is, most of the time, meaningless.

To illustrate the argument, note that George and Smoke find it necessary to qualify their notion of value-free policy research:

> When necessary, the policy analyst should indeed urge that the objectives of current and contemplated policy be redefined to make them more consistent with what he perceives to be the final goals of the policymaker. However, he does not assert his own "final" goals or values (except perhaps negatively by declining to assist in implementing certain policies).[9]

Quite apart from the admission that scholars may, after all, seek to influence "final" goals negatively (logically no different a matter from trying to do so "positively"), the authors recognize that policy scientists can engage in goal manipulation—it all depends on the level of the goal.

All of this might lead one to suggest that academics should engage in *no* policy-relevant work, but this is not tenable: barring scholars from a discussion of both ends and means places restrictions on the academic enterprise that are disturbingly broad, and that bear no correspondence with actual academic practice—past, present or, in all likelihood, future. If social scientists could not comment on links between ends and means, most of their work would be vacuous. The sensible approach is to place no constraints whatsoever on what the social sciences can examine. This does not eliminate the possibility that work with a policy-orientation may fall short of ideals of scientific inquiry. Consciously or not, scholars in this area may be found to interpret facts in light of values, or to twist analyses to encourage acceptance of particular objectives. How much of a problem this in fact is, and whether such problems are likely to be especially common in policy-relevant work or are shared by scholarship of a less applied sort, is further discussed elsewhere in this volume.

The Issue of Peer Evaluation

Another argument against policy-relevant work is that it may vest power to evaluate scholarship in hands other than those of academic peers, threatening the intellectual integrity of the social sciences. The natural sciences have staunchly resisted non-peer evaluation, a steadfastness deemed crucial to their record of achievement. If this principle were relaxed even slightly, some people fear, scholars might respond to the concern of either the lay public, or policymakers, or both, implicitly agreeing to allow those segments of society to judge the quality of their contributions. Were this to happen, the growth of innovative and empirically verifiable knowledge would likely be impeded.[10] Still, the issue is not clear-cut: it all depends on which aspect of the scientific product is externally evaluated.

Certainly, it is unacceptable to place the authority to evaluate scholarship's *epistemological* merit in any hands other than those of scientific peers, since such merit can be judged only according to the canons of scientific inquiry, and only by those who have accepted and mastered these canons. But this does not exhaust the issue, because the purpose of scientific inquiry cannot merely be to demonstrate epistemological virtue. Its ultimate mission is to answer meaningful questions about the natural or social world, and any judgment on the value of a scholarly product must, in addition to epistemological considerations, be concerned with the significance of the questions it addresses (as this chapter's second section will further argue). This significance may be grounded in the applications to which the new knowledge can be put, but it may also have nothing to do with practical considerations. According to sociologist Scott Greer, three sorts of problems, or questions, typically engage the attention of social scientists,[11] and the appropriate judges of the importance of the issues addressed may depend on the category of question involved.

A first category involves "policy" issues, i.e., social problems to which some practical urgency attaches. Practical in this context means that a problem is, in principle, amenable to solution. Urgency suggests that some segments of society want it to be resolved, sooner rather than later. The second category of problems are those of "general social philosophy," originating from a need to conceive of social existence in terms of a meaningful system of institutions and relations, and to harmonize that belief with actual experience. Here, scholarly problems usually stem from a clash between accepted world views and apparent evidence. The purpose of the inquiry, then, is to resolve the discrepancy, either by integrating the new evidence or new ideas within an existing frame of reference or by creating one that is more satisfactory. Problems of the third type are those "intrinsic to developing scientific disciplines." These concern the internal consistency of scientific theories, as well as their match with observable evidence; the problems to be resolved under this heading come from challenges to the validity of existing theories or to their empirical accuracy. These three categories are not mutually exclusive, and any one of them can lend significance to scholarly inquiry; but the appropriate judges of the importance of the questions addressed by scholarship may vary according to the category of question involved.

The third class of issues—problems intrinsic to developing scientific disciplines—are rarely recognized outside the scholarly community. Even if they were more broadly recognized, neither their scientific importance nor their methodological integrity can easily be judged by those without the theoretical background and training needed to interpret the implications of relevant evidence. Consequently, the importance of this sort of scholarship typically must be judged internally, by the professional peers of those conducting the inquiries. But the same conclusion does not apply to the other two classes of problems.

To begin with, scholars cannot be considered the *only* proper judges of the importance of issues of general social philosophy they choose to address. Gaps between social and political world-views and actual practice may be recognized at various levels of society and by those directly con-

cerned; such awareness can be as meaningfully rooted in the daily experience of ordinary citizens as in the academically sanctioned writings
of professional social scientists. Thus, for example, the importance of
economic globalization may legitimately be evaluated by those who experience its effect. Similarly, many though not all segments of the lay
public can evaluate intellectual efforts at bridging gaps between ideals
and reality. This is not to say that anyone could provide a satisfactory
solution to such gaps, but that many people other than the peer reference
groups of professional scholars can form a reasonable opinion of the value
of scholarly efforts in this area. Consequently, excluding non-peers from
judging the substantial value of social scientific attempts to deal with
problems of general social philosophy is hard to justify, even if those
outside the scholarly community cannot say much about the epistemological merits of scientific work.

This conclusion also applies to the first of Greer's three categories of
problems addressed by social scientists—those relevant to *policy*. It is hard
to believe that scholars are necessarily the best judges of the practical urgency of policy issues. It seems that those who stand to be affected are in
as good a position to estimate the urgency of problems addressed. For this
reason, segments of the lay public may legitimately judge the practical
value of the scholarly effort, assuming it is epistemologically sound. It could
further be argued that those who are charged with implementing a policy—
i.e., the society's policymakers—are apt to have a pretty good idea of the
feasibility and implications of possible solutions: at least as good an idea as
many professional academics. Engineering, rather than basic science, may
be the more appropriate model here. Under the circumstances, it is reasonable to open evaluation of the value of policy-related inquiries by social
scientists to members of non-peer groups.

Because many objections to non-peer evaluation invoke the example of
the natural sciences, it is necessary to observe that, in fact, the natural
sciences do not provide a satisfactory parallel with regard to the role of
non-peer groups. The closest analogy to policy-related questions within the
natural sciences are those involving the technological implementation of
knowledge produced by basic science. In most cases, only engineers and
technicians are in a position to estimate the feasibility of developments that
lead from scientific principles to practical applications.

Analogies between the social and natural sciences break down completely where other categories of issues are concerned. If it is possible

within the social sciences to speak separately of "general problems of social philosophy" and of the substantive problems "intrinsic to developing scientific disciplines," this is because there is assumed to be a class of theoretical questions validly addressed by both scholars and non-scholars, and another falling within the former's exclusive purview. While this may be an appropriate view, it is hard to find a parallel in the natural sciences, where virtually all theoretical matters, because of the highly specialized conceptual foundation and intellectual tools involved, are within the domain of none but those who have mastered them professionally. Consequently, it is understandable that the scope for non-peer evaluation should be much more restricted in the natural than in the social sciences, a conclusion that applies to the *importance*[12] as well as the soundness of scholarship.

We conclude that a concern for policy relevance will neither impair SIR scholars' links to their society nor damage the integrity of the standards by which their work is judged. A lingering worry, however, is that their ability to produce good scholarship might be damaged by more basic incompatibilities between knowledge designed for practical application and that pursued as an end in itself.[13] Accordingly, the next section asks whether the quality of international relations scholarship, especially its theoretical foundation, is likely to suffer from efforts to make it useful.

The Consequences for Theoretical Development

Like the previous section, this one has two parts: the first describes what we estimate to be the principal attributes of "good" theory; the second inquires whether these qualities might be impaired by an emphasis on policy relevant knowledge.

Theory is a set of general propositions about the same subject, connected by relations of conjunction and implication, that, by embedding knowledge in a meaningful structure, allows relevant properties of that subject to be explained and predicted.[14] There are many conceptions of the items that should be placed on a scorecard of theoretical worth, but no consensus defines a common set, particularly not in the social sciences.[15] Nevertheless, we will not stray too far from most perspectives by suggesting that the desirability of theory can be judged at two levels: their *soundness* and their *value*.

Sound Theories

The main functions of theory are to explain and predict, and a sound theory is one that competently discharges both functions. There is little controversy about the meaning of prediction: it is the business of anticipating a future condition, by establishing a link between it and an antecedent condition.[16] The antecedent condition may be as simple as a prior value of the property that is being predicted, or it may involve a complex pattern of multivariate causation; but the meaning of prediction is relatively uncontroversial.[17]

The relation between explanation and prediction is more complex, as is their respective place in empirical theory. The logical structure may be quite similar in the two cases, but it need not be, since prediction is possible without prior explanation. For example, the ability of ancient astronomers to anticipate the movement of celestial bodies far outstripped their ability to explain why these movements occurred as they did. With regard to everyday experience, most people can predict that speaking on one end of an open telephone line will result in their words being reproduced at the other end, even if they lack a grasp of the processes involved. Of the two, therefore, explanation is the more demanding task and, by extension, the more ambitious scientific achievement. It is also apparent how a prediction differs from an explanation. Aside from the fact that prediction (unlike explanation) involves some reference to the time of the assertions contained in the premises, explanation rests on at least one theoretical generalization linking an antecedent and consequent condition, while prediction requires, in principle, no more than the observation of some empirical regularity. (For example, one could predict that Britain and France will not fight each other because, since the Napoleonic wars, they have never done so. Similarly, my voice will be reproduced at the other end of the telephone line because this has always been the case, for me and everybody I know).

While an ability to predict says little about a capacity to explain, the obverse rarely applies: in the vast majority of cases, we are well placed to predict that which we are in a position to explain. To take an example discussed in chapter 5, if one can explain why war is very uncommon, if not unheard of, among mature democracies, one would be in a good position to predict the consequences for war as political liberalization proceeds. The bottom line is that, while even prediction alone may be very useful, a theory which allows no more than this is a comparatively modest accomplishment (no matter how sophisticated the analytical tools marshaled for the purpose), while the production of generalizations capable of explaining is a more ambitious and valuable attainment.[18] Because of this, and while predictive power alone may characterize an adequate theory, the measure of a superior theory is its ability to *explain* classes of phenomena that we have some reason to care about. (Accordingly, we are adopting a conception of theoretical purpose that is closer to the "realist"[19] than to the "instrumentalist" position in the philosophy of science.[20])

Two key attributes stand behind a theory's explanatory ability: (a) the truth of its premises (are they empirically correct?), (b) its completeness (in the sense that no propositions crucial to the task of explanation are missing).

True Generalizations   According to the dominant "correspondence theory"[21] of truth, truth is an objective property of statements (e.g., C, I, or G), determined by the correspondence between that statement and observable data. In other words, a statement is true to the extent that it corresponds with reality.

To some extent, the implications of a requirement that the premises of theoretical arguments should be true depend on whether the logical structure of the argument behind the theory is deductive or inductive. Although an inductive argument is sometimes thought of as one that moves from the specific to the general, while a deductive argument starts from general premises, this is not a strictly accurate basis for distinguishing between the two (except, for example, in the case of induction by enumeration). From a strict epistemological point of view, the distinction is this: a deductive argument is one whose premises fully support its conclusion, while the premises of an inductive argument support the conclusion, but less than fully.[22] A correct mathematical derivation, for example, embodies a deductive argument; most reasoning by analogy, as well as most statistical arguments, represent inductive arguments. While the basis for the conclusion of a deductive argument is always logical, that of an inductive argument is always empirical. In the former case, conclusions follow from necessity; in the latter case they rest on probability. Obviously we need both. Inductive arguments add to our store of knowledge new empirical truths. Deductive arguments allow us to maintain consistency among our propositions. Still, they involve truth in different ways.

If the premises of a deductive argument are true, then, as long as the argument is logically valid (e.g., a valid syllogism), the conclusion is implied by logical necessity. In other words, in a valid deductive argument, true premises necessarily imply a true conclusion. But the converse does not apply, for a deductive argument containing one or more false premises may, nevertheless, produce a true conclusion. For example: all chairs have two legs, George W. Bush is a chair, therefore George W. Bush has two legs. From a deductive point of view, this argument is perfectly valid, and the conclusion is undeniably true; nevertheless, both of its premises are false. The problem is that nothing in the process of deduction *itself* can tell us whether a true conclusion was produced by false premises—a situation that is obviously perilous to explanatory endeavors. More obviously, false premises may produce a false (though perfectly valid) conclusion: if validity were to be confused with truth, the consequences for knowledge-creation would be obvious.

Closely related to this point, in discussing the respective merits of prediction and explanation, we should consider the argument occasionally made by social scientists of a deductive bent, one made in Milton Friedman's much-quoted article on "The Methodology of Positive Economics."[23] In this piece, Friedman claims that the value of a theory depends on how useful it is at predicting certain outcomes, whether or not the assumptions behind the successful predictions are correct. Since, as we have seen, it is logically entirely possible for false assumptions to yield accurate predictions, the statement is not completely indefensible. Nevertheless, two caveats are necessary. The first is that it is much more likely that an accurate prediction would be produced by a valid argument based on true premises than on false premises, since the prediction's accuracy (its truth value) could be merely coincidental in the latter case. Because of this, attentiveness to the truth of one's assumptions is likely to enhance the quality of one's predictions. The second observation is that, even though false premises may coincidentally yield correct predictions, they certainly provide no basis for *explaining* the outcomes they seek to predict; in fact, they may lead us *away* from correct explanation. Accordingly, arguments yielding correct predictions from erroneous premises must be judged a less ambitious achievement than arguments that, proceeding from true premises, provide both an explanation *and* a prediction of some relevant outcome.

The premises of an inductive argument typically involve statements that are, explicitly or implicitly, conditional or probabilistic. Accordingly, and unlike the deductive case, true premises need not produce true conclusions in an inductive argument—all that can be said here is that true premises are more likely to yield true conclusions, and vice-versa. (Although rigorous statistical tests may, when appropriate, give us a reasonably good idea of the probability that our conclusions are in fact true.) Thus, while we cannot be certain that true premises lead to true conclusions in the inductive case, false premises less often lead us to true conclusions here than in the deductive case. Our ability to both explain and predict, on the basis of generalizations inductively produced, becomes a matter of degree; and this ability is enhanced to the extent that our premises are true.

Clearly, then, whether primarily deductive or inductive, the explanatory value of a theory benefits from true premises: in the deductive case, it ensures a true conclusion; in the inductive case, it makes it much more likely. Under the circumstances, the empirical correctness of the premises of a theoretical argument is an important condition of the theory's ability to do an adequate explanatory job.

Theoretical Completeness   A complete theory is one that omits no general propositions needed to explain the phenomenon it addresses. This sounds straightfoward, but the pursuit of completeness requires careful judgment. In international relations, as elsewhere in the social sciences, consequences rarely possess a single cause or lack secondary effects; and in a world of intricate causal patterns and multiple layers of implication, boundaries tracing perfectly complete theories can rarely be drawn. Moreover, as parsimony is equally a measure of good theory, the typical strategy is to stay well within these hypothetical boundaries.

These caveats notwithstanding, it is desirable that theories should have no debilitating gaps: full explanations are obviously preferable to partial explanations, and the predictions they yield are correspondingly intellectually satisfying as well as more accurate. Explanatory incompleteness can assume two forms. The omitted influence may have a bearing on the phenomenon to be explained while, at the same time, being unrelated to other influences with such bearing (e.g., in statistical analysis, the case of orthogonality). If so, the explanation would be impoverished by ignoring this influence, but the estimated impact of the causal factor(s) encompassed by the theory would not necessarily be biased empirically—it is just that the picture would be incomplete. If, however, the causal factor(s) included were related to those that were not, even this partial picture could be distorted, for what is attributed to the first may actually be reflecting the operation of the latter. In other words, even the partial explanation is misleading. Consequently, and while an elegant theory is preferable to one that is cumbersome, aesthetic appeal cannot be weighed equally with completeness. A sound theory, one that does a good job of explanation and prediction, is likely to be based on true premises and encompass most pertinent causal propositions.

Valuable Theories

Because a theory can be both commendably sound and disappointingly banal, it must be evaluated not only in terms of its epistemological virtues but also by the added intellectual value it provides. Value, in turn, has both a qualitative and a quantitative dimension, since a theory may be valuable because of: (a) the *scope* of the phenomena it accounts for, and, (b) the *significance* of the phenomena it addresses.

Theoretical Scope   A complete theory is one that neglects no significant component of the explanation behind an outcome. By contrast, a theory of great scope is one from whose premises many *implications* may be drawn. Theories that correctly account for many phenomena that had previously been poorly understood, or that suggest new paths to explanation, are obviously better than those which illuminate a very narrow range of questions or questions to which we already had satisfactory answers. Accordingly, a theory's scope is a first measure of its value.

This criterion is consistent with Imre Lakatos' dictum that bodies of related theory ("research programs") should be evaluated in terms of how "progressive" or "regressive" they prove to be.[24] In Lakatos' view, theories are rarely rejected just because some of their premises appear untenable. Rather, most have a "hard core" of assumptions and hypotheses considered irrefutable, in the sense that they cannot be questioned without opting out of the research program. The hard core is shielded by two sorts of rules. The first (the "negative heuristic") defines this core by specifying which assumptions and hypotheses are unassailable. The second (the "positive heuristic") indicates how the research program may expand and develop, consistent with the hard core's assumptions.

Thus, the research program establishes a "protective belt" of generalizations and assumptions, subject to a range of permissible modifications in light of the evidence. If observational evidence is at odds with the hard core, the explanation and the remedies are to be found in the protective belt. By adjusting the protective belt, a theory can be modified to yield a product that continues to resemble itself, but without some of the problems and inconsistencies of the original theory—permitting it to remain part of the research program, with a family resemblance ensured by the negative heuristic shielding the hard core. For example, Marxism may be considered a research program, one which in many eyes entered a degenerative phase some time ago. When its initial predictions of a rising rate of surplus value extracted from labor in response to declining rates of profit, and of a correspondingly intensifying class conflict, failed to be vindicated in the early part of the twentieth century, Lenin's *Imperialism*[25] sought to demonstrate how profit rates could be maintained without increasing the rate of surplus value extraction: by means of imperialist expansion. With the aid of additional assumptions, Lenin attempted to rescue the essence of Marxist political economy from falsification by events. Similarly, political realism can be considered a research program, whose neorealist variant, as devised mainly by Kenneth Waltz,[26] was intended to develop an additional layer of assumption (an expanded protective belt) meant to cope with flaws in the classical realism of authors such as Hans J. Morgenthau.[27]

But how far can one go in adapting the protective belt? In other words, when does a research program become too burdened with ad hoc assumptions and exceptional conditions to justify further fidelity to its basic premises? According to Lakatos, research programs remain progressive as the new assumptions *expand* the range of phenomena that the theory can explain. A research program that continues successfully to account for novel phenomena satisfies this condition and should be kept alive. One that does not is a "degenerating" program and it deserves to be abandoned. Similarly, when two competing research programs within the same field of inquiry are compared, the one that is more progressive—i.e., the one that explains what the other does and then some—is to be preferred. In our case too, and in a related vein, a theory with a wider explanatory reach is to be considered preferable to one with a narrower reach, other attributes being equal.

Significant Theory   In addition to conditions of scope, a theory's importance is also defined by what may loosely be termed its significance: the knowledge it provides must be knowledge worth having. For this to be the case, and as we are dealing with empirical theory, its concepts must refer to world states that exist or that could exist, and for which an acceptable operational definition is provided; in other words, the concepts must be empirically meaningful.[28] The "righteousness" of policy is not an empirically meaningful concept, but the "the cost" of a policy is. Moreover, a concept may be empirically meaningful in one area of the social sciences, but not in another—simply because the empirical content may not carry over from one to another. The issue is pertinent to much political science, where concepts developed in other social science disciplines sometimes are uncritically imported, yielding categories bereft of much empirical meaning upon transplantation.[29] Beyond this, judgments about significance are rooted in values and expectations rather than in the canons of scientific inquiry. Because the knowledge produced within the field of international relations, especially that cast in quantitative and formal terms, is sometimes charged with triviality, we must begin with an overview of the foundations on which such charges rest.

Triviality can assume at least two forms. If a theoretical argument involves a question whose answer we have no reason to care about, we are in the presence of a pure form of triviality. The reasons for our indifference may be pragmatic. Since we tend to care about knowledge that affects our well-being, a judgment of triviality could result from a perception that the question involved does not concern our well-being in any discernible fashion. But, as Cardinal Newman pointed out in his celebrated work, "There is a knowledge worth possessing for what it is, and not merely for what it does."[30] Justifications for the humanities rarely rest on pragmatic grounds, and even scientific results need not provide implications for action to be considered important. For example, most people would regard as meaningful theories that contribute to our understanding of human evolution, although it is unlikely that many practical implications would be drawn from even the best evolutionary theories. Similarly, geological theories on continental drift would scarcely be judged trivial, even though they contain few guides to action. Thus, even relatively "useless" knowledge may be considered important if it addresses questions that culture, human experience, or natural curiosity lead us to seek to answer. If we simply do not care, the knowledge is intrinsically trivial, no matter how sound the theory behind it, or how broad the scope of meaningless phenomena it addresses. For reasons discussed in chapter 1, in the traditional SIR era—for example, the work of Morgenthau, Wolfers, Bull, or Fox—the scholarship could hardly ever have been charged with triviality.

In addition to intrinsic importance, the significance of conclusions is sometimes measured by how surprising they are in terms of initial expectations. Generally, the interest that a statement of theoretical relation, like a statement of fact, generates is inversely proportional to its antecedent plausibility, since it is usually deemed more important to demonstrate the unexpected than to confirm the self-evident.

It may be objected that, while it could seem trivial to confirm what most people would have in any case expected, it is often a good idea to do so—simply because the contrary finding, though unlikely, would be extremely interesting.[31] For example, although most people would yawn at the finding that U.S. presidents dislike Communism, it would be highly intriguing to discover that, contrary to expectations, some do not necessarily feel this way. This argument makes a useful point, but it assumes that the question to which the anticipated answer is provided is of considerable *intrinsic* importance; otherwise, it could not be considered important, even if its antecedent plausibility had been very low. The degree of triviality, therefore, *jointly* depends on the intrinsic significance of the question and on the antecedent plausibility of the answer: it is inversely proportional to the former and directly proportional to the latter.

Having defined desirable theoretical knowledge as that which is both sound and valuable, each being further defined by two properties, we may ask how these qualities could be undermined by adding, as an additional requirement, that the theory be policy-relevant. This implies an overview of the forms that relevance can take, since its implications for the growth and quality of theory may depend on the type we have in mind.

Theory and Relevance: Is There a Tradeoff?

Would a quest for policy relevance impair the quality of theory? Since "disinterested" scholarship provides the standard of comparison, the question is whether policy relevant theory is likely to do less well than its disinterested counterpart in terms of soundness and/or value. There are two reasons to think that this might be the case. The first is *epistemological*: is there something intrinsic to the logic of inquiry of the two sorts of theory that favors the soundness and/or value of the disinterested variant? The second concern is essentially *sociological*: it springs from the possibility that the professional incentives by which the two sorts of scholars—relevant and disinterested—are driven may favor the soundness and/or value of the latter's work. Figure

4 catalogues the possibilities for theoretical impairment, and an answer to the question posed in this section requires a comparison in these terms.

A first observation is that there are no purely *epistemological* reasons for thinking that either type of theory should fare better with regard to *soundness*. In either case, the irreducible function of theory is to explain, an ability logically independent of whether the phenomenon to be explained involves a policy outcome or not. As Philip Melanson has pointed out, "relevance is a perspective applicable to the focus of research and not to the epistemic quality of inquiry."[32] But there may be something about the patterns of inquiry associated with relevant or disinterested theorizing that could affect the *value* of their respective contributions. It is also conceivable that the professional incentives and culture proper to the two types of scholarly work could affect differently their soundness and/or value.

Truth and Relevance If the substance of a conclusion matters more to a scholar than its empirical correctness, the argument's premises may be

Source of Impairment	Truth		Completeness		Significance		Scope	
Internal Logic	Relevant		Relevant		Relevant		Relevant	
		Basic		Basic		Basic		Basic
Professional Incentives	Relevant		Relevant		Relevant		Relevant	
		Basic		Basic		Basic		Basic

FIGURE 4 Comparison of Relevant and Basic Theory

distorted, consciously or not, to justify the desired inference. The incentive to distort could spring from partisan objectives or ideological blinders. Inducements to delude could infect most forms of relevance, but one suspects that they are most to be feared in the instrumental case, for it is there that desired outcomes are involved most directly. Incentives to mislead could also be found in estimates of direct or secondary costs, if a scholar's commitment to certain policies should cause their costs to be minimized. The possibility of tendentious distortions in policy-relevant theorizing cannot be dismissed, but a search for concrete instances turns up very little,[33] suggesting that the concern may be overstated. In any case, this form of corruption cannot be considered the monopoly of relevant theory, since ideological values and political predilections may color *any* scholarship that engages political values. A statement about the viability of socialism or, say, about the peacefulness of Islam might reflect a scholar's political inclinations, whether or not that statement had any obvious bearing on policy choices.

An incentive to deceive could also be linked to the narrow professional interests of scholars, rather than to their political beliefs. For example, the problem may be rooted in a desire to create maximum scholarly impact, either by challenging a broadly held assumption, by seeming to fill a widely lamented gap in knowledge, or by scoring points in a visible academic debate. While it cannot be denied that such objectives weigh heavily on many scholarly minds, or that, in exceptional cases, truth may be twisted accordingly, there is again no reason to suppose that such incentives are more likely to infect policy-relevant work than scholarship with no concern for policy.

It is important to remember here that truth may also suffer from problems that have no basis in an incentive to distort. In inductive work, the problem may stem from a necessarily arbitrary operational definition of theoretical terms. Thus, whether or not it is true that democracies don't fight each other may depend on whether or not one accepts the convention that defines war as an interstate conflict involving at least 1,000 battle deaths.[34] Similarly, findings about international inequality that are true when national wealth is measured in conventional (GNP per capita) terms may have to be modified if a broader measure of quality of life is substituted.[35] The risk here is not that truth is misrepresented, but that sometimes it is difficult to agree on its exact boundaries. Similar problems may be produced by imperfect measuring instruments and procedures, which, if the measurement error should be systematic rather than random, may bias the generalizations produced by the research. But there is no reason to think that systematic, though wholly unintended, measurement errors are more apt to impair the truth of theories that try to be relevant than of those that do not.

Truth may also be undermined by simplifications designed to foster theoretical parsimony and elegance, a problem more often encountered in deductive than in inductive work.[36] Simplifications that strip away redundant layers of meaning or that ignore idiosyncratic deviations from common tendencies are integral to theory-building. But when simplifications play havoc with the truth of the premises employed, the implications for explanatory generalizations are debilitating, even where interesting conclusions follow as valid deductions from dubious premises. An illustration is provided by realpolitik's claim that the pursuit of power is a dominant aspiration of states, one that pervades their conduct of international affairs. In the "classic" realism of Hans Morgenthau, the power drive is rooted in one of those "elemental bio-social drives by which in turn society is created."[37] In the neorealism of Kenneth Waltz, a concern about relative power flows from the anarchic structure of the international system, and the pervasive security dilemma this creates.[38] Certain predictions, especially about the way in which nations acquire and manage power, follow naturally from this premise, and gratifyingly elegant models of international politics have been derived from this foundation. But the truth of their assumptions is tenuous; as an empirical matter, one can identify many nations that, linked to other members of the international system by objective conflicts of interest, are keenly attentive to power considerations. But it is equally easy to compile long lists of countries that are not troubled by security fears, and whose policies indicate no great concern with power. Yet so influential is political realism, so convenient are its assumptions for theory, and so many professional careers have been built on these assumptions, that there has been little incentive to test their empirical correctness. This is unfortunate. Given the ultimate implausibility of many of these premises, one may doubt their truth.

Significantly, contemporary realism's assumptions are unrelated to attempts at relevance. While Morgenthau was concerned with the practical applications of his precepts, Waltz's contribution to neorealism displays no great interest in policy implications; his objective is a pure theory of international relations.[39] It seems that misleading simplifications, with their corresponding impairment of explanatory ability, are likely to occur wherever parsimony is more valued than truth. It is likely that deductive research compares unfavorably with inductive work on this basis, but it is not likely that the problem weighs more heavily on relevant theory than on disinterested academic efforts.

To some extent, truth may also fall victim to the imperative of theoretical novelty that is a weighty element in the academic reward structure. This novelty may be substantive, but too often in recent years it has been displayed mainly in the forum of new research techniques. As we argued in chapter 1, trudging over well-charted paths does little to enhance scholarly reputations or the growth of knowledge. As one observer noted:

> There exists the possibility that in some fields of science, where many basic truths are fully known, the emphasis on novelty will detach itself from social utility and come to constitute its own reward. . . . A considerable gap between truth and novelty seems to have materialized in the field of political studies.[40]

Even though the exact impact of a quest for novelty on the truth of explanatory propositions is hard to determine, it would seem less likely to affect policy-relevant than disinterested work. With the former, pragmatic purpose is likely to outweigh pure novelty as a measure by which scholarship is judged. This is clearly the case with demand-driven theory; in the supply-driven model, the only instance where this may not be so is with basic theory that becomes relevant only in light of some subsequent problem (and where theory is not developed in response to a practical challenge). In either case, it is hard to have a significant and sustained influence on policy with conclusions or premises that are wrong.

The Goal of Completeness   An emphasis on policy usefulness could conceivably limit the comprehensiveness of theoretical explanations, especially if there was some demand-driven urgency for a particular study. Even so, the magnitude of the problem depends on how broad a conception of relevance is adopted, as well as on the pattern of incentives behind the analytic endeavor. For example, the policy tools included in the instrumental relations outlined by the scholar could be determined by an estimate of how effectively they could be acted upon, neglecting those which, while causally significant, are less malleable. Similarly, although recourse to certain policy instruments might also be precluded by domestic politics, or cultural constraints, or might not be affordable in terms of their direct costs and secondary consequences, this does not make them less necessary to a theory accounting for the desired outcome. Scholars might also be led to emphasize policy instruments that promise to have the greatest causal impact on the desired outcome, disregarding those whose influence is less weighty, with similar costs to theoretical completeness. Accordingly, if the analyst is guided by a narrow notion of short-term practicality rather than a broad conception of what policy-relevant knowledge should encompass, the explanatory structure behind the policy recommendations may be weakened by significant gaps.

Afflictions of this sort are possible, but the problem is not rooted in the intrinsic *nature* of policy-relevant work. Because soundness is a necessary condition for meaningful theoretical relevance, and since theory must be reasonably complete in order to be sound, a proper view of the analyst's job precludes omissions of this sort. Thus, in a satisfactory program of policy-relevant theorizing, the instrumental relations would encompass a comprehensive statement of links between policies and outcomes, an adequate survey of pertinent contextual considerations, as well as a discussion of direct and secondary consequences. Influences that in a vision bounded by narrow practicality might be neglected become variables whose values are explicitly accounted for.

On grounds of both truth and completeness, risks to soundness cannot be entirely neglected, but they appear modest and, where they cannot be dismissed, their source is more likely to lie in misguided professional incentives than in the logic of inquiry inherent in relevant theory. By the same token, there is nothing to suggest a bias toward incompleteness on the part of disinterested theory, particularly with general propositions empirically derived on the basis of an examination of observational data, as in statistical models whose success is partly measured in terms of variance explained. Some grounds for concern can be found in deductive work, where elegance and parsimony are often purchased at the cost of theoretical completeness. But the problem, if there is one, is not grounded in the logic of deduction per se, but in incentives that are more aesthetic than genuinely epistemic.

Thus, there is little grounds for believing that relevant theories are likely to be less sound, qua theories, than those rooted in a disinterested agenda. But, since this does not exhaust the standards of merit for theory, we must ask whether relevant theory is apt to be less valuable than is pure theory.

Relevance and Theoretical Significance   The first issue is whether policy-relevant theorizing asks questions that are intrinsically at least as meaningful and interesting as those addressed by scholars with a commitment to disinterested theory. We believe that it does. A question that claims the attention of a policy-relevant theorist typically involves the pursuit of some desirable objective; while it is logically possible that objectives of trifling importance would be addressed, plainly this is unlikely. Lacking much incentive in the form of professional rewards to be relevant, scholars usually embark on such work because of the importance attached to the issues involved, an importance typically measured by the consequences of failing to attain the policy objective.

However, because intrinsic importance need not be measured exclusively by pragmatic criteria, issues addressed by disinterested theory may be even more significant. In fact, it is sometimes assumed that the really important scientific questions can only be tackled with a wholly disinterested frame of mind, unfettered by practical concerns. Abraham Flexner expressed a widely held view when he maintained, decades ago and in a subsequently muchquoted article, that:

> Throughout the whole history of science most of the really great discoveries which had ultimately proved to be beneficial to mankind had been made by men and women who were driven not by the desire to be useful but merely by the desire to satisfy their curiosity.[41]

We believe that this view rests on a romanticized view of scholarly curiosity and of the manner in which questions are selected for scientific examination in the academic community. As we discussed in chapter 1, in most of the social sciences, where professional recognition depends largely on the apparent sophistication of the research tools and conceptual categories employed, questions are often selected according to the methods and concepts that can plausibly be employed in their analysis. These are not criteria that have much bearing on the intrinsic importance of the issues addressed, and some loss may be expected here. Often too, issues are selected because, for whatever reason, a critical mass of colleagues has already decided to deal with them. In part, this view stems from an understandable conviction that a question addressed by a large number of colleagues must be worth addressing. It also springs from the fact that an intensely studied issue implies the easy availability of empirical information (say, a useful data set) upon which research can readily be conducted. Partly too, it is because incorporation into a vigorous stream of scholarship stands to promote the visibility of associated work by embedding it in a lively pattern of mutual citation, promoting the professional visibility of participating scholars. These are circumstances better explained by the sociology of knowledge than by the canons of scientific method, and experience indicates that either significant or trivial issues may occupy scholarship in the process.

In principle, issues that are not currently very meaningful may become so subsequently, as new information becomes available or new needs or interests emerge. However, to be at all plausible, the justification requires that the currently trivial does, in fact, often prove significant with time. Whether or not this is so in the natural sciences may be debated; it would be a debate complicated by the difficulty of disentangling the various strands of scientific work, both pure and applied, that precede most useful discoveries in these areas. In the social sciences, instances of trivial work for which value has later come to be found do not readily come to mind—what was trivial decades ago is likely to be every bit as trivial today.

In the field of international relations, charges of triviality are also directed at conclusions that appear self-evident. Here, the claim of banality can be refuted if the importance of a correct answer is great enough to make *any* uncertainty intolerable. The claim can further be undermined in inverse proportion to the conclusion's antecedent plausibility (not all expectations are equally firmly held). Controlling for intrinsic importance, the task is to decide whether policy-relevant thinking is more or less prone to confirming the expected than is basic-theoretical work.

Such concerns are at least plausible. For example, it might be feared that political rewards—in forms ranging from public acclaim to access to power—may sometimes be proffered to scholars who prove the obvious, because even that which is apparent may be hotly denied in political debates. But actual instances of such intellectual corruptions do not suggest themselves, and it is hard to be impressed by an abstract possibility supported by so few concrete examples. As far as disinterested theory is concerned, there are no reasons intrinsic to its logic to lead us to expect the banality of high antecedent plausibility. Nevertheless, this form of triviality could be (and sometimes is) the byproduct of academic agendas wherein the significance of conclusions matters less than the appeal of the analytical methods employed. Where this is the case, there is no reason to expect that the substance of the work would be especially interesting (except, perhaps, on purely meth odological grounds).

Relevance and Theoretical Scope   Since the scope of what scholars seek to explain is restricted by the questions asked, we might wonder whether disinterested scientific curiosity yields a greater range of questions than does policy-relevant work. Again, such concerns are at least plausible. Except in some supply-driven instances, questions generated by policy-relevant theory tend to be limited by the objectives sought by policymakers. In turn, policy objectives are guided by current interests and values, and these may be bounded by shifting and parochial considerations, in addition to ideological agendas.[42] Nevertheless, the gravity of the problem depends on the category of policy-relevant knowledge involved.

It could be argued that concerns loom largest with cases of demand-driven relevance where theories focus on instrumental relations alone, and that, if the enterprise were broadened to encompass contextual relations, as well as direct and secondary consequences, the resulting theoretical edifice might be very encompassing. A counterargument might be that in policy-relevant work, the starting point is always given by the policy objective, and that the theory's scope cannot extend very much beyond its confines. Assuming that this is so, the criticism does not distinguish theory that seeks to be useful from that which does not, since there is no reason to think that the latter's explanatory structures are less firmly rooted in the outcomes to be explained than the former's. The only issue that really matters here is whether either type of theory concerns itself with a wider range of outcomes than the other, a question whose answer would require careful examination of the two bodies of scholarly literature. Again, and we have no a priori basis for predicting what conclusions would be reached.

It must be observed that degenerative research programs—those that keep expanding their protective belt of ad-hoc assumptions and auxiliary hypotheses with no corresponding increase in the range of phenomena explained— are unlikely to be compatible with policy-relevant work. Here, pragmatic incentives make an understanding of policy outcomes (both the causes and implications) the principal justification for theoretical development, and the measure of its success is whether, with regard to these outcomes. These research programs explain the range of the possible and the implications of choices. Where observational data indicate that a theory cannot explain these matters, it will probably be modified or abandoned. Here, then, usefulness provides a direct incentive to create and maintain well-performing theory. Concerns extraneous to its objectives—for example, the faddishness or apparent sophistication of the analytical tools used—are unlikely to sustain an unsuccessful theory. Therefore, considerations that sometimes ensure the longevity of degenerative theory are less likely to afflict relevant than disinterested work, and the former's explanatory scope may benefit accordingly.

Conclusions

The impact of a quest for relevance on the quality of international relations theory will continue to be debated,[43] but certain claims must be challenged. There is little reason why relevance should distort the proper relation
between scholar and society, either in terms of unwelcome academic intru-
sion in discussions about the society's ends or by placing the evaluation of
scholarship in nonprofessional hands. The more closely these claims are
examined, the less conviction they carry. Most important, there is little reason to assume that policy-relevant scholarship must fare less well than its
disinterested counterpart in terms of either soundness or value. The possibility that relevance would corrupt knowledge by twisting it to conform with
ideological biases, as at one time the natural sciences were hobbled by being
tethered to theological agendas, may reasonably be set aside; it is highly
implausible so long as professional scholarly peers act as watchdogs on issues
of theoretical soundness. And while it is of course possible that weak arguments or empirical evidence might be used to justify certain policies, few
cases can be found of SIR that is corrupted in such a fashion over any
significant period of time. In a liberal society the competitive marketplace
of ideas makes it likely that such ideas will be detected when they are used
in this way.

Other threats may be entangled with a quest for relevance, but they are
hardly unmanageable; in any case, similar problems afflict disinterested theory. Truth, completeness, and explanatory scope could, in principle, suffer
from the professional incentives of relevant theorists, if these incentives were
to lead them to generalizations that favor simple, direct, and immediately
workable guides to action, of the sort that may be most appealing and com-
prehensible to policymakers. But in the nature of things, this is a problem
more plausibly encountered in policy *advocacy* than in policy-relevant *scholarship*. These are very different types of work. Moreover, the structure of
professional rewards facing the scholar unburdened by a concern with relevance seem at least as often to be based on criteria external to the quality of
the explanations offered. Whatever qualms about relevance one may enter-
tain, they tend to be rooted in assumed professional incentives, not in the
nature of the explanatory enterprise. Moreover, these incentives are often
compared to an overly idealized conception of the drives behind the development of disinterested theory.

If it is not likely that theoretical development would be harmed by relevance, it may actually benefit from a concern with practical implications. In other words, the very *opposite* of what is sometimes maintained may be true.

In an observation as apposite to the field of international relations as to other behavioral sciences, Abraham Kaplan observed that inquiry related to practice

> has the advantages of providing anchorage for our abstractions, and data and tests for our hypotheses. For behavioral science the advantages are especially great, counteracting the tendency to empty verbalizations characteristic of some sociologies, or the self-contained formalism of certain economic theories.[44]

In a similar vein, Joseph Ben David, a distinguished sociologist of science, has observed that an intellectual grounding in the world of practice may lead to considerably more innovative and interesting work than scholarship shaped exclusively by the ethos of ivory towers:

> Practice . . . is an invaluable guide in locating relevant problems — rather than finding illusory ones, which happened not infrequently in the history of academic thinking. . . . The problems of practice are always real, and it usually possesses a tradition which is the result of a long collective process of trial and error and which may suggest the way toward new theory and new methods.[45]

Nurtured both by a comprehensive view of usefulness and an insistence on high standards of scholarship, relevant scholarship may produce premises and thus conclusions that are more likely to be empirically true than those yielded by disinterested theory. It is less likely to be rooted in those conceptual issues that have little connection to a meaningful empirical reality, even though they provide vehicles for the advancement of academic careers. It may also stand a better chance of being valuable: by definition, it deals with matters of practical significance; matters that are no less likely to be intrinsically important, from a theoretical standpoint, than those addressed by theoretical efforts unconcerned with usefulness.[46] Accordingly, both soundness and value may benefit.

We must, finally, remain open to the possibility that the pursuit of useful knowledge actually may produce theory of a *better* quality, because it would be empirically more meaningful and more focused on the truth of its premises, than a program of knowledge-creation dominated by the reward structure of disinterested theory.

5 The Inter-Democratic Peace—Theoretical Foundations and Policy Implications

In this chapter and the next, we discuss the practical policy implications of some recent international relations scholarship: namely, the literature surrounding the democratic peace and that associated with institutions and international cooperation. Our aim is to determine what guidance, if any, this knowledge might provide to practitioners, and to examine its strengths and weaknesses in this regard. An obvious question at this point is why we selected these two bodies of scholarship rather than others. Three considerations drove the decision. First, we wanted issue-areas that would be broad enough to encompass a variety of specific problems and relationships American decisionmakers face. Many foreign-policy problems turn on when and under what conditions the United States should collaborate with others, as opposed to going it alone, while many others turn on how to prevent conflicts from erupting in the first place. The literature on institutionalized cooperation should help address the first set of questions; work linking democratization with pacific international behavior should illuminate the second. Second, we looked for topical areas in which there was enough scholarly literature to provide a basis for an extended discussion, including exchanges across competing points of view. Third, we sought a body of scholarship sufficiently mature in terms of the solidity of its empirical and theoretical foundations, i.e, one that has been thoroughly vetted by the profession over a substantial period of time.

In this chapter, we analyze the implications of the proposition that democracies are much less likely than autocracies to engage in international hostilities, at least against other democracies. This assertion has achieved widespread (though not universal) acceptance, and has generated a virtual cottage industry of empirical research by international relations scholars.

The proposition can also be embraced on ethical grounds. Many policies connected with peace and security have implied tools with unpleasant connotations that could be justified only, and reluctantly, by the end they were supposed to promote. For example, alliance politics and nuclear deterrence were regarded as unavoidable evils required by an exalted objective. In the present case, however, the clash between the ethical content of means and ends disappears, as the instrument (democracy) is intrinsically as desirable as the objective (peace).

The notion that democracies behave differently on the world stage is especially consequential at a time when the cold war's termination, along with an extensive spread of democracy, presage a new era in international relations, requiring that long-accepted policy assumptions be substantially revised. As Bruce Russett asks: "Does the post–Cold War era represent merely the passing of a particular adversarial relationship, or does it offer a chance for fundamentally changed relations among nations?"[1] The possibility that the second answer is correct leads us to inquire what, if anything, the United States can do to promote this transformation, and what contribution scholarship can make to understanding the link between democracy and peace and the ways of ensuring that it is realized. We will begin by placing the proposition in its broader theoretical context.

The Intellectual Context

Traditionally, the notion that a nation's form of government shapes its attitude toward military force has not been the dominant academic belief. More often, it was been thought that either properties common to all states, or else compelling attributes of the international system, lead nations to behave uniformly in most important respects—irrespective of their internal political differences. This position has characterized scholars identified as political "realists," for whom foreign policy reflects a primary concern with security and power in a threatening world, a concern unaffected by domestic political proclivities.

Hans J. Morgenthau, a founder of modern realist thinking, observed that statesmen "think and act in terms of interest defined as power. The aspiration for power being the distinguishing element of international politics."[2] For Morgenthau, this is natural, since the drive to "dominate" has the status of an "elemental biosocial drive" that is "common to all men."[3] International politics reflects the imperatives of power, and war is avoided only by adhering to realist tenets of international behavior (e.g., by respect for an international balance of power).

In more recent, "neorealist," variants of this doctrine, the need for power does not appear as an inherent drive, but as a response to *anarchy*: the defining property of the international system. Anarchy implies insecurity and the need for self-help, from which it follows that national security and sovereignty must rest on power. If peace is to prevail, power must be acquired and managed internationally in such a way that aggression is discouraged. Domestic politics are neither here nor there: foreign and security policies stem from international circumstances too compelling to allow much variation rooted in regime characteristics.

The opposite position has also had adherents. Some have questioned the notion that anarchy necessarily breeds a security dilemma among nations, requiring power-based responses. It has been argued, since the eighteenth and early nineteenth centuries, that insecurity could be mitigated by fostering economic interdependence among nations—a view held, inter alia, by theorists of the French enlightenment,[4] and the Manchester School in England.[5] Similarly, a number of scholars have argued that international organizations can foster cooperation among nations, substantially mitigating their sense of insecurity. In some views, political federations could even be created among nations, virtually removing the possibility of war among them.[6]

Most significantly for our concerns, it has been argued that war-proneness does vary from nation to nation, depending on the political system—in particular, that nations with governments subject to popular control are less inclined to resort to force in their external dealings. The French *philosophes* disapproved of political cultures that glorified military conquest and balance of power—cultures viewed as pathologies of despotic governments—and they felt that freely expressed public sentiment would not countenance such values. This feeling was most influentially expressed by the Marquis de Condorcet. Best known by political scientists for his "jury theorem" and "Condorcet equilibrium," he also argued that international peace required a profound restructuring of domestic politics.[7] People (unlike monarchs) were peace-loving; the challenge was to ensure that their preferences prevailed.

International treaties (especially involving military alliances) should require legislative ratification at the level of electoral districts—to ensure that they contain no nefarious designs.[8] War should require a declaration by the legislature (and even this would be permitted only if the other side had instigated hostilities).[9] To further guarantee that the popular will would prevail, Condorcet urged that new elections be held as soon as feasible after war had been declared, allowing voters to ratify the legislature's decision, or to refuse to do so.[10] The effect would be a substantial reduction in the incidence of war.

In a similar and currently better-known view, Immanuel Kant[11] argued that peace required governments based on republican constitutions,[12] which would ensure three things: (1) the respect of individual freedom; (2) a common source of legislation, and the separation of executive and legislative authority, and, finally, (3) the political equality of citizens. In turn, a collectivity of free and equal citizens exercising control over executive decisions would not countenance executive wars.

> The republican constitution . . . provides for this desirable result, namely perpetual peace, and the reason for this as follows: If (as must inevitably be the case, given this form of constitution) the consent of the citizenry is required in order to determine whether or not there will be a war, it is natural that they consider all its calamities before committing themselves to so risky a game. (Among these are doing the fighting themselves, paying the costs of war from their own resources, having to repair at great sacrifice the war's devastation, and, finally the ultimate evil that would make peace itself better, never being able—because of new and constant wars—to expunge the burden of debt.) By contrast, under a nonrepublican constitution, where subjects are not citizens, the easiest thing in the world to do is to declare war.[13]

The implication of Condorcet's and Kant's views is that democracies are far less likely to opt for war than autocracies, and that domestic political arrangements may matter more than the character of the global system in accounting for war and peace.[14] These arguments impressed a number of statesmen, including many of the U.S. Founding Fathers, who agreed that popular control over major foreign policy decisions would promote the cause of peace.[15] More recently, Woodrow Wilson, whose ideas on foreign policy were deeply rooted in philosophical convictions acquired before entering politics, claimed a link between peace and democracy. These convictions included the virtues of free debate and popular opinion, and a belief that democracy alone offered the promise of "the establishment of the most humane results of the world's peace and progress."[16] When a post–World War I international order was contemplated, he declared that "The world must be made safe for democracy. Its peace must be planted upon the tested foundations of political liberty," emphasizing that "A steadfast concert of peace can never be maintained except by a partnership of democratic nations."[17] More recently still, a number of U.S. statesmen of the cold war period have stressed the dependence of peace on democracy and the inherent aggressiveness of Communism—although the line between empirical observation and rhetorical flourish was often blurred during those decades.

While earlier thinking on the implication of democracy for peace was grounded in casual and impressionistic assessments of the popular and legislative impact on executive actions, modern research methods and extensive data have produced knowledge of a more rigorous sort.

During the 1960s, a series of related efforts, using for the most part large aggregates of data, explored the possibility that either the incidence or the intensity of international conflict may be predictable on the basis of the political systems of countries involved. The evidence indicated that this was the case.[18] A study by Michael Haas[19] found evidence that democratic states were less often party to conflicts than nondemocracies, a finding confirmed by several subsequent studies.[20] In the 1970s, Rudolph Rummel of the University of Hawaii, published an extensive, five volume, study of war, arguing that democracies, or libertarian states, are more peaceful than autocracies, because of:

> the responsiveness of elected leaders to domestic interest groups or public opinion, which ordinarily will oppose violence, tax increases and conscription . . . Domestic interests set limits and libertarian leaders lack the power or the will to take violent initiatives or make moves escalating violence, unlike their authoritarian or totalitarian counterparts.[21]

Most research during the 1960s and 1970s suggesting that democracies are more peaceful than autocracies took the *nation state* as the unit of analysis—computing the number of wars engaged in by various countries, then comparing those numbers on the basis of political systems. However, this said little about the political systems encountered in the warring *pairs* of nations, which requires identification of the dyads involved (In order to find out which political systems fight most, but also what kind of political systems they tend to fight).

An early study of this kind by Stephen Chan[22] took as its unit of analysis the dyad-year (i.e., each possible pair of nations examined on a per-year basis). It found that nondemocratic dyad-years showed proportionately less war involvement than those including two democracies. In a subsequent, and much quoted study, Zeev Maoz and Nasrine Abdolali[23] provided what is now the most widely accepted statement of the democratic peace. Examining all pairs of states for the period 1816–1976, they found that although democratic states were no less war-prone than nondemocratic states, none of the 332 dyads engaged in war were *jointly* democratic. This yielded the conclusion that, while democracy does not guarantee peaceful behavior in general, democracies will not fight each other. These findings were confirmed by several subsequent studies, including one by Maoz and Bruce Russett that considered the war-democracy relation in the context of a number of possible intervening conditions.[24]

The finding about the disinclination of democracies to fight each other has since gained much academic support; by one reckoning "the absence of wars between democracies comes as close as anything we have to an empirical law in international relations."[25] Two broad theoretical explanations for this finding have been proposed. The first, "normative" or "cultural" explanation, maintains that democratic political culture—based as it is as on bargaining, negotiation, and compromise in its domestic politics—will be extended by democracies to their external relations, especially when dealing with countries that subscribe to similar political norms.[26] A second, "structural," explanation finds the source of the democratic peace in legislative, public, and other constraints on the ability of government to initiate war. While it may not be immediately obvious why these constraints should account for less war *among democracies*, as opposed to more pacific policies in general by democracies, an explanation can be offered. As Michael Doyle points out, domestic constraints on war involvement are likely to be relaxed only if the war is to be fought for a popular reason, and wars against nondemocracies are far more likely to be popular than against nations which share one's democratic structures and values.[27] This is because they should be harder to legitimize domestically.

Although advocates for the supremacy of one or the other explanation can be found, it is nearly impossible to disentangle the respective effects of the cultural and structural attributes—since both simultaneously

characterize democracies. The most credible conclusion is that, while, in-
dividually, either could account for the democratic peace, their combination
provides its strongest guarantee.

The Democratic Peace and the Policymaking Community

Given the empirical evidence, theoretical plausibility, and ethical appeal
of the claim that democracies do not fight each other, it is not surprising
that the proposition should have been embraced by policymakers. The policy theme drawn by the Clinton administration (the first fully post–cold war
administration) was the need to move from a strategy of containment to one
of *enlargement*, i.e., of expanding the community of nations adhering to
political democracy and free market principles. In a public address in September 1993, Anthony Lake, the President's National Security Advisor, explained that:

> During the Cold War, even children understood America's security
> mission; as they looked at those maps on their schoolroom walls, they
> knew we were trying to contain the creeping expansion of that big,
> red blob. Today . . . we might visualize our security mission as pro-
> moting the enlargement of the "blue areas" of market democracies.[28]

The justification for enlargement was not only couched in terms of democracy's domestic virtues, but also of its international benefits — including
the democratic peace, which was initially accounted for in terms of a largely
cultural explanation. According to President Clinton, in his first major foreign policy address,

> Democracy is rooted in compromise, not conquest. It rewards tolerance,
> not hatred. Democracies rarely make war on one another. They make more
> reliable partners in trade, in diplomacy, and in the stewardship of our global
> environment.[29]

Soon, the foreign policy of the United States came to be defined by the
coupled concepts of *engagement* and *enlargement*: the first involving active
internationalism, the second encouraging democracy and market economies
in those parts of the world in which they had not fully taken root. These two
themes provided the title of the administration's 1996 national security report, stating that, "Our national security policy is . . . based on enlarging the

community of market democracies while deterring and limiting a range of threats to our nation, our allies, and our interests."[30] Democracy was to be promoted because "Democracies create free markets that offer economic opportunity, make for more reliable trading partners *and are far less likely to wage war on one another*."[31] (Our emphasis.) Deputy Secretary of State Strobe Talbott further explained, enumerating the various objectives of U.S. foreign policy, that:

> We will advance all the objectives I have just enumerated, and others as well, if we also strengthen associations among established democ-racies and support the transition to democracy in states that are emerg-ing from dictatorship or civil strife. Democracy, in short, is the one big thing that we must sustain and promote wherever possible, even as we deal with the many other tasks that face us.[32]

The commitment went well beyond rhetoric, and the administration could indeed point to numerous examples of its efforts at enlargement. These included vigorous support of the quasi-public National Endowment for Democracy, aid to a democratizing Russia and to several newly indepen-dent states of the former Soviet Union, and to a number of Eastern and Central European nations. Policies included support for South Africa's dem-ocratic transformation, and for similar (though much less successful) efforts in Cambodia. Enlargement ranged from the military intervention designed to restore democracy in Haiti, to such actions as hosting the Summit of the Americas, which reaffirmed the members' commitment to democracy.

Surprisingly in light of the above, the national security reports submitted in the following two years[33] no longer explicitly referred to the goal of en-largement, subsuming it under the more general heading of engagement. Moreover, references to the international benefits of democracy no longer mentioned the fact that they do not fight each other. The explanation for this shift is interesting from the perspective of policy-relevant knowledge. According to a National Security Council official with substantial respon-sibility in this area, there were two reasons for this change of emphasis.[34] The first was the finding that although democracies are unlikely to fight each other, they are not more pacific overall. The second was the more recent suggestion by a number of political scientists that, independently of what may apply to established democracies, nations going through the pro-cess of *transition* from autocracy to democracy may be quite war-prone.

Under the circumstances, the benefits of enlargement would have had to be presented in far more qualified and ambiguous terms, probably accounting for the decision to shift the focus of official statements of U.S. foreign policy.

Significantly, then, a large part of the original justification for the policy of enlargement, and the reason it was subsequently downplayed by U.S. foreign policy doctrine, appear grounded in academic findings. Thus, work on the democratic peace represents a vivid example of policy-relevant thinking (rooted, in this case, in supply-driven scholarship), and we must evaluate the extent to which the proposition that democracies do not fight each other is a reliable foundation for policy.

As we have seen, relevance may assume various forms, and appraisals must be specific about which is at issue. Since the most basic form is *instrumental* relevance, we will begin by evaluating the democratic peace proposition from that perspective (is it really true that democracies do not fight each other). Secondly, social science may help us understand how democracy itself can be promoted, adding *contextual* relevance to its contribution to our grasp of the range of the possible. Finally, it can shed light on the *costs*, if any, of pursuing global democratization, expanding our understanding of the consequences of the actions we take. We will examine each variant of relevant scholarship in turn.

Instrumental Relevance and the Democratic Peace Scholarship

Instrumental relevance concerns the association between policy and desired objective. Here, the objective is international peace, the instrument is democracy. The credibility of any proposition that claims instrumental relevance is proportional to the faith that can be placed in its truth—in this case, that democracies do not fight each other. Despite considerable academic support for this proposition, both the quality of the research and the theoretical assumptions that stand behind it have been questioned. With regard to the former, a number of methodological challenges have been directed at the correlation between joint democracy and dyadic peace. With regard to the theory, it has been suggested that the correlation may be an artifact masking other, more basic, influences on peace.

Methodological Challenges

Two complaints about the quality of the research are most often encountered. The first concerns the significance of the failure, by most scholars working in this area, to find any instance of a war between two democracies. The point is that war, among *any* two nations at any given time, is very unlikely. Even if these things were governed by chance alone, the proportion of wars between democracies, as well as those involving autocracies, would be very small. Therefore, it may be hard to assign much substantive significance to the absence of any instance of war between democracies. As one critic points out, the probability of winning the lottery is extremely small, so the fact that none of his immediate relatives ever won it cannot be imputed to anything specific about his family.[35]

Thus, Maoz and Abdolali, while finding no instances of wars in their democratic-dyad years, also found that only 0.10 percent of the nondemocratic dyad-years witnessed a war; and, if this were governed by chance only 0.12 percent of the democratic dyads would have experienced war. Obviously the difference between 0 percent, and either 0.10 percent and 0.12 percent is very small, as is the difference between those two figures. Thus, even a slight change in the way either democracy or war is measured could wipe out that difference.

A second problem with much of the democratic peace research is more technical. The issue is that the dyad-years used as the basic unit in most of these studies are not statistically independent—in the sense that the probability of war for one dyad is not unrelated to the probability of war for another—while the assumption of independence is required by the vast majority of statistical tests of association. The problem is evident both cross-sectionally and across time. Cross-sectionally, many of the war dyads are part of *multilateral* wars, meaning that individual dyadic wars are not independent events. For example, during World War I, the war between Russia and Germany was not independent of the war between Russia and Austria-Hungary, even though they are so considered for purposes of the statistical analysis. Across time, too, it is obvious that the war between Russia and Germany in 1916 is not independent of the war between the same two countries in 1917. When the assumption of independence is violated, the significance of any statistical relation found tends to be inflated—implying that the apparent relation between democracy and peace may be an artifact of the dependence of the dyad-years.

Thus there are two main criticisms of the quality of research under-pinning claims of a democratic peace: the sensitivity of the findings to mea-surement error and the statistical dependence of the units of analysis. How disabling are they?

Qualms regarding measurement procedures are hard to evaluate in a definitive manner. The variables directly involved are democracy and war. Measures of democracy typically are multivariate—as, for example in the frequently used Polity-II data set,[36] or in the data on freedom and democracy computed by Freedom House.[37] Generally, the measures encompass (a) the existence of free elections, (b) a meaningful measure of democratic account-ability, and, (c) constraints upon executive authority. These indicators are sometimes further weighted in the computation of the extent to which two nations are *jointly* democratic.

Although the exact threshold that divides democracies and nondemocra-cies is inevitably subjective, the conclusion that democracies do not fight each other has followed from studies using somewhat different operational definitions. In any case, as Alex Inkeles has observed: "indicators most com-monly selected to measure democratic systems generally form a notably coherent syndrome, achieving high reliability as measurement scales. . . . In the real world they are so intimately linked as to almost perfect substitutes for each other."[38] We recognize that there may be plausible ways of mea-suring democracy that could wipe out the finding that democracies do not fight each other, but we also feel that they would be no less plausible than those that confirm it.

As for war, it is generally measured by criteria established by the Corre-lates of War (COW) project, which assumes that the conflict is between two independent nation states (excluding civil, revolutionary, or colonial wars) and that the level of violence goes beyond the level of a minor skirmish. The threshold of violence required for a conflict to qualify as a war is a minimum of 1,000 battle deaths. While this comes close to a definition that most people would accept, the 1,000 figure is not inherent in any conceptual definition of war, such as would be found in a dictionary. Furthermore, different thresholds might yield different results. For example, a study by Erich Weede,[39] found that different conclusions on the democratic peace could be reached if the threshold were 1,000 battle deaths than if that thresh-old were 100.[40]

Obviously, variations in operational measurement of either democracy or war might yield exceptions to the proposition that democracies never fight

but, even so, plausible exceptions are few and far between.[41] Most fundamentally, this criticism reflects the fact that neither of these two terms has
a conceptual definition so precise in its ordinary meaning as to eliminate
all uncertainty at the level of operational measurement. From a policy perspective, the implications reach no further than this. Criticism regarding
chosen measures matters only to the extent that policymakers' understanding
of the meaning of either war or democracy are significantly at variance with
the meaning implied by those measures. It is unlikely that this would be the
case very often; thus, measurement issues should not affect the utility of
policies seeking to promote peace by encouraging the proliferation of democracies.

The more significant criticism concerns the lack of independence among
the dyad-years which most studies examine, and several solutions to this
problem have been suggested. Stuart Bremer[42] considered only the *original*
belligerents, and only the year in which the war began. While this obviously
limits the number of dependent dyad-years, it also leads to such implausible
anomalies as reducing World War II to the fighting between Germany and
Poland in 1939. A better solution is to treat the dependence as an expression
of conflict-*diffusion*, and to study it accordingly. This was done by Raknerud
and Hegre[43] who treat inter-dyad dependencies as diffusion of war effects.
In addition, they question the assumption of "stationarity" implicit in most
previous work—i.e., that the relation between dependent variables and predictor variables (in this case the probability of war and the presence or absence of democracy) does not change with time (e.g., that it is the same in
1830 as in 1980). In a sophisticated model incorporating these new assumptions, the authors confirm that, at the dyadic level, democracies are in fact
less likely to fight each other, but that they are no more pacific than autocracies in terms of their overall war involvement (while politically mixed
dyads are especially conflict-prone). A large part of the explanation, they
reckon, is in the different war-*joining* behavior of autocracies and democracies: while democracies do not go to war with each other, they are particularly likely to join other democracies in their wars with autocracies. This
information has obvious policy implications, since decisionmakers can benefit from knowing that, when involved in conflict, a democracy is more likely
to get help from other democracies than an autocracy is from other autocracies.

The finding that democracies do not fight each other implies that a world
with more and more democracies is likely to be a correspondingly peaceful

world; it establishes that regime type matters when it comes to foreign policy, and it casts substantial doubt on the claims of political realism, a doctrine that both scholars and policymakers are now increasingly questioning. Max Singer and Aaron Wildavsky, for example, argue that realist assertions must be challenged

> by the new reality of no war among the democratic great powers. . . . Relations among these countries will not be influenced by the need for military allies. Nor will they be concerned with the balance of military power among groups of democracies. . . . [D]emocracy is a basic long-term hope for achieving general peace.[44]

Within the policymaking community, Deputy Secretary of State Strobe Talbott, criticized traditional thinking that, under the heading of realism, focused foreign policy on matters of raw power, drawing the policy implications of the evidence in support of a democratic peace: namely, "that there is a hard-headed, national-interest based rationale for the promotion of human rights and democracy into the fabric of our diplomacy as a whole. It is, precisely, an imperative of 'realpolitik,' not just of 'idealpolitik.' "[45]

What light scholarship sheds on the possibilities of actually promoting democracy is information of a contextual sort, and we will address the issue presently. But it will be useful to linger on the generalization that democracies do not fight each other, to see whether this bivariate relation holds when a variety of ceteris-paribus circumstances are controlled for. In other words, we ask whether the relation does not mask other, more basic relations which, when taken into account, would make regime-type appear less relevant to the incidence of war. By understanding the influences that intervene between democracy and peace, as well as those that may mask the link, scholars help policymakers understand the why's and wherefores of a theoretical relationship of great practical moment.

Theoretical Challenges: Intervening and Confounding Conditions

It has been pointed out that the democratic peace may simply be an artifact of the cold war. The point is that during the cold war's 45-year duration, democracies as a group were linked by their common conflict with the Soviet Union and its allies. Social scientists understand that social entities faced with a common enemy are less likely to engage in conflictive behavior among themselves,[46] and it may be that many differences among Western industrialized democracies were muted during the period when they were linked by an overriding common cause. In other words, it is possible that that the Soviet threat, rather than anything intrinsic to democracy, accounts for much of the evidence in favor of the democratic peace.

One could argue that there were few, if any, wars among democracies at *any* time, not just during the cold war. Nevertheless, results such as those reported by Maoz and Abdolali would probably seem less persuasive if the cold war years, and thus the bulk of the democratic dyad-years, had not been part of the research. Moreover, research by Oneal and Russett, which covers only the 1950–1985 period (and which focuses on militarized disputes, not just wars),[47] finds that, while democracies are less likely to engage in such disputes, the existence of an *alliance* (several of which linked democracies during the cold war), also makes conflict less likely.[48]

A second issue is whether the lack of wars (or militarized disputes) among democracies is not a consequence of their economic interdependence — that trade and investment, not regime type, account for their disinclination to fight each other. A substantial body of theorists has argued that security dilemmas can be trumped by economic links among nations — rendering the opportunity costs of fighting too high. Again, the most valuable research is that of Oneal and Russett;[49] it reports that economic interdependence does indeed make a difference, without, however, wiping out the effect of regime type. Democracy continues to matter, but its pacific impact is amplified by economic openness and by trade interdependence. Of course, the exact nature of the causal relation may be debated — since democracies are also more likely to have open economies than are autocracies, and because they may be more inclined to trade with each other. Thus, even if regime-type makes a difference to the prospects for peace for cultural and/or structural reasons, it may do so *additionally* by the economic incentives it creates.

A final possible intervening variable, political stability, is also significant, because of its implications for policies to encourage the spread of democracy. It has been asserted that governments facing high levels of domestic disorder may seek to unify the society by involving it in a common struggle against an external enemy.[50] Moreover, if disorder is rooted in governmental performance, a foreign quarrel may deflect attention from its failures, and it might provide government with an excuse to tighten the reins of domestic control (say, by censoring the press, introducing martial law, etc.). Accordingly, a stable government may be less likely to initiate war.

Not only may unstable polities be tempted to start wars, they may also be *victims* of aggression—because they could seem incapable of mobilizing society for a fully effective defense. There is some evidence that the impact of regime type on war involvement at the dyadic level is lessened when political stability is also brought into the equation. For example, in a study that introduces an explicit control for stability, Maoz and Russett conclude that "Stable states are far less likely to fight one another than expected, regardless of their regime type."[51]

If so, the correlation between political system and peace may be spurious. Since it is well-documented that established democracies are more stable than nondemocracies,[52] stability may account both for flourishing democracy and for a disinclination to fight (at least with other democracies). However, it is also possible (and somewhat more likely) that democracy promotes stability, and that stability in turn promotes peace. If so, the relation would not be spurious—stability is simply an intervening variable. Even so, policy implications are apparent, for this conclusion suggests that, if a way could be found to ensure stability even in the absence of democracy, and if peace were the ultimate imperative, the incentive to promote democracy could be reduced.

We see that social science has not only provided the generalization about the democratic peace, of which policymakers took careful note, but also the caveats and ancillary propositions on which thoughtful policies could be based. In this way, it has shown relevance of an instrumental sort—describing the link between democracy and peace and defining the faith that should be place on it—and, to some extent at least, it has shaped the policy debate accordingly. Of course, it is not enough to know that the spread of democracy may promote peace; it is also useful to know how this proliferation could be encouraged.

Contextual Relevance: Foreign Policy and the Promotion of Democracy

The benefits of scholarship to policymaking extend beyond establishing ends-means relationships. Social science may also shed light on the context of instrumental relations, most notably by explaining how the means of policy (and even the intervening variables) may, in turn, be affected, and how their values may be anticipated. No part of the context of the democratic peace appears more important, from a decisionmaker's perspective, than the issue of how democracy itself can be promoted.

An exception not long ago, democracy has become the world's dominant political system. Not all countries have fully embraced all of its attributes, but few governments do not feel compelled at least to pay lip-service to the democratic idea, and few can claim legitimacy on the basis of any other principle.

Despite the recent diffusion of democracy, it is not obvious that the process is one of linear progress. Samuel Huntington,[53] reckons that the spread of democracy moves in cycles, and that we are currently experiencing its third wave. The first was witnessed between 1820 and 1920, when democracy spread through much of the Western industrialized world (and parts of Latin America). A second wave crested in the decades immediately following World War II, when decolonization often was associated with the adoption of the colonial powers' political forms. The third wave appeared in the mid-1970s, gathering momentum in Latin America, Eastern Europe, and to an extent in Africa, in the 1990s. However, as the previous two waves demonstrated, the process is not irreversible, and one may ask what can be done to ensure the expansion and consolidation of democracy?

From the perspective of the scholarship, the task is logically twofold. It should illuminate the objective conditions in which democracy is most likely to take root and flourish. Having done so, it should indicate to what extent and how these conditions can be molded by U.S. activities.

The Conditions of Democratic Transition: Insights of the Social Sciences

Although disagreements appear at the margins, and while scholars may disagree on the respective causal weights to assign to each, a broad consensus attends the general foundations of democracy,[54] and these may be grouped into several categories.

Economic prerequisites: No correlates of democracy have been as extensively studied, or accorded a more basic role, as those of an economic character. In Seymour Martin Lipset's early and influential view (1960, revised 1981): "The more well-to-do a nation, the greater the chances that it will sustain democracy" (p. 31 of 1981 edition), and numerous scholars agreed.[55] A large part of the reason for this view is that economic growth (presumably based on market principles) goes hand-in-hand with a growing and educated middle class, which generally eschews political extremism while embracing the fundamental tenets of the democratic process. As long, then, as disparities of wealth are reduced along with growth, society avoids a "runaway cycle of ever-increasing inequalities" wherein:

> a small minority with superior resources develops and maintains a hegemonic political system (often headed by a single dominant ruler) through which it can also enforce its domination over the social order and hence strengthen the inequalities even more.[56]

The notion that the outlook for democracy improves with economic growth came to be referred to as the "all good things go together" perspective,[57] it guided U.S. foreign assistance programs in the 1960s, and, in one view, it has "generated the largest body of research of any topic in comparative politics."[58] However, this research has produced a few caveats to the Lipset thesis, and these may provide useful contextual guidance to policymakers.

One caveat is that the outlook for democratic transition does not increase linearly with growing affluence. Alex Hadenius observes that the degree of democracy rises from low to somewhat higher levels of development but flattens out thereafter.[59] Przeworski and Limongi (1997) find that transitions from authoritarian to democratic regimes become more likely with increases in per capita income, but *only* to a level of about $6,000. "Above that, dictatorships become more stable as countries become more affluent."[60] In other words, beyond a certain threshold, added affluence may be *counterproductive* to a democratic transition.

Just as importantly, Przeworski and Limongi have shown that Lipset's argument probably is misspecified. The point is that two models may be implied by the notion of a democratic transition. The first is that economic development itself creates the conditions for the demise of authoritarian regimes—the implication being that policies that encourage development accelerate their dissolution (Lipset's thesis). The second is that economic development holds no privileged position in accounting for the *collapse* of authoritarian regimes, which can be the result of a variety of economic or noneconomic circumstances (war, for example). The role of affluence is felt *after* the collapse—in ensuring the survival of the democracy established at that point. Evidence amassed by these two authors supports the second model, suggesting that, whatever may cause the dissolution of authoritarian rule, the major function of affluence is to help ensure that it is not re-established.[61]

The policy implication is that encouraging economic development may not be enough to promote democracy, that increased wealth may actually strengthen authoritarian regimes after a point, and that other possible conditions for their demise should be addressed.

The Socio-Cultural Context: The structure of society and the character of the national culture may also shape the prospects for a country's democratization. To begin with, and related to the matter of economic development, a society not overly inegalitarian is a better candidate for democracy than one that is. According to many, this translates into the requirement for an educated middle class—a bourgeoisie. As Barrington-Moore put it: "No bourgeois, no democracy."[62] It is also considered desirable that the society should be functionally differentiated, with a strong service sector. In fact, Hadenius observes that the proportion of a society employed in the service sector is an even better predictor of democracy than are raw measures of economic development,[63] since a society with a developed service sector is also likely to be a well-educated society with a substantial middle class.

Political culture matters very much, as well, especially with regard to the value it places on civility in political discourse, its tolerance for a pluralism of beliefs, and its commitment to the primacy of process in collective decisionmaking. Samuel Huntington has further argued that not all religious cultures are equally conducive to democracy: Protestantism, in his opinion, is most so; Catholicism's case is more ambivalent, Islam, Confucianism, and Buddhism are hospitable to authoritarian rule. The crux of the matter is the extent to which a culture is "consummatory" in character—a matter determined by the degree to which intermediate and ultimate ends are connected, and how difficult it is to segregate politics from religion, and process from outcome.[64] Obviously too, the extent of a country's ethnic diversity, as well as the experience these ethnic groups have of each other, is a crucial facet of the socio-cultural context and predictor of the likelihood that democracy would prosper.

While a nation's socio-cultural attributes are not easily and directly malleable from without, understanding their nature may guide policy in two ways. First, by providing an appreciation of the limits of the possible, and by implication, a better predictive grasp of the international environment within which U.S. national goals must be pursued. Second, by indicating what, if any, *indirect* levers may be available for the purpose of shaping the socio-cultural context. In this regard, scholarship's insights on the way in which such contexts are shaped by economic growth may be most relevant. Nevertheless, an understanding of socio-cultural context's hold on political life may serve a cautionary function for the policymaker, since a facilitating political culture is not likely to take root in a society characterized by extreme inequality, or by deep ethnic or religious cleavages.

Institutional Foundations: We know that institutions shape political outcomes, and social science has cast considerable light on those upon which democracy rests. The importance of political parties to democratic development has, in particular, been extensively documented. We understand that parties are the key institutions for organizing political participation,[65] and that they perform their democratic function when they are a stable reflection of the interests of a meaningful segment of society, rather than an instrument of the personal ambitions of restricted elites.

Scholars have also examined the ways in which democracy requires properly constituted bureaucracies. Since Max Weber's seminal work on the subject, bureaucracy is recognized as a component of modernization, as a basis for *rational legal authority*.[66] We appreciate the extent to which nonpartisan bureaucracies are essential to the implementation of democratic decisions, and for ensuring the political system's procedural integrity. We also recognize that they cannot occupy too strong and independent position within the political system but must be accountable to representative institutions,[67] nor can they be mainly a vehicle for political patronage. A bureaucratic culture rooted in the ideal of a civil service is required, and the manner of bringing this about has been addressed by academics.[68] Similarly, but more obviously, democracy cannot function unless its military and police service operate on the basis of a professional, nonpartisan culture. While the military have played a significant role in the politics of the developing nations in recent decades, the conditions of their withdrawal from politics also have been the object of academic scrutiny.[69]

Accidents or Patterns: Background, macro-structural circumstances of the sort discussed above affect the likelihood that authoritarian rule will be challenged, and they probably improve the outlook that the democracies by which they are displaced would endure. Still, it has been observed that democratic transitions rest on many events that cannot be anticipated and on decisions whose implications cannot always be foreseen. As the editors of the most thorough current examination of the process observe, an adequate theory of transitions

> would have to include elements of accident and unpredictability, of crucial decisions taken in a hurry with very inadequate information, of actors facing irresolvable ethical dilemmas and ideological confusions, of democratic turning points reached and passed without an understanding of their future significance. . . . this is not to deny that the macrostructural factors are still there." . . . At some stages in the transition, in relation to certain issues and actors, those broad structures filter down to affect the behavior of groups and individuals. But even those mediations are looser, and their impact more indeterminate, than in normal circumstances.[70]

The important point, however, is that what appears accidental may not really be so, since systematic scrutiny often reveals structure where things initially seemed random. While the substance and consequences of human decisions appear less predictable than the impact of the sorts of macrostructural conditions discussed above, the task of the social sciences is to seek regularities where they are not immediately apparent, allowing them to provide policy guidance where none previously had appeared feasible.

Democratization and the Levers of Policy

Given an appreciation of the conditions that foster democracy, what guidance can scholarship provide U.S. policymakers concerning *specific* steps to promote such conditions? Focusing on the four classes of conditions surveyed above, the socio-cultural foundations of democracy are the least plausible candidates for external manipulation; the economic bases, on the other hand, are those about which most has been said. As one influential study notes, "at the current time . . . and no doubt in many previous decades, the most important international influences on prospects for democracy in developing countries appear to be economic ones."[71]

Because of its global economic sway, the United States is in a strong position to affect the course of democratic transformations. Here, scholarly contributions have generally kept in step with (but rarely preceded) the dilemmas identified by policymakers; associated work has been driven by explicit or implicit demand rather than by an initially disinterested supply.

Much as academic discussions on the impact of growth on democracy shaped the justifications for U.S. economic assistance policies in the sixties, the more recent emphasis on multilateral economic assistance has placed the spotlight on the policies of major international lending agencies—the IMF in particular—and on their social and political consequences for developing nations. During the 1980s, much social- scientific commentary on IMF policies concerned its insistence, as part of its conditionality agreements, on tight monetary policies, and on the removal of "structural impediments" to growth: usually in the form of large government deficits, monopolies, and excessive governmental regulation of economic activity. Academics examined the socio-political consequences of these priorities, consequences flowing from reduced government subsidies and other transfer payments, high interest rates, bankruptcies of companies denied government assistance, and increased unemployment with fewer programs to mitigate its most immediate consequences.[72]

More recently, discussion of IMF policies has focused on the consequences of its insistence on unfettered globalization—particularly with regard to international capital flows. It has been observed that, while the IMF has sought to free these capital flows in the 1990s, the volatility implied for many developing economies has amplified capital flight during economic downturns, causing exchange rates to collapse, and leading to the bankruptcy of firms unable to pay their foreign debts. The direct consequences for democracy have been examined,[73] and these appear as disruptive as those of the earlier, and never entirely abandoned, IMF conditionality requirements. Since the United States' is the single most important voice within the IMF, and as the organization's priorities produce socio-political consequences within recipient countries, scholarly scrutiny of these matters consequences bears directly on the impact of U.S. policies on democratization in the developing world.

Beyond economics, the U.S. is also in a position to strengthen the *institutional* bases for democracy in many nations, through direct assistance and in the context of international organizations—the United Nations in particular. Programs at building or rebuilding administrative structures, legislative and judicial bodies, and internal police forces have encompassed nations as diverse as El Salvador, Cambodia, and Haiti. Nonetheless, academics have not extensively explored the conditions attending the success or failure of such programs.[74] Yet, as with economic conditions, these are matters most competently examined by those whose expertise lends itself to the systematic study of regularities, and to rigorous inferential reasoning. This, then, is an area where scholarly contributions have not risen to meet policy needs, but where they are in a position to help shape national policy.

Earlier, we observed that part of what determines the success or failure of democratic transitions can appear as a series of apparently random events—usually in the form of choices that may or may not be taken and whose consequences, at the time, seemed almost impossible to foresee. Moreover, decisions by external actors, including the United States, are sometimes taken at these critical junctures, leaving a record of their impact for scholarly scrutiny, allowing a search for system where much had appeared random.

Thus, during the weeks and days in February 1986 when, following the fraudulent Philippine presidential elections, a variety of U.S. actions may have tipped the balance of power away from President Marcos and toward Corazon Aquino. A few days after the U.S. Senate and House condemned the electoral fraud, Philippine Defense Minister Enrile and Deputy Chief of Staff Ramos quit the Marcos government, took over defense headquarters, and called on Marcos to resign. The next day, the White House also called for Marcos to leave office, and offered to fly him to a safe haven in the United States (ultimately, spiriting him off to Hawaii). Three years later, when renegade troops sought to mount a coup against Aquino, President Bush declared that U.S. aid would be cut off in the event of its success, while U.S. warplanes based in the Philippines flew air cover for Government forces. The rebellion was quelled. In a related vein, in late April 1996, it appeared that Paraguay's first democratically elected president in half a century, Juan Carlos Wasmosy, was about to be overthrown by a coup led by his cashiered army commander General Lino Oviedo. A swift response by the Organization of American States, spearheaded by the United States, threatened Oviedo with economic and diplomatic isolation if he carried through his designs. This show of hemispheric clout, along with pro-Wasmosy demonstrations in Asuncion, may have made a decisive difference to the outcome.

We are unaware of much systematic examination of the link between critical events and critical U.S. decisions, but the need exists. The point is not only that what appear to be random critical junctures may yield a structure when subjected to scientific scrutiny, but also that there may be a pattern to the types of outcomes that U.S. activities produce in different circumstances. Causal empiricism and ordinary knowledge may not be enough to discover the underlying structures, and the tools and resources of scholarship may be called for.

The Costs of Seeking Democracy

We argued, in chapter 3, that the policy-relevance of knowledge can extend beyond its assistance in charting, via expanded instrumental and contextual understanding, the possibilities for foreign policy: it can also improve our grasp of the costs and consequences of various policies. While the direct costs of trying to forge democracy abroad may not be particularly high, the secondary cost, in terms of present gains foregone, i.e., opportunity costs, may be more significant. Moreover, present benefits may involve future costs, which may also have to be included in the decisional calculus. What light, if any, can the social sciences shed on these costs?

Opportunity Costs and the Politics of Linkage

During the cold war, the United States was often deterred from pressing too diligently for democracy by a fear of the geostrategic costs this might entail. The promotion of freedom at Communism's expense was translated into military and geopolitical goals that, in many cases, displaced their own ultimate objective — promoting the global democratic interest. This displacement of the end by its means was evident in Latin America, much of Asia, and parts of Africa, where particularly vicious right-wing dictatorships frequently were embraced by the United States as allies in its anti-Communist crusade. The preference for right wing dictatorships over left-leaning democracies in the developing world reflected a conviction that the geopolitical struggle could be jeopardized by attempts to reform totalitarian or authoritarian allies. Pressing for their democratization was a risk that the stakes did not appear to justify.

In a post–cold war context, the issue no longer involves a tradeoff between the promotion of democracy and global political objectives. If a tradeoff exists, it seems to be between the former and the pursuit of U.S. *economic* gain. Clearly, the nation's willingness to encourage democracy in oil-rich Saudi Arabia falls short of its willingness to do so in, say, Haiti. Similarly, the strength of U.S. dedication to democratic political rights in Cuba far exceeds its commitment to those rights in China. In both cases, fear of an *economic* cost accounts for the seemingly tepid interest in furthering democracy within certain countries.

Officials responsible for these policy choices usually deny that democracy is subordinated to a more tangible, but less lofty, concern. In their view, the best policy—the one they have chosen—is to *separate* the two pursuits, the nature of the link being such that attainments on either objective may suffer if made conditional on achievements on the other. Thus, according to former Secretary of State Madeleine Albright, "We determined some time ago that it was not a good idea to link human rights and trade, and that we actually make better progress in both when they are not linked."[75]

In principle, there are three possible approaches to the democracy vs. economic benefit dilemma, and rigorous scholarship may help clarify the choices. The first is to neglect the promotion of democracy within economically important authoritarian regimes, while trying to extract the utmost economic benefit from the relationship with them. The second, is to place a similar priority on both economics and democracy, without linking the economic relationship (from which both sides presumably benefit) to improvements in the partner's domestic politics (benefiting the desires of the U.S. government, but not its partner's). The third possibility is to link the economic relationship to progress at democratizing the partner's domestic political arrangements.

The choice of strategy depends on two sorts of awareness, while scholarship's contribution concerns the second of the two. The first type of awareness concerns the values to be placed on the foreign policy objectives of democracy promotion and economic gain, respectively, and this includes the matter of determining the acceptable terms of tradeoff between the two (to the extent that they are at all incompatible). In terms of the three strategies discussed, the first assumes that fostering democracy is considerably less important than the pursuit of U.S. material gain; the third implies that these priorities are reversed (because of a declared U.S. willingness to sacrifice economic gain if democracy does not advance sufficiently); the second strategy gives them equal weight. These are normative, not empirical, matters; and decisions at this level are appropriately made by a democratic process of weighing and aggregating societal preferences. Here, it is not obvious that scholars have any particular comparative advantage over other segments of the polity.

The desirability of a strategy depends not only on the relative preferences of U.S. society but also on the actual tradeoffs it faces. These are determined by the economic partners' responses, which, in turn, depend substantially on their own acceptable tradeoffs. A grasp of these preferences and calculations is an *empirical* matter, involving our second level of awareness; here, scholarship can make a considerable contribution by establishing the empirical logic on which U.S. decisions would depend.

The first of the three strategies assumes not only that economics is more highly valued than democracy-promotion by the United States but also that the other side objects to its own democratization more intensely than it values the economic relationship, and that it would sacrifice the latter to avoid the former. Accordingly, a tradeoff implying an economic loss to the United States is assumed. The second strategy assumes that the other side can be encouraged to pursue democratization even in the absence of economic incentives. Finally, the third strategy implies that the other side values the economic gain from the relation more than it objects to the costs associated with democratization, that it will accept the latter to enjoy the former. Here, the presumption is that there are other tools that the United States can use to promote democracy that would not cause the other side to disrupt the economic relationship. Plainly, each strategy makes different assumptions about likely preferences and calculations by the other side.

Scholars can help policymakers navigate this sort of dilemma by pointing to the logical implications of certain linkages, but more importantly by assessing their empirical truth or falsity. We need rigorous, general propositions about what leads nondemocratic governments to accept certain tradeoffs between desired internal political arrangements and economic gain offered by partnerships with the United States. These propositions must identify the conditions that influence how tenaciously such governments will cling to established political structures, as well as those that determine how badly they may want the benefits of an economic relationship offered by the United States. Only competent social-scientific research can produce credible generalizations of this nature.

To provide policy guidance in concrete instances, these generalizations must be supplemented by information on applicable initial conditions (the I's of explanation), since such information determines whether the circumstances specified in the general propositions are indeed met in the particular case. While scholars may contribute to the fund of knowledge bearing on initial conditions, it may often be the case that a statesman's sources of information may rival those of the social scientist. Although academia's comparative advantage lies with theoretical generalizations, it has not shed much light on economic and other costs implied by policies pressing for democratic reforms by major economic partners. This is an area of potential, not actual, scholarly contribution, and we present it as a gap that could profitably be filled.

Future Benefits and Present Costs: The Issue of Inter-Temporal Tradeoffs

As we argued in chapter 3, costs can be assessed not just in terms of tradeoffs between objectives, but also across time. Future interests can be sacrificed for present benefits, or vice-versa, and policy-relevant scholarship should also cast light on costs thus conceived; here, the literature offers more than it did in the previous case. The issue is that, while the process of building stable democracy should decrease the likelihood that states would fight, the transitional period may actually yield an *increased* likelihood they would do so. In two journal articles, one widely read by top policymakers, Edward Mansfield and Jack Snyder argued that, even if established democracies do not fight each other, countries in the process of democratization may be particularly war-prone.[76]

It is probably true that a world where more countries were mature, stable democracies would be safer and preferable for the United States. However, countries do not become mature democracies overnight. More typically, they go through a rocky transitional period, where democratic control over foreign policy is partial, where mass politics mixes in a volatile way with authoritarian elite politics, and where democratization suffers reversals. In this transitional phase of democratization, countries become more aggressive and war-prone, not less, and they do fight wars with democratic states.[77]

Examples of transitional democracies engaged in war are not limited to parts of the former Soviet Union and Yugoslavia, they include mid-Victorian England in the Crimean War, the wars engaged in by France at the time of Napoleon III, World War I and Wilhelmine Germany, and so forth. The explanation for the frequent readiness of transitional democracies to fight must, according to the authors, be sought in the nature of domestic political competition following the collapse of autocracy. Elites associated with the old order compete among themselves and with the new political elites. Struggling for public support to further their rival interests, they appeal to popular, often nationalist symbols. The passions thus unleashed can drive the nation to war, even where this was not the initial intent.

The authors provide a quantitative analysis of the relation between war and regime transition (relying of COW data for the first, on Polity-II for the second), reporting that, "On average, democratizing states were about two-thirds more likely to go to war than were states that did not experience a regime change."[78] The policy implication follows naturally: "In the long run, the enlargement of the zone of stable democracy will probably enhance the prospects for peace. But in the short run, there is a lot of work to be done to minimize the dangers of the turbulent transition."[79]

While Mansfield and Snyder's research was cast at the monadic (not dyadic) level, examining the general propensity of a state to fight, the argument about the dangers of democratic transition created a stir both within the policymaking and the academic communities. It encouraged the Clinton Administration to downplay the role of democratic enlargement in public statements of U.S. foreign policy. It also led scholars to examine the proposition about democratization and war, yielding a number of qualifications to Mansfield and Snyder's conclusions, and, by extension, to the policy implications of their work.

A study by Ward and Gleditsch examined the impact of key properties of regime transition on the probability of war involvement.[80] The authors asked to what extent this probability is affected by: (a) the *direction* of the transition (from autocracy to democracy or the other way), (b) the *magnitude* of the political change implied by the transitions, and, (c) the *smoothness* of the change (the extent to which the change is linear, rather than characterized by oscillations and reversals). Their conclusions are more nuanced than Mansfield and Snyder's, agreeing that, if the sole focus is on whether a change toward democracy has occurred or not (a binary statement of the issue), it can indeed be said that democratic transitions may encourage fighting (as might, for that matter, autocratic transitions). But the magnitude of the change is also very important, since changes of large magnitude in the democratic direction are associated with significantly *smaller* probabilities of war than are more modest steps. At the same time, rocky changes toward democracy heighten the likelihood of bellicosity (bolstering the hypothesis that stability may be as important as regime type in this respect).[81] The policy implications are that democratization need not be feared if peace is the ultimate objective—it all depends on whether the transition is substantial and smooth enough. Accordingly, changes of a large magnitude are to be encouraged, and all possible steps should be taken to discourage backtracking.

Even these findings are not fully conclusive. Like Mansfield and Snyder, Ward and Gleditsch examine the general bellicosity of democratizing nations, but unlike most of the work in democratic peace literature, they do not ask against what sorts of states (democratic or autocratic) this is apt to be directed. Thus, we do not know whether, during the transition process, the war-prone democratizing states would fight other democratizing states and full democracies. Another necessary observation is that this work establishes only the bivariate relation between the onset of war and the transition characteristic; unlike much research of the dyadic sort, it does not consider the possibility of intervening variables that may modify the impact of regime transition on war involvement.

Oneal and Russett,[82] however, examine both dyadic relations and intervening variables. They focus on the dyadic level of analysis, they control for number of intervening influences in addition to economic interdependence (e.g., territorial contiguity), and they examine the direction of regime change (either from autocracy to democracy or vice-versa). Their conclusion: "We find no indication that a dramatic change in regime type, either from autocracy to democracy carries an added risk of dyadic conflict."[83] At the same time, the intervening condition of economic interdependence remains significant. Thus, the only study so far to examine the impact of regime transition on dyadic conflict casts further doubt on Mansfield and Snyder's finding, suggesting it does not provide firm grounds for retreating from an active policy of democratic enlargement.

The policy implication is that worries about the short-term consequences of democratization must be taken with a large grain of salt: the process may not encourage external conflict if certain conditions are controlled for (economic interdependence, in particular); at most, a concern with ensuring the smoothness of the transition may be called for. This research also highlights scholarship's role in discouraging a belief that the world is simple, and that certain, easily grasped, causes invariably lead to clear-cut consequences. Democracy and peace do appear related—*under certain circumstances*. Democratization, despite the administration's concerns, may not imply war-proneness. The opportunity costs to the United States of insisting upon democracy on the part of economically valuable partners *depend on the assumptions* one makes. By insisting on causal complexity, social science's contribution may not always be what decisionmakers most desire, but it may provide what they frequently need.

Conclusions

There is little doubt that basic assumptions about world politics color the foreign policy strategies of U.S. decisionmakers. Much as the realism of the postwar period shaped (and legitimized) the cold war policies of containment and deterrence, so the democratic peace proposition influenced the Clinton administration's strategies of engagement and enlargement. Scholarship on the democratic peace influenced Clinton's formative foreign policy doctrines, and subsequent academic reservations about the proposition led to a recasting of the doctrine of enlargement.

Some of the academics associated with this body of work, while aware of its practical implications, have undertaken it for professional reasons largely unrelated to the pursuit of relevance. Others, (e.g., Bruce Russet, Rudolph Rummel) have been more explicit about the value of their research to policymaking. In any case, the impact of the democratic peace proposition is an instance of supply-driven relevance, demonstrating how concerns originating largely within the Ivory Tower can come to influence choices made in the corridors of power.

As theoretical propositions, the statements regarding the democratic peace and its various corollaries represent some of the best that social science has offered in recent years. From the standpoint of validity, conclusions follow from assumptions by logically compelling inference. From the standpoint of truth, the credibility of the propositions is buttressed by rigorous methods of empirical analysis and by explicitly operationalized variables. Generalizations about the cultural and structural characteristics of democracy provide a broader explanatory foundation for the democratic peace proposition. Moreover, the value of this body of work is evident—it is highly interesting from the perspective of knowledge per se, and it is of substantial practical value (proving that the two are not incompatible desiderata). Thus, work on the democratic peace, while policy-relevant, also rates very highly as theory (higher than much wholly disinterested international relations theory).

Not only has it helped mold statesmen's basic conceptions of the desirable and the possible, it also demonstrates to those willing to learn that a number of ceteris paribus conditions (e.g., economic interdependence) mediate the direct instrumental relation between democracy and peace. It alerts them to the particular dangers associated with democratic transitions, while indicating why such dangers must not be overstated (as the Administration may, implicitly, have done). In addition, and with a direct bearing on policy decisions, social science sheds light on the conditions that promote the transition to democracy. It has provided broad theoretical generalizations, but it also has helped qualify them in a manner relevant to the concerns of decisionmakers (as in the proposition about the threshold beyond which the link between wealth and democracy may no longer hold). Admittedly, it has not had enough to say on the manner in which specific U.S. policies can, in turn, affect these conditions; but it is well suited to address these issues and may well do so—perhaps in response to a specific demand originating from the policymaking community.

Most importantly, this body of work has demonstrated how knowledge and policy interact, and it has shown that both the quality and value of scholarship may benefit from tackling questions that are substantively meaningful.

6 International Institutions and the Possibilities for Cooperation: Theoretical Foundations and Policy Implications

Having explored the policy relevance of scholarship on the inter-democratic peace, this chapter inquires whether a second body of SIR, one focused on international institutions, has important policy implications. The challenges of dealing with a tightly interconnected international system are increasing, and national policy goals can rarely be attained without substantial international coordination. In principle, well-designed international institutions provide a way to develop and implement common policies to deal with collective problems, and it is hard to find an international issue that has *not* become increasingly institutionalized in recent decades.

Especially since the end of the cold war, intergovernmental organizations (IGOs) have become key vehicles for promoting democratization, human rights, open markets, and the transfer of advanced technology across sovereign borders. Not surprisingly, however, some international institutions are better equipped than others to deal with these problems. One scholar claims that "in recent years, we have gained insight into what makes some [international] institutions more capable than others—how such institutions best promote cooperation among states and what mechanics of bargaining they use."[1] If this is so, the theoretical and empirical literature on international institutions should carry important practical implications. Our purpose in this chapter is to examine these implications.

U.S. leaders appear vexed by the tradeoffs attending multilateral collaboration. As the world's only superpower, the United States has a clear stake in an orderly international environment, one that fosters effective international coordination and burden-sharing. For example, Americans prefer sanctions against rogue states to be imposed through international organizations, and U.S. officials have come increasingly to rely on agencies such as the World Bank and International Monetary Fund to manage the world economy and spread U.S. influence abroad.[2] Yet acceptance of international norms constrains national autonomy. Because the U.S. is less vulnerable to some international problems than other states and at times adopts a take-it-or-leave-it stance toward cooperation, U.S. officials periodically opt out of multilateral solutions to international problems. Washington's lack of enthusiasm for a proposed International Criminal Court—a seeming anomaly for a country rhetorically devoted to the rule of law—is a recent example. Such tradeoffs are not new: the unilateralist-multilateralist dilemma has been a recurring theme in U.S. foreign policy for more than a century. But it is thrown into sharper relief today, as deepening globalization and its attendant problems coexist with a domestic backlash against multilateralism.

If scholarly work on international institutions can shed light on these issues by illuminating the opportunities, constraints, and consequences of multilateral action, it should help officials shape external pursuits through multilateral means. Our discussion will proceed in four steps. First, we discuss the historical and intellectual context in which international organizations have developed over the last century and a half, focusing on the way in which scholars' analytical frameworks have colored their interpretations of these institutions' impact and effectiveness. Second, we examine what contemporary scholarship tells us about the instrumental links between foreign policy objectives and international institutions. Third, we explore the broader context in which these relationships operate, and we discuss some of the direct and indirect costs of multilateral institutions. We close the chapter by briefly examining the influence these ideas have had on policy analysts and policymakers.

The Historical and Intellectual Context of International Institutional Development

As used in this chapter, the term *international institutions* refers to routinized patterns of multilateral and bilateral practice that define acceptable behavior. Such institutions include informal as well as formal international regimes and intergovernmental bureaucratic organizations. Regimes can be defined as the norms and rules that regulate behavior in specific issue-areas involving international activities. Although the direct parties to these institutions are typically governments, the actors that are regulated may be non-state entities (such as the oil tanker owners and operators who have been the targets of the oil pollution discharge regime).[3]

IGOs generally constitute the administrative arm of international regimes and are responsible for their day-to-day operation and long-term development.[4] IGO secretariats service the interstate meetings through which regimes operate and support their ongoing work, often in ways that have a cumulative impact. For example, the extensive body of trade case law built up since the 1950s has mainly been a product of the legal expertise housed within the GATT and WTO secretariats. Because a good deal of international activity is regulated on a problem-specific basis, many of the examples in this chapter will be of regimes that provide a framework through which states seek to achieve specific policy goals.

IGOs and regimes have become a very visible feature of modern international policymaking. There were fewer than 40 IGOs in the decade before World War I; now there are more than 400. In the middle of the nineteenth century, when the first modern IGOs were established, they sponsored two or three interstate conferences a year; today, close to 4,000 meetings are held annually under the auspices of international institutions.[5] Not only national governments, but also multinational firms, trans-state lobbies, and domestic political groups try to capture these institutions for their own purposes, and IGO officials also try to shape their own environments. Because these relationships are complex, observers, including IR scholars, differ over how much international institutions affect states' actions. To appreciate the issues involved, it is helpful to provide some background about when and why international institutions emerged and scholars' differing interpretations of that story.

The Historical Context

Four major developments have catalyzed the growth and development of international institutions since the nineteenth century. The first was the Concert of Europe system, a product of the 1815 Treaty of Paris that ended the Napoleonic Wars. It established the precedent that the major powers would deliberate about the region's stability, even in the absence of a war or a crisis, and would act together when possible. Although barely institutionalized by contemporary standards — the Concert was strictly intergovernmental in nature, with no administrative structure aside from its governments — its meetings broadly foreshadowed the Group of Seven summits that began in the 1970s and planted the seeds for more fully institutionalized arrangements down the road.

The second development consisted of the creation of several "Public International Unions" beginning in the mid-nineteenth century. These interstate agencies took up such problems as the trans-border standardization of telegraph communications, improvements in the efficiency of interstate mail delivery, the standardization of international patent and copyright protection, and many other such tasks over time. In coordinating such tasks, they supplemented the existing administrative responsibilities of national governments in areas where states were becoming increasingly commercially and technologically interdependent.[6]

The third development began at the turn of the twentieth century, when governments began sending representatives to conferences at the Hague for the purpose of creating and codifying the practices of warfare. The Hague system, as it came to be called, was halted by World War I, but resumed in the 1920s and again after the end of World War II in the late 1940s. The fourth development, the creation of global, multipurpose IGOs, involved more ambitious security objectives. The League of Nations and the United Nations were designed as global collective security bodies, intended to deter aggression by the expectation of a concerted response from member states. To make that kind of response palatable, all members were given a veto in the League Council, while in the UN the five permanent members of the Security Council had to agree for joint action to take place. But global collective security has at most worked only once as fully intended, in the 1991 Persian Gulf War. Both bodies have nonetheless made other major contributions to world order. Under their auspices, international regimes and IGOs designed to solve problems in areas such as labor standards, the liberalization of international trade, and the financing of international development have developed.

Except for the period just after World War II, the largest number of IGOs has been created to foster interstate trade. For many years the next largest group focused on conflict management, though by the 1980s economic development IGOs had become more numerous. Nevertheless, wealthy states are represented disproportionately in contemporary IGOs.[7]

Not surprisingly, these institutions have had a mixed record of achievement. The League failed to uphold the principle of collective security during the interwar years, but fostered economic, social, and human-rights work quite advanced for its era. The United Nations has played a key role in decolonization and development. Its officials nurtured the development of peacekeeping, a form of conflict management in which neutral forces monitor agreements between warring parties and seek to prevent new violence. But it has also been plagued by a bloated bureaucracy and public forums more noted for bombast than content. The two agencies chiefly responsible for management of the world economy, the International Monetary Fund and World Bank, have mainly been praised by the wealthy countries, but have often been castigated by the poorer ones on grounds of insensitivity to their needs. Overall, international institutions have broadened the agenda of international politics and have affected the way in which many international problems, especially socioeconomic ones, have been handled. And even though the UN and other global IGOs with broad mandates have often been seen only as "talk-shops," the organizations and regimes with narrower mandates have been more effective.[8] At the same time, international institutions rarely acted decisively on major security issues during the twentieth century[9], and there is little reason to think that this pattern will soon change.

The Intellectual Context

The two major theoretical traditions within IR interpret this record quite differently, a difference that reflects deep disagreement about the possibilities for international cooperation. Liberals—those who believe that common values or interests can induce states to work together—take an optimistic view. They believe that governments can commit themselves to common norms, standards, and institutions that facilitate joint action even in the absence of centrally enforceable international rules. In this view, international institutions can be used to increase or stabilize the benefits of peace, such as economic interdependence, and to raise the costs of war, perhaps through collective punishment of aggression. By contrast, Realists expect little from international cooperation other than that based on shared security fears. International institutions, they say, are either ineffective in restraining behavior or just legitimize the position of powerful states. When states' objectives conflict, Realists argue, so will their behavior—regardless of prior commitments to institutions.

At least since the eighteenth century, much of the debate about international institutions has been framed by these two broad views. A third and more recent view examines how people's social identities and norms may be fostered by their institutionalized relationships. Because interests here are seen to grow out of social relationships, rather than as analytically prior to them, it is neither *a priori* optimistic or pessimistic about the possibilities for institutionalized cooperation.

The Liberal Tradition and International Institutions   Liberal thinking about the prospects for institutionalized cooperation has gone through three major phases. This evolution has taken Liberals from a position that featured grandiose objectives, but lacked a plausible mechanism to achieve them, toward a more practical approach grounded in the concrete objectives of national policymakers.

The first phase began in the fifteenth century, when a number of writers began offering plans for interstate organizations they hoped would control or even end war in Europe. Notable proposals came from the duc de Sully (who served as chief minister to Henry IV of France), Emeric Cruce, Hugo Grotius, William Penn, the abbé de Saint-Pierre, Jeremy Bentham, and Immanuel Kant. All of their plans called for a voluntary association of states that would be represented within a central body. For these thinkers, the balance of power had never led to peace and was inherently incapable of doing so. Just as individuals had escaped the dangers of stateless societies by contracting to form governments, they reasoned, states could likewise delegate some autonomy to institutions that could mediate or otherwise reduce conflicts among them.[10] Kant focused less than the other writers in this group on the coercive role of international institutions; for him, effective interstate institutions would emerge, if they did at all, out of an international civil society comprised of republican states.[11] But these writers shared core assumptions, which constitute the Idealist school within the broader Liberal tradition. They believed (1) that progress is possible among states just as it is within them, (2) that human agency can significantly move humankind down a progressive sociopolitical road, and (3) that there is a natural harmony of interests among states.[12] The third assumption implies that any conflicts that do arise among states reflect actors' temporary misunderstandings rather than fundamentally incompatible state objectives. Based on these premises, each of these thinkers saw an important role for institutionalized interstate cooperation in bringing humankind closer to perpetual peace (the title of Kant's famous essay, discussed in more detail in chapter 5).

These proposals were very impractical and had little impact on European rulers of the day. Except for Kant's plan, the league of states they called for was supposed to be able to control or coerce governments that violated group norms.[13] How this was to be achieved within a voluntary body was never spelled out. Behind all of these plans was the presumption that the practices of power politics *must* be tamed by force of institutionalized rules, since failure was simply unacceptable. Such thinking was revived by the horror of World War I. In referring to the League, Woodrow Wilson offered no reasoned argument about how it would help prevent future wars; instead, he said "if it won't work, it must be made to work."[14] Not surprisingly, when universal IGOs were built during the twentieth century, they did little to undermine the anarchic structure of the international system.[15] If anything, in affirming the importance of juridical sovereignty, they reinforced the basic logic of self-help at the state level. In this sense, the most optimistic thinkers about war, peace, and institutionalized international cooperation have repeatedly been disappointed.[16]

A second phase in the evolution of Liberal thinking on these issues came with the realization that the Idealists' goals had been too ambitious. According to this line of argument, the institutions likeliest to succeed were not those with grand political objectives. Effective institutions would be those that served specific practical functions—namely the coordination of rule-making and implementation for technical problems common to many states. This summarizes British Functionalism, a school of thought with a strong and enduring contribution to SIR beginning in the nineteenth century.[17] It began with Jeremy Bentham, Richard Cobden, and John Stuart Mill—classical Liberals who believed that the same community of interests linking individuals could be created among states, provided that voluntary exchanges across boundaries were unhindered. International order would reflect a harmony of interests, but only on bread-and-butter issues. This harmonious result would be created through a spontaneous, bottom-up process that operated through transnational civil society. It would require little organizational guidance or coordination from governments.

After the Great Depression, this laissez-faire argument was replaced by one that recognized the major welfare functions of modern states. International welfare, it was argued, would be best served by integrating the functions states were now performing, rather than by wishing state functions away.[18] A key proponent of this idea was David Mitrany.

Mitrany's thinking was driven by a belief that war stems from socio-economic problems such as poverty, illiteracy, and economic insecurity. But he rejected international solutions that involved a frontal challenge to sovereignty. He proposed instead that efforts to improve the quality of life be task-specific, "each [task] according to its nature, to the conditions under which it has to operate, and to the needs of the moment."[19] The "Functionalist" argument that followed from this premise meant that each effort's organizational form would be dictated by its specific function. Over time, Mitrany reasoned, cooperation would flourish through a twofold process. As people's socioeconomic needs were met across national jurisdictions, the tasks would be expanded. For example, successfully preventing crop erosion in a poor country might stimulate other efforts to make farmland more productive. Cooperation would also "spill over" into new areas: as farm yields grow, pressures to manage commodity export prices might grow as well. As people across states joined in these activities, state institutions would lose much of their *raison d'être*, and thus their practical and emotional grip on individuals and groups.[20] In this way, Mitrany believed that "the artificialities of the zoning arrangements associated with the principle of sovereignty would be broken down."[21] Not only would people live better, regardless of *where* they lived or *who* they were, but their attachment to particular states was expected to weaken as state functions were transferred, bit by bit, to transnational bureaucratic management.

But Mitrany's scheme had a serious flaw: it tried to bypass politics. "In many fields," he claimed, "arrangements between states have been settled and developed directly in conferences attended by technical experts representing their respective technical departments, without passing through the complicating network of political and diplomatic censors."[22] But even if senior officials at times delegate technical issues to lower-level officials, they do so at their own discretion. Mitrany was naive to view political and diplomatic considerations as "complications" when politicians or diplomats would often be held directly accountable for the consequences.

A Neofunctionalist school of thought emerged in the 1960s, in part as a response to the Mitrany's technocratic determinism. Ernst Haas, one of its leaders, agreed with orthodox Functionalists that task-specific programs could enhance international welfare, if they were kept organizationally separate from broad ideological disputes. But, unlike Mitrany, he viewed the process and consequences of international collaboration as *inherently* political. For lessons learned in one functional area to be applied to others, political actors would have to make that choice for self-interested reasons. They could just as easily learn *not* to deepen or broaden their cooperation. Related to this, Neofunctionalists expected that politically disinterested technical expertise might be ignored. Unless experts' recommendations were tied to concrete benefits that mattered to politically relevant constituencies, those ideas would likely be of little use.[23] From a Neofunctionalist perspective, the prospects for building viable international institutions were slighter than Functionalists had hoped or expected. Neofunctionalists were thus not surprised that the institutions created in the twentieth century had such a mixed record.

Neofunctionalism was not just a reaction to the naivete that characterized orthodox Functionalism. It also tried to account for an intriguing puzzle: the slowing of what had been seen in the 1950s as a trend toward integration at the regional level. When that process stalled in Europe beginning in the mid-1960s and failed to catch on elsewhere, analysts tried to explain why Functionalist "logic" had escaped so many policymakers. But observers soon had another puzzle to explain, one for which Neofunctionalism had no ready answer. During the 1970s, the world economy suffered a number of serious shocks. Oil prices skyrocketed, the Bretton Woods exchange-rate system disintegrated, and North-South economic relations became notably more acrimonious. Yet in some issue-areas, international institutions were more of a presence than in others or were performing better in managing the situation. The international monetary regime made a transition from fixed to floating exchange rates, in the process creating a new role for the International Monetary Fund as a broker of privately supplied liquidity to insolvent governments. The oil-importing states created the International Energy Agency to manage shortfalls in petroleum supplies. At the same time, there was no international regime for foreign direct investment, which had become an area of increased contentiousness, and the norm of nondiscrimination in the international trade regime had become honored in the breach almost as much as in practice. How could these uneven patterns of international regulation and regulatory effectiveness be explained?

This question stimulated the third phase of Liberal thinking about international institutions. Neoliberal Institutionalists noted that certain aspects of the international environment seem to inhibit bargains governments otherwise would want to make with one another. First, sovereignty means that property rights—actors' ability to possess and exchange assets with the knowledge that they can make liability claims if their rights are violated—are fragile across state lines. Second, because information about others' behavior is costly and unevenly distributed, governments may be uncertain about which policies will benefit them. Third, negotiating many separate issues on an *ad hoc* basis rather than under the aegis of general standards can be inefficient. Political Scientist Robert Keohane argued that international institutions can help states address all of these problems, making it easier for them to cooperate where they otherwise might not.[24]

From a Neoliberal perspective, international institutions serve governments by setting agreed-upon standards and monitoring compliance with them. Enhancing the quantity and quality of information is central: without knowledge about others' intentions, officials will have doubts about whether agreements will be honored. This tends to inhibit costly commitments, even those that might serve a state well. International institutions address this problem by making governments' behavior more transparent and by stabilizing expectations through the development of common standards. This occurs in several ways. Dealing with the same set of issues and actors over time tends to tie actors' reputations to their compliance records. By monitoring governments' compliance behavior and by publicizing it, asymmetries of information that can hurt some parties relative to others—and thus inhibit agreements—are evened out. Enforcement may also be easier within an international institution than it is bilaterally: common norms provide a standard against which to hold others responsible and, if necessary, punish them. Finally, institutions also lower states' bargaining costs by clustering issues together. Doing so obviates a need to invent new rules for each issue and makes it easier for negotiators to link concessions across issues within the same overarching regime. For all of these reasons, Neoliberals expect international institutions to become more numerous and relevant as interdependence deepens.[25]

Neoliberal Institutionalism made an important contribution in showing how regimes help states deal with uncertainty and commitment problems. These problems are inherent in mixed-motive situations—those where the parties' interests are partly compatible, yet partly competitive. Theorists agree that mixed-motive conditions are more typical of social life, including international relations, than completely harmonious or totally conflictual situations. But they present policymakers with significant tradeoffs. Overlapping goals provide a reason to make agreements; the conflicts provide reasons to cheat or otherwise gain unilateral advantages over others. In showing how international institutions can help governments manage these problems, Institutionalists helped explain how states are able to act on their complementary interests when there are also reasons not to do so. In this way, Neoliberalism helps explain why institutions are capable of outlasting the particular intergovernmental bargains that produced them—something Neofunctionalism is hard-pressed to explain. But Neoliberal theorists were able to achieve these results only by narrowing considerably what they have tried to explain. In their argument, institutions stand out as useful tools *given* a set of overlapping state interests. If interests themselves are more open-ended,[26] the Neoliberal approach is less compelling.

In sum, Liberals explore how institutions can be used to realize complementary yet latent benefits across societies. At times, the benefits themselves, such as species preservation or nonproliferation, can be achieved only if everyone's actions are predictably restrained. Cooperation can also foster risk-sharing and burden-sharing. Fundamentally, Liberals take such shared goals for granted and ask how barriers to cooperation can be minimized. While Liberalism has been the main intellectual context within which international institutions have been discussed, two other traditions, Realism and Social Constructivism, have also had a role in the conversation.

The Realist Tradition and International Institutions   In contrast to Liberalism, Realism offers a fairly bleak perspective on the order-producing potential of international institutions. From a Realist perspective, progress toward intersocietal cooperation is limited by power politics. States cannot trust one another enough to stop competing. The only significant exception to this generalization is joint action to deal with a shared security threat. These constraints, Realists believe, typically give officials little flexibility to work together.[27] In this environment, institutions can do little to foster or upgrade common international interests.

Two processes produce this pattern.[28] First, international institutions remain weak because states control the only real leverage in world politics. States have authoritative control over all behavior on their territories, which means that international institutions are weak trustees of state purposes. These institutions have little political or legal life of their own. Since at least the seventeenth century, anything approaching supranational authority outside of the European Union has been summarily rejected. Because the United States has refused to pay millions of dollars in assessments, the UN is insolvent; even the International Monetary Fund, regarded as one of the most capable institutions, is tightly dependent on the wealthy states for contributions.

The failure to implement a collective security system in the League or the UN can also be seen, from a Realist perspective, as a reflection of states' determination to remain autonomous. Aside from the way it is institutionalized, collective security is prone to serious collective-action problems: even states that would prefer a strong regime capable of deterring aggression are often tempted to let others supply the forces or take the casualties that the commitment requires. But a strong distrust of powerful intergovernmental bodies puts the objective even further out of reach. The standby military forces that UN Security Council members pledged to commit for enforcement purposes have never been put at the organization's disposal. As a result, to fight the Gulf War, a coalition had to be constructed largely *ad hoc* by the United States.

Realists also highlight a second constraint on international institutions: a tendency for state officials to define their international interests competitively. As Kenneth Waltz put it,

> When faced with the possibility of cooperating for mutual gain, states that feel insecure must ask how the gain will be divided. They are compelled to ask not 'Will both of us gain?' but 'Who will gain more?' . . . [T]he impediments to collaboration may not lie in the character and immediate intention of either party. Instead, the condition of insecurity—at the least, the uncertainty about the other's future intentions and actions—works against their cooperation.[29]

By Waltz's reasoning, this problem constrains states from cooperating more powerfully than the first, since nothing about sovereignty *per se* requires that its present meaning remain fixed. If all that was at stake for states was their status as autonomous actors, they could decide that realizing complementary interests across societies was of prime importance and pursue this objective by delegating some authority to IGOs. But according to Realists, the competitive logic of self-help is a tight constraint on states that care about their security; it inhibits any cooperation that could create more capable state rivals down the road. From this vantage point, any mutual restraint that is evident has little to do with institutional rules or norms, and is simply a byproduct of competitive power considerations. Beyond this, cooperation is likely to be much less frequent than Liberals believe. Realists thus conclude that "what is most impressive about international institutions . . . is how little independent effect they seem to have on state behavior."[30]

Conversely, Realists contend, when we *do* see extensive institutionalization it tends to reflect the interests of a dominant state. Hegemonic states are able to shape international relationships in such areas as security, trade, and monetary affairs; in return, such states subsidize or protect their junior partners. They tolerate uneven burdens, surmounting collective action problems by indulging free-riding.[31] For example, the United States fostered extensive institutionalization in Western Europe in the 1950s as a way to harness German military and economic resources in the cold war. The geopolitical situation in East Asia made it less crucial for Japan to become a regional military power at that time, so Asian relationships were less formally institutionalized.[32] If institutionalized relationships have taken on a life of their own, particularly in Western Europe, one may need Liberal insights to explain contemporary behavior. But even Neoliberal analysts agree that uneven power resources are crucial at an institution's early stages as a way to reassure vulnerable states, subsidize poor ones, and guarantee key commitments.[33]

Social Identities, Norms, and International Institutions   Unlike Liberals and Realists, adherents of sociological approaches assume that policymakers' objectives are malleable, not largely fixed, and that they are affected by the transnational society in which they and their states are nested. This society (or the parts of it with which officials and domestic groups identify) shapes the ideas, norms, and identities that resonate with decisionmakers.[34] Just as Kant assumed that republican states would constitute a society with values quite different from those in a monarchical society, contemporary discussions of democratization and human rights could be interpreted to reflect transnationally defined (and often hotly contested) notions of how "the public good" should be defined. Values, from this point of view, are "constructed" out of a dynamic process of social learning and interaction.

The issue of how social groups politically shape individual actors politically lies at the heart of this approach. What people want depends on whom they interact with, how attached they are to those groups, what they learn from the interaction process, and how they legitimate their preferences and knowledge claims to others. Social structures, such as the Indian caste system or the hierarchy of elites that manages the international monetary system, embody particular norms, and the actors that operate within those structures learn preferences through socialization into the group. Two propositions follow from these assumptions. First, the more attached people are to group-defined notions of legitimacy, the likelier they are to accept policies and decisionmaking procedures they might otherwise reject on grounds of individual self-interest. Second, as people's understanding of legitimacy or the nature of their community change, so will their fundamental preferences.[35]

From a Constructivist perspective, international institutions play two roles in these processes. Because these institutions often embody shared causal and prescriptive meanings, what counts as a legitimate rationale for behavior within them must be justified in terms of those meanings.[36] An official trying to explain behavior inconsistent with World Trade Organization rules cannot say her government dislikes the rule at issue; some extenuating circumstance or countervailing norm must be offered. To understand state behavior, the analyst therefore takes note of what is being justified and how others interpret it. Out of such dialogue, international institutions become forums within which norms are applied, interpreted, and evolve.

International institutions can also serve a more active role, as propagators of norms. Sociologists have long noted how organizations such as schools, hospitals, and business firms socialize students, medical personnel, and employees; the organizational culture becomes a part of their value-set. Martha Finnemore has shown similar processes at work in the interaction among international organizations and states. IGO officials have socialized governments to accept new goals and values in areas such as governmental organization of science policy and the choice of appropriate development strategies for poor states.[37] Of course, IGOs have limited leverage in these situations, since governments remain free to reject any such advice. But from a Social Constructivist perspective, it may be hard to understand why they would accept it—especially, as Finnemore argues, when at times there were important practical reasons not to do so—unless the institutions involved were seen as carriers of persuasive and legitimate standards.

As we have seen, there is an extensive body of theoretical work on the role that international institutions play in fostering cooperation. In examining whether this work can help decisionmakers, we begin by exploring its instrumental relevance. If international institutions operate in the ways just discussed, how could policymakers use them? We then discuss whether the conditions necessary for these instrumental relationships to operate are in fact likely to exist, which opens up the possibility that the work just discussed might have contextual relevance.

Instrumental Relevance: International Institutions as Direct Facilitators of Cooperation

Although they have not focused very explicitly on policy implications,[38] Neoliberal Institutionalists have implicitly explained the existence of international institutions in instrumental terms. In their account, these institutions are useful because they can minimize incentives to defect from agreements and provide incentives that make cooperation more likely. They do this by helping officials monitor and enforce their commitments and by facilitating efficient, productive bargaining across various sets of issues. In both ways, institutions help to lengthen what scholars call the "shadow of the future"—the degree to which future benefits from cooperation are taken into account when decisions are made about honoring present commitments. When governments take this seriously, they sacrifice immediate benefits in the expectation that others will reciprocate over an indefinitely long future. Effective regimes thus institutionalize a set of practices based on long-term restraint and reciprocity, making it easier for states to achieve their complementary interests.

Institutions as Tools for Monitoring and Enforcing Agreements

SIR emphasizes three ways in which international institutions facilitate monitoring and enforcement. First, they establish rules that define permissible behavior. In so doing, institutions help stabilize people's expectations, reducing the uncertainty that may foster instability in a relationship or become a source of decisionmaking stress for the participants.[39] As a result, behavior becomes more predictable.

These benefits appeared during the long truce that separated the 1956 and 1967 Arab-Israeli wars. After the 1956 war, a tacit security regime prevented a conflict that neither Egypt nor Israel wanted. It was implicitly agreed that Egypt would not blockade the straits of Tiran at the tip of the Sinai peninsula, and that its offensive forces in the Sinai would remain limited. Egypt also agreed to accept UN peacekeepers on its territory. From

Israel's perspective, any change in these arrangements, and especially any redeployment of the Egyptian army, would have signaled a dangerous change in Egyptian intentions. But as long as the Israelis could monitor those forces, they believed they could detect key changes in Egyptian behavior. Over an eleven-year period, these arrangements allowed expectations on both sides to stabilize, making it easier to manage the truce.[40]

Second, institutions provide significant information to its members. In areas where the parties understand important implications of their own actions, their behavior may be modified in desired ways. For example, international institutions established to slow the proliferation of weapons of mass destruction house substantial technical expertise, much of it dealing with the dangers that accompany the transfer of dual-use technologies. States often use this data in formulating their export-control policies. Likewise, governments may need mechanisms to share and discuss intelligence about how well an institution's rules are working. Similarly, the extent to which the procurement policies of threshold nuclear-weapons states are constrained by export restrictions is a key concern. For example, the elaborate foreign procurement network Iraq built to obtain weapons technology went undetected until the International Atomic Energy Agency (IAEA) and the UN Special Commission on Iraq (UNSCOM) combined their data. This suggested that the controls and the information about them that had been collected up to that point had been inadequate.[41]

Information about members' compliance can be vital when there are temptations to cheat. In the case of nonproliferation regimes, exporting prohibited items may be attractive: to help defense producers (and thus domestic employment) and to strengthen ties with recipient governments (thus increasing the exporting nation's influence in a particular region).[42] Former British Trade and Industry Secretary Nicholas Ridley framed the problem bluntly. Speaking about his government's exports of sensitive materials to Iraq, he claimed that restraint would only benefit Britain's commercial competitors, "since we have no evidence that they take as restrictive a view [of export restrictions] as we do."[43] Especially if the chance of detection seems slight, it may hard to dissuade states from acting on such temptations.

Mutual restraint under these conditions is possible only if behavior can be monitored closely enough. A lack of high-quality information about others' capabilities and behavior raises suspicions that some parties will cheat or otherwise gain unfair advantage. For example, many industrial states will follow dual-use export-control rules only as long as they believe that most others are doing so. To this end, requiring dual-use technology suppliers to furnish information on their nuclear, chemical, and missile-component export policies may deter some violations or lax internal control procedures,[44] perhaps by encouraging domestic bureaucracies to police the situation better themselves to avoid embarrassment. By collecting the relevant data and furnishing it to all members of a regime, an international institution can help address these concerns.[45]

Third, international institutions help enforce rules (another function emphasized by SIR), although this function is performed less directly than the other two. These institutions typically have no power over their members other than a capacity to foster mutually beneficial behavior and, if the right information about compliance is collected, a capacity to identify defectors. Yet therein lies their enforcement leverage, according to Neoliberal scholars. All else being equal, if governments value others' cooperation on other issues down the road or value their own reputations as trustworthy partners in future agreements, they will tend to comply with their commitments today, even if they have incentives to cheat.[46] Of course, decisionmakers must believe in the possibility of future benefits and believe that violations today are likely to be detected, putting future benefits at risk. Neoliberal analysts take the first belief as common, if not a given. They see a complex world consisting of many interconnected issues, offering many opportunities for joint welfare to be improved through mutual restraint and cooperation. Whether decisionmakers also hold the second belief depends significantly on how international institutions are designed. To the extent that clear standards for behavior are identified and pertinent information about compliance is pooled, states' reputations for compliance should become common knowledge.

This line of argument suggests four variables, all of which can be manipulated, that affect how well international institutions monitor and enforce agreements. Officials can ask how cooperation problems might be mitigated by collecting and pooling certain kinds of information. Policymakers can try to craft rules that will be relatively easy to enforce. It may be possible to limit the number of participants so as to ease monitoring and enforcement problems. Finally, officials can determine how elaborate the rules and monitoring procedures must be to maximize the likelihood of compliance.

First, policymakers can take remedial action if they find that cooperation is likely to be inhibited because of inadequate information. For example, the right kind of information may be able to keep governments or firms from working at cross-purposes in cases where a lack of coordination would quickly become counterproductive. By monitoring international oil stocks and developing contingency plans for emergencies, the International Energy Agency helps governments act together during an oil emergency. These procedures may have helped prevent panic buying by both governments and firms during the 1980 oil crisis.[47]

Scholars have also pointed out that the way information is collected may be open to choice, depending on the degree of intrusiveness the parties will accept and the available inspection technology. For example, whether the parties must submit regular evidence that they are complying with the rules or simply submit to inspections upon allegations of noncompliance is open to some discretion.[48] There would seem to be a tradeoff: the greater the damage a party would suffer quickly if another violated an agreement, the more transparent an inspection system would have to be. On the other hand, the more demanding the inspections, all else being equal, the less likely governments are to accept such procedures. As technology evolves, the degree of intrusiveness required for effective inspections might drop. Underground nuclear tests can now be detected reasonably accurately without on-site inspections, something that was much more difficult during the early cold war years. But detailed on-site inspections are still needed to verify compliance with the Chemical Weapons Convention, since prohibited materials can easily be stored in many places.

It may also be possible to craft rules in ways that induce compliance. When the type of behavior that is singled out for regulation is highly transparent, it is easy to detect violations. When governments or private actors they deputize have particular incentives to identify violators, more will be found. And when most violations can be prevented in the first place by effective monitoring, it becomes unnecessary to detect and punish them after the fact. In short, designing regulatory burdens so that the actors have incentives to comply will significantly enhance compliance. These principles were successfully implemented during the 1970s in an international regime designed to control discharge of waste oil at sea by tankers. Rather than sanction discharges after they had occurred, rules were crafted to require that tankers carry equipment that cleans the waste material on board. This made it easier to detect noncompliance before any violation occurred. By delegating the task of certifying the cleaning equipment to private actors who had incentives to report honestly, rather than leaving the reporting of discharges to ship operators or governments that have financial stakes in the oil or tanker businesses, violations dropped significantly.[49]

Of course, these lessons will not be applicable in every regulatory situation. In the waste-oil pollution regime discussed above, the key considerations for governments and firms were economic, and all of these incentives made it attractive to regulate the problem in one particular way. Where different types of incentives are simultaneously at work, it may be harder to devise regulatory procedures that line up the parties' costs and benefits so neatly in one direction. Depending on the issue, for instance, it may be difficult to write rules in ways that make violations highly transparent. Still, even a more limited application of these lessons would probably increase the likelihood of compliance.

Furthermore, since monitoring and punishing violators is easier when there are not many participants in an institution, limiting membership may increase the likelihood of compliance. There are two reasons for this. The larger the number of participants, the harder it becomes to identify violators. Even when violators are identified, free-riding often makes it difficult in large groups to punish those members who have defected, since there are strong incentives to let "the other fellow" bear the burdens of secondary economic sanctions or other costly actions designed to enforce international obligations.[50] It may be impossible to keep an institution's membership small, if the problem to be addressed is global in scope. But where membership can be limited, enforcement will usually be less problematic.

Finally, policymakers can select the kind of institutional structure appropriate to the problem they face. If governments seek simply to avoid a specific outcome, the desired behavior should be largely self-enforcing once a few simple rules are laid out. Since only modest regulation is necessary in these cases, it should be easy to build effective regimes. But if the goal is that the parties behave in certain ways where there are complex temptations to act otherwise, very precise rules, careful monitoring, and credible penalties for noncompliance are needed. In such cases the parties may have incentives to renege on their obligations in various ways, or particular aspects of the underlying bargain may be vulnerable to noncompliance. These sorts of problems typically require a formally institutionalized regime, serviced by an administratively effective IGO.[51] The difference between the kind of arrangements needed to reduce the risk that nuclear weapons can be launched without proper authorization (an objective presumably shared by every relevant government) and one needed to stem the flow of ballistic missile technologies to eager would-be buyers captures this point.

One general and important policy implication emerges from scholarship on bargaining and cooperation: Effective enforcement should be emphasized whenever a new institution is created or a new agreement is contemplated. Unless monitoring and enforcement problems are seen as manageable, the parties will expect an agreement to collapse, undermining their commitment to cooperation.[52]

Institutions as Facilitators of Efficient, Productive Bargaining

Aside from their value in policing agreements, many SIR theorists[53] agree that well-designed institutions can ease the procedural and political barriers that often inhibit bargaining, and thus the likelihood of reaching agreements in the first place. In this sense, international institutions give national officials efficient forums in which to negotiate solutions to ongoing common problems. Available scholarship suggests that these benefits are achieved in three ways. First, institutions can help officials reach agreements by providing mechanisms for dealing with a variety of issues under a single set of rules and bargaining procedures. Second, repeated use of particular institutions tends to create bargaining principles and precedents that make it easier over time to reach new agreements. Finally, by making the costs of "no agreement" high and salient, the use of valued institutions creates a bias toward cooperative solutions rather than discord.

The number of international institutions has mushroomed over the last few decades, presenting a puzzle to Realists, though not to Liberal thinkers. From the latter perspective, increasing economic, social, and strategic interdependence among states creates more distinct issues that need regulation. Interdependence also multiplies connections among those issues, such that solutions to some requires that others be dealt with as well. As contemporary Neoliberals see it, these trends often make it cost-effective for states to deal with interconnected issues within stable international institutions.

According to Robert Keohane, the greater the number of distinct issues within a given problem area, the more interconnected they tend to become. Few states can consider the economic implications of widths of territorial waters without also considering the military ramifications; as we saw above, the economic and security implications of various dual-use technologies are tightly linked. Thus, agreements on any issue increasingly imply agreement on others, as interdependence grows. A government may, for example, agree to limit its exports of missile guidance-system technologies only if others restrain exports in dual-use sectors where they have a comparative advantage. From this perspective, dealing with related issues under a common set of norms and negotiating procedures is cost-effective in two ways. It obviates a need to reinvent the regulatory wheel for each new issue that arises. And in bringing negotiators together to deal with a set of issues, it allows them to trade concessions more easily than would be possible if each issue were handled separately. Thus, the more distinct issues there are in a given policy area, the more efficient it will be to handle them under a common set of norms and negotiating procedures.[54]

Institutions also facilitate bargaining by creating precedents that indicate how issues should be resolved. Since the mid-1980s, the Russian-American arms control regime has progressively chipped away at the strategic instability problem created by fixed-based, multiple-warhead ICBMs. With each successive round of negotiations, the presence of such weapons has diminished in both states' arsenals. Perhaps any repeated bargaining situation would create such norms and expectations. But the likelihood is higher within explicitly recognized institutions, since it is here that particular notions of legitimacy and order become codified.[55]

By raising the costs of failing to reach agreement, institutions foster mutually productive bargaining in a third way. If the above arguments are correct, regimes repay the investment made in their creation by providing a varied stream of benefits over time. But the other side of this coin is that they then become publicly valued assets whose reputations are at stake every time they are used. The implication for political leaders, whether in the context of the WTO, NATO, or any other high-profile institution, is that anyone who appears responsible for a breakdown in key negotiations is putting the institution's reputation, and thus its future usefulness, at risk. Especially during protracted rounds of trade talks, such pressure has helped to spur agreements.

As in connection with monitoring and enforcement, the preceding discussion suggests several instruments of policy. For example, different issues can be bundled together, so that they form a package within an institution.[56] Creating an international institution around some set of issues or broadening the scope of an existing issue-package makes sense when doing so carries fewer organizational or political costs than making *ad hoc* agreements for each separate issue. U.S. officials realized as long ago as the 1930s that individual trade agreements with one country could harm trade with many others. Their solution was a rule—unconditional most-favored nation trade status—that in principle would be applied to all states with which the United States has "normal" trade ties. Over time most commercial matters, including exchange in areas as diverse as manufactured goods, commodities, and services, have been brought within the trade regime under this norm, largely for reasons laid out in the Neoliberal argument.[57]

How issues are organized internationally may also matter. Issues dealt with by different international institutions—such as trade and money among economic issues and nuclear proliferation and dual-use technologies among security issues—are often managed by different bureaus at home.[58] If a government believed its partners would handle certain issues differently were they managed through different domestic bureaucracies, repackaging the international arrangements regime might change the substantive results. The United States, for instance, might prefer that issues relating to host-nation support for its military forces be managed by foreign rather than defense ministries, under the premise that the former would emphasize the diplomatic stakes rather than the financial costs. That might suggest an effort to switch the international channels through which financial offsets are negotiated.

To some extent, one's choice of partners in joint undertakings can also be manipulated. Neoliberal scholars argue that keeping the number small facilitates monitoring and enforcement. But limiting participation can also promote agreement in the first place. In a world of divergent interests, few global institutions achieve ambitious goals.[59] Identifying a relatively small number of states that share important interests may be preferable to deadlock over the scope or terms of an agreement. To avoid legitimizing exclusionary practices, such arrangements should allow for the eventual inclusion of all interested parties.[60] But there may be advantages in bringing particular states inside a regime sooner than later. China's strong interest in joining the WTO has given Washington unusual leverage in pinning down many commercial commitments from Beijing, leverage that did not exist before Chinese leaders became committed to regime membership.[61]

This raises the issue of problems for which any effective regime would have to be broadly inclusive. In observing bargaining over a global-warming regime, James Sebenius inferred that participation in such arrangements is best broadened gradually. Agreement on basic principles should first be reached among a small, like-minded group of states. Then, Sebenius suggests, selected others can be induced through various incentives to accept the necessary commitments. The enlargement process would continue over successive rounds of bargaining until something near universal participation has been reached.[62] These suggestions harken back to the Neofunctionalist idea that cooperation might "spill-over" to new problems and constituencies. What differs in this approach is more explicit attention to the contingent nature of the enlargement process and a careful bargaining strategy.

Contextual Relevance: Examining Actors' Preferences for Institutional Solutions

Neoliberals' conclusions about the purposes of international institutions ultimately assume that actors' goals coincide enough to produce cooperation, as long as the processes of making and verifying agreements can be facilitated. In this section, we ask whether these premises are justified and, if so, whether they suffice to generate policy-relevant understanding. We begin by unpacking the ceteris paribus clause in Neoliberal arguments, asking whether conflicts over the relative shares from cooperation are likely to spoil many efforts to achieve it. We then scrutinize some common assumptions about the key sources of support for international regimes. Do major states in fact have a large, continuing willingness to invest in international institutions, as this work contends? The answer to this question should shed light on whether the policy tools identified in the previous section will actually be available. We further unpack the ceteris paribus clause to ask a more fundamental question: What might institutionalized cooperation look like if the parties share a deep commitment to norms, identities, or shared knowledge? Following a discussion of each set of assumptions, we examine some of the major policy implications.

Are National Interests Really Complementary?

At some level, shared national objectives must exist if international institutions are to be useful. But what if this requirement cannot be taken for granted? What policy guidance would then follow? In arguing that national interests are essentially competitive, Realists reject as inapplicable the relationships discussed in the previous section. They force us to examine how much the Neoliberal *ceteris paribus* clause might qualify the link between institutions and cooperation. Depending on the impact of these variables, it might be useful to examine *their* causal antecedents.

For Realists, the "typical case" in international relations is one in which states seek gains at each others' expense. It follows that few international

security institutions exist, since "security" usually means being more powerful than an adversary. As the Concert of Europe and Russian-American
strategic arms control arrangements suggest, it typically takes a strong and
shared fear of war for even limited security regimes to emerge. Even so, as
the Israeli-Egyptian regime illustrated, the behavioral restraints tend to be
fragile. According to Realists, international issues reflect competition over
the distribution of scarce goods, not the prospects for joint gains. In examining global communications issues, for example, Stephen Krasner found
no evidence that joint gains were achieved through institutional means. In
two issue-areas, radio broadcasting and remote sensing, there are no international regimes because powerful states have achieved their goals unilaterally. Telecommunications issues are regulated internationally, but the regimes in this area have evolved in response to changes in relative power.[63]
To Realists the general point is clear: international institutions are arbiters
of relationships that ultimately depend on the distribution of power; their
instrumental value in fostering latent common interests is correspondingly
slight.

   This argument has prompted two major responses. First, there is no "typical" IR case, since a concern for relative gains does not follow simply from
the existence of an international system based on self-help. Anarchy *per se*
does not force states to be power-seekers. Whether they become so depends
on specific features of their environment. For example, bipolarity is likelier
to induce competitive behavior than multipolarity, since gains for one party
in a two-power configuration come chiefly at the other's expense. Power also
becomes an objective only to the extent that gains accruing to one party at
some period can be used against others subsequently.[64] But these environmental characteristics represent only specific types of situational configura-
tions, not any universal attributes. Absent some such condition, neither
policymakers nor analysts would necessarily expect states to be motivated by
relative power.

   Does competitiveness define the "typical" IR case? If an official were
willing to make this assumption—perhaps because in her experience, struggle has characterized important international relationships—she would follow the logic of Krasner's analysis. If not, she could seek policy guidance in
the argument that what varies across situations are the particular environmental constraints under which actors operate, not any general preference
for either relative power or joint gains. For example, geographic or technological conditions that make it easier to attack territory than defend it would
put a premium on relative gains, since military investment would have direct

implications for one's coercive power or battlefield success. Conversely, when force is unlikely to be used offensively, perhaps because geography or technology makes it easier to defend than attack, there is no quick return to coercive potential. In that case, states would not compromise their security through cooperation, even if their partners gained relatively more from the bargain.[65] Such arguments could help Group III or Group IV analysts diagnose the strategic situations they face and assess at least one major risk of institutional participation.

A second response to the Realist critique focuses on the political purposes behind power. It assumes that actors pay attention not just to others' capabilities, but also to their goals and the presumed time-frame of the interaction. The logic here is that the strategic importance of power *varies* with the compatibility of actors' objectives. It is not a constant, as Realists assume. The more incompatible policymakers expect their substantive goals and norms to become over time, the more competitive their international strategy will be, and vice-versa.[66] By this logic, governments pondering whether to cooperate with others ask not just if others will gain more, but how *likely* it is that any such gains would be used against them.[67]

It follows, then, that a policymaker can accept the value of international institutions at low risk *if* she can assume that others' goals will be compatible over the long term (applying, perhaps, some discount rate to the future). Having made that assumption, officials may believe that investing in a regime can change others' preferences—or even the nature of their internal institutions or values—through the relationships fostered by the regime. This has been a key argument in favor of using regimes such as the WTO instrumentally to nudge China in a liberal direction.[68]

How Assured Is the Hegemon's Support for Institutionalized Order?

Even if policymakers accept Neoliberal premises about compatible interests, they may not want to pay, or be able to pay, the price of effective international institutions. Especially for large states, these institutions carry nontrivial "maintenance" costs. Even under the lower assessments the United States is seeking from the United Nations, it would still pay one-fifth of an annual UN budget of well over $ 1 billion. Objectively, this is a small sum in a U.S. Federal Budget of more than $2 trillion. In fact, the entire United Nations system has a smaller annual budget than the government of a typical large city.[69] Nevertheless, the U.S. dues have never been less politically popular in Congress, nor has financial support for the IMF or discretionary peacekeeping operations ever encountered more resistance there. What then can be assumed about continuing American backing for international institutions?

The question matters because Neoliberals and Realists agree that a hegemonic state (under foreseeable conditions, the United States) often has long-term reasons to subsidize key international institutions. As discussed earlier, hegemonic states appear willing to pay for the public goods on which many regimes depend. They open their markets more than do those they trade with, subsidize others' security, and in general invest heavily in international order. They do so not for altruistic reasons, but because the benefits—the prosperity that comes from trade, the stability and the deference from allies that accompany military protection—accrue largely to them. Some of these costs need be paid only intermittently. Heavy institutional startup costs must be paid only once, and effective institutions can repay that initial investment over a long period of time, especially if, as in NATO, attractive new goals can be found when the original ones disappear.[70] But startup costs are not the only major expenses involved. Institutions require a constant flow of resources to keep them running. Consensual, multilateral institutions also require a hegemon's continuing willingness to live by the rules to which it holds others, even when inconvenient. In short, none of these institutional obligations is cheap or easy, even for a very strong state. If international order depends significantly on such hegemonic commitments, and those commitments are seemingly made on a contingent, instrumental basis, are they indefinitely sustainable?

In an important theoretical argument, John Ikenberry, an SIR scholar, answers in the affirmative. In return for supporting the web of contemporary international institutions, he argues, a hegemonic state gets a commitment from others to embrace the essential principles and rules of the existing international order. For their part, small and weak states understand that security and economic institutions lock larger states into predictable courses of action, reducing the possibilities of coercion and the hegemon's ability to act unilaterally. Although NATO, the IMF, and the WTO all have their roots in the 1940s, they persist, from this point of view, because they limit and channel the behavior of all parties in mutually predictable, beneficial ways. Moreover, since these institutions have become embedded in the domestic structures of the key member states, they have become more durable over time. The bargain—powerful states agree to act within institutional norms in return for similar restraint from others—is thus dependable over the long term. Ikenberry concludes that core U.S. commitments to contemporary international institutions are really *not* contingent, so long as they yield these benefits.[71]

Yet even if this fundamental bargain is durable, the terms on which the hegemonic state subsidizes others may be less so. Even as the United States has fostered closer economic, social, and technological ties with the rest of the world, its opposition to institutionalizing these relationships in expensive or constraining ways has hardened. The end of the cold-war consensus on foreign policy has made it difficult to justify international institutions in terms of stark U.S. national interests, and sharper partisan divisions have made it more difficult to fashion a renewed consensus. Foreign resentment at these developments jeopardize U.S. ability to organize multilateral foreign-policy coalitions in cases where U.S. leaders cannot act unilaterally.[72] In 1999, U.S. officials were brought up short when, after proposing an extension of a peacekeeping project, the reply was "What do you care? You don't pay anyway."[73]

This assessment suggests two policy implications. For the foreseeable future, U.S. officials will want to act abroad when they cannot act alone, and will need to attract foreign coalition partners. To be enticed, potential partners must see Washington make reasonable contributions to joint projects and abide by the norms to which it holds others. To that end, U.S. domestic politics cannot pose a high bar to multilateral cooperation. Former UN Ambassador Richard Holbrooke thus tried to reframe the rationale for UN participation to domestic audiences, chiefly Congress. He justified U.S. contributions to UN peacekeeping efforts in cost-effective security terms: because the U.S. will not be the world's policeman, yet has a large stake in effective conflict management, the UN needs effective peacekeeping capabilities. Such capabilities require American support. Even if the presence of American soldiers in such contingents is smaller in the future than it used to be, it must be visible and dependable.[74] Unless such an appeal can succeed the United States cannot credibly bind itself to international institutions.

Over the longer term, Holbrooke's successors would be in a stronger position to make this case domestically if the international system depended less on U.S.-supplied goods. If key regional states were to take over some security and economic responsibilities now borne largely, even within multilateral contexts, by the United States, free-riding might become less of a problem, and create less resentment within the United States.[75] Europeans are now beginning to discuss creation of a local defense capability, housed within NATO, that would allow Europeans to act alone when the United States did not want to be involved. The U.S. has complained for decades about the lack of a single European defense partner with whom to share burdens and coordinate policy. Based on the above reasoning, it should now support Europeans' apparent efforts to create one.

International Institutions as Carriers of Common Norms, Identities, and Knowledge

The Realist-Liberal assumption that national interests are formed by states more or less on their own, with little discussion with other states, may provide a reasonable first approximation. But if, as Constructivists argue, actors shape the context in which they operate through their social relationships, then international institutions come to reflect the norms, identities, and shared knowledge they acquire via those institutions. Under certain conditions, according to this perspective, international communities can be built out of such relationships. While this challenges the Realist view that communities exist only *within* nations; it is at odds with Liberal arguments that see institutions *simply* as means to attaining autonomously formed state goals.

Much SIR scholarship would suggest that institutions transform the context of international interaction in three ways. One is by codifying and augmenting legal norms. The UN has accomplished much in this area by making explicit a good deal of customary international law and by sponsoring multilateral treaties in new areas of the law. Second, as Constructivists note, the norms institutions embody empower certain actors to make legitimate claims with respect to others.[76] For example, as the UN's human rights organs have become more assertive, nongovernmental organizations (NGOs) have been empowered to make claims against governments that were ruled out of order several decades ago. Even if the UN cannot enforce those norms, they may become a standard by which future behavior is assessed. Third, as Constructivists emphasize, if international issues are defined through a process of interaction, preferences may evolve through confrontation with other points of view. This suggests that what political leaders want to achieve, how they define their reference group, and what they assert to be causally true about the world might be influenced through conversations that occur within international institutions.

Contemporary IR scholarship points to scenarios that illustrate these processes, especially the third. One set of examples focuses on community building at the regional level. The Organization for Security and Cooperation in Europe (OSCE), a successor to the cold war–bred Conference on Security and Cooperation in Europe, is now being used to build a deeply rooted European community. The OSCE has fostered many face-to-face interactions among private and public groups in technical, political, and practical areas. In this way, the "we-they" feeling already shared by many European political and professional elites has penetrated more broadly throughout civil society. Outside of a shared aversion to war, the glue that is creating a common identity out of many disparate national societies is the belief that "Europe" is an inclusive community of democratic societies. To the extent that policymakers take this common bond seriously, they are acting on the basis of the Kantian Idealist notions discussed above. Seen through Constructivist eyes, the OSCE's community-building practices have been important beyond Europe; they have influenced regional integration schemes in the Asia-Pacific region, Africa, and even in the multilateral Arab-Israeli peace negotiations.[77]

Another set of cases involves the impact of shared knowledge on international policy coordination. Trans-state groups of scientific specialists can become influential in policy circles by virtue of their professional agreement and the legitimacy it imparts to their recommendations. Known as "epistemic communities," they are most influential when policymakers are uncertain about how to deal with a technical problem, there is a strong technical consensus, and technical advice is highly institutionalized. Under these conditions, technical expertise can help frame issues for public and elite debate, spread knowledge throughout the relevant technical communities, and help officials cut through complex issues in making policy choices.[78] Thus, groups of policy specialists may create a seamless web across the lines separating Groups II, III, and IV, as discussed in chapter 3. This argument has been applied to areas as diverse as nuclear arms control, stratospheric pollution, and the convergence of regulatory ideas among central bankers.[79]

One might ask what this formulation adds to Functionalist thinking, since the conclusions are so similar. From a Constructivist perspective, it clarifies how social knowledge affects ends and means. When technical specialists clarify causal linkages in a problem area, decisionmakers may discover new goals or new ways to solve old problems. Anticipating these results in their concept of spillover, functionalists remained unclear about why experts' opinions are validated in some problem areas rather than others. The epistemic communities argument helps plug this gap. It suggests that when a technical consensus is convincingly married to policy objectives, certain technical solutions acquire a special legitimacy. The result is a socially coherent group of experts with a stake in solving particular problems. As this consensus broadens, an important kind of community may be built or reinforced across borders.

When international institutions become carriers of strong norms, identities, and knowledge, the political effects can be significant. Leaders may use relevant knowledge to think through problems at the national level and to conform to prevailing international standards when the social or material costs of noncompliance are high.[80] Institutions that embody community norms and knowledge can therefore be used to do important things. By discussing issues such as human rights and environmentally sustainable development, inclusive bodies such as the UN General Assembly draw markers around legitimate state conduct. The International Court of Justice and the Special Tribunals formed to investigate and prosecute war crimes committed during the 1990s can be used to educate governments and concerned private groups about the incidence of unacceptable behavior and strengthen the underlying norms.[81] Even more ambitiously, as the OSCE example suggested, institutions might be used to nurture new international communities. But even the most committed policymaker must have raw material with which to work. In world politics, shared norms and identities are typically weak *relative* to national values and identities. Unless there is evidence of some common normative structure across states—whether it derives from a shared objective, such as sustainable development, or a commitment to broader values, such as pluralism and democratic rule—one might begin by assuming that community standards are weak.[82] Thus, caution in using institutions in this way is warranted; only if a strong normative seed has been planted can institutions incubate and represent community values.

The Costs and Consequences of Acting Through International Institutions

SIR can also clarify the costs and consequences of using international organizations for national policy purposes. For poor states, the scarce funds spent on dues and official representation in international bodies may matter most. Consequently, policymakers in such nations may ask whether institutional participation yields them more—in resources transferred to their societies or in expanded opportunities for international coalition-building—than they spend. Scholars agree that poor states on balance tend to be well served by their involvement in international institutions. They are often able to use their voting power in plenary IGO bodies to secure agreements and create international programs they could not achieve through non-institutionalized diplomacy.[83]

Wealthy states typically focus on different kinds of costs. The money they spend on participating in IGOs is small relative to their overall government budgets, and they depend less than poor countries on international institutions as a source of bargaining power. What at times irks political and policy elites in rich states is the loss in national discretion that accompanies international commitments. This has been true in the United States, and particularly so within Congress. Woodrow Wilson's inability to convince the Senate to ratify the Versailles Treaty stemmed mainly from concerns about the perceived curtailment of national autonomy that membership in the League of Nations would imply for the United States. Fear of this sort of consequence are behind much opposition to the United Nations. As Edward Luck has documented, the United Nations is, "a favorite target of those [U.S.] legislators concerned about threats both to American sovereignty and to congressional prerogatives."[84] As the protests directed toward the International Trade Organization, IMF, and the World Bank suggest, fear of unanticipated constraints on national autonomy and sovereignty fuel distrust of other multilateral institutions as well.

International relations scholars over the last few decades have helped to clarify the real costs and tradeoffs here. Some national discretion *is* necessarily yielded in specific policy areas in the process of international collaboration. Whether the purpose of an international agreement is to achieve results that no state can achieve on its own, or simply to make the actions of other states more predictable, national officials cannot achieve the objectives unless they follow certain rules. In this sense, they cannot have their cake and eat it too.[85] But, most international relations scholars agree that contemporary international institutions do not represent a threat to sovereignty, understood as the final legal right of independent states to undertake or reject international commitments as political leaders see fit. Just the opposite seems to be true. International institutions are *not* designed to implement centrally enforced rules, as would occur if those bodies came to constitute a genuine world government. Instead, they are designed to stabilize governments' expectations and coordinate their joint efforts, so that common *agreed-upon* state purposes can be served.[86] No piece of contemporary SIR has found evidence that IGOs might somehow gobble up sovereignty from national governments that are asleep at the switch, as the original Functionalists once hoped. If anything, the basic norm that states are legally responsible to no outside, supra-national authority is as strong as it was in the sixteenth and seventeenth centuries, when it evolved as a way to end internecine religious warfare in Europe. This norm, of course, might eventually decay. But it is hard to see how the exchange of specific pieces of national discretion for specific international agreements could bring about supranational institutions under anything resembling current political conditions.

What SIR cannot authoritatively address are matters of values. People may legitimately prefer that decisionmaking and implementation remain at the national level, even if an international institution could discharge some function more effectively. Decisions, here, must rest on a process of democratic aggregation of societal opinion, not on social science. What SIR can do is help responsible officials and opinionmakers separate the false questions and concerns from the real ones, and provide the empirical information on which value judgments sometimes rest.

International Institutions and the Policymaking Community

Immanuel Kant argued that "the opinions of philosophers on the conditions of the possibility of public peace shall be consulted by those states armed for war."[87] While this is unlikely to happen, some forms of consultation can be expected. During the cold war for example, scholars specializing in arms control and nuclear strategy had a real impact on U.S. defense-policy. More recently, as we saw in chapter 5, assumptions about an interdemocratic peace have influenced U.S. and European foreign-policy communities. Yet nothing this dramatic has happened in the area of international institutions and institutionalized cooperation.

The reasons are straightforward. Most of the ideas discussed in this chapter are more subtle those explored in chapter 5, and all of them are more controversial. Even if contemporary Neoliberal theorists are correct, the link between institutions and cooperation does not afford much policy leverage, being limited to situations wherein states already agree on ends. Compared to the dramatic difference democracy apparently makes on the central issue of war, the policy effects produced by variables discussed in this chapter are fairly slight. The arguments examined here are also more controversial: unlike the empirical findings reported in chapter 5, which scholars have largely accepted, none of the generalizations discussed here enjoy full academic support. It is no surprise that theoretical work on international institutions has had less practical impact outside the ivory tower.

One partial exception has been Functionalism. Its influence is reflected in the specialized agencies of the United Nations, each designed to complement the main body's broad focus on peace, security, and development. More dramatically, Functionalist precepts shaped the design of the post– World War II Western European order. Jean Monnet, a French official and one-time League of Nations employee with extensive wartime experience in joint production and planning, found himself perplexed by the problem of Franco-German relations in the late 1940s. France was determined to constrain German power enough to ensure that no military threat would ever again surface; Germany, aided by the United States, was in the early stages of its postwar economic recovery. To reconcile these objectives and bind them to peace, Monnet reasoned that constraints on both states' industrial autonomy was necessary. He proposed to put their coal and steel firms under joint supranational control. As his one-time aide George Ball put it, the objective was to force gradual integration of the two economies:

> All of us working with Monnet well understood that it was quite unreasonable to carve a single economic sector out of the jurisdiction and subject it to the control of international institutions. Yet . . . Monnet recognized that the very irrationality of his scheme would compel progress and might then start a chain reaction. The awkwardness and complexity resulting from the singling-out of coal and steel would compel member governments to pool other production as well.[88]

Quite consciously, spillover was programmed into the EU's institutional design.

Beyond this, the practical influence of scholarly ideas in this area is hard to trace. As a one-time scholar of politics, Woodrow Wilson was probably influenced by Liberal Enlightenment thought, though the precise link is unclear. Today, at least some policy specialists interested in coordinated interstate action seem aware of the regimes literature,[89] though the impact on policy choices or governmental bargaining positions is cloudy. What is clear from this chapter is that *if* officials want to work together, there is a long tradition of theoretical work—and some increasingly precise causal propositions—from which they can draw guidance.

Conclusions

Contemporary foreign-policymakers must manage extensive interdependence in a diverse, fragmented world. In principle, the literature on international institutions has a long pedigree, and it should shed light on this problem. Because this subject goes to the heart of war and peace, every major IR tradition has something to say about it.

Why, then, has this literature not had a larger impact on policy? Perhaps the practical payoff has seemed too low. Unlike the work on the democratic peace, there is no analytic "smoking gun" here—no single malleable variable affording high policy leverage. Instead, the work on international institutions is filled with qualifications and debates. Sorting through these is difficult enough for scholars, much less policymakers! Yet the instrumental knowledge offered by Neoliberals is impressive, provided one assumes that the underlying conditions are met. Among the industrial democracies at least, there are enough overlapping interests to view this work as a rough strategic guide for managing interdependence. When combined with other theoretical propositions that help unpack some of the key qualifications, it adds up to an impressive body of knowledge—even if it is a messier package than the democratic peace literature.

It is worth noting that the one intellectual argument that *has* resonated among policymakers and elites was specifically designed to be practically useful. For all its weaknesses, Functionalism identified core problems and key pieces of solutions to them. As scholars strive to understand international relations, they could do far worse than seek to emulate these objectives.

7   Useful Knowledge: Value, Promise, and Limitations

      The gap between international relations scholars and decisionmakers has assumed a character of ineluctability—a condition that is surprising in a field created less than a century ago with the express purpose of shedding light on pressing policy problems. Although scholars and policymakers have different professional goals, both have a strong interest in understanding the processes and parameters of international relations. One would therefore expect sound analysis from inside the Ivory Tower to find resonance within the corridors of power. Good "ordinary" knowledge provides, at best, a partial basis for policy, and there are many ways in which it can be misleading. And policy relevance, as we have seen, goes far beyond relevance of a directly instrumental sort. Moreover, since there are no precise historical analogies to current international developments, practitioners need analytic help more than ever before.

    Five key arguments have found form in this book. They suggest that international relations theory can be useful in more ways than is commonly thought, and with little or no cost to the quality of scholarship. They further specify what shape relevant knowledge can assume, the settings in which it can originate, and the paths by which it can be brought to inform policy. Taken together, these arguments provide a foundation for reorienting our thinking on the practical value of scholarship in international relations and foreign policy. We begin by summarizing the book's five major arguments, following which we will suggest some tentative steps via which a process of bridge-building between academia and government might be initiated.

What Have We Learned About Useful Knowledge? The Five Arguments

Our first argument is that SIR naturally has policy implications, and that the profession has lost sight of that fact for reasons lacking intellectual justification. Except in policy schools, university-based IR scholars have come to focus more on technical refinements and winning intellectual turf battles than in making sense of significant real-world developments. SIR was created for quite different reasons. Reflecting on the tragedy of World War I, a group of public intellectuals in the 1920s set out to give future foreign-policymakers analytic assistance in confronting issues of war and peace. Like the other major social-science disciplines, SIR soon found a place in university curricula on the assumption that it could contribute to improved policy. Hans Morgenthau, E. H. Carr, Inis Claude, and Arnold Wolfers saw no reason why good scholarship should not also address the major foreign-policy issues of their times. But beginning in the 1960s, the scholarly study of IR increasingly veered away from the interests and concerns of most foreign-policymakers, especially in the United States. The new emphasis on methodologically rigorous inquiry had value, but it came to be pursued at the expense of substantive significance.

Rather than help thoughtful practitioners interpret the world, SIR has become almost entirely self-referential. PhD's are trained to speak only to each other, and to train future PhD's. Unless they deliberately seek projects or professional experiences forcing them to confront real-world dilemmas (for example, via the Council on Foreign Relations Fellowship Program), they spend their careers wholly within the confines of internally defined problems. Because the status of professional scholars rests on how their work is received by their peers, scholarly fashions—including those that discourage policy-relevant work—become powerfully self-reinforcing.

The cornerstone of relevance is a quest for valuable knowledge, whereas the sociology of academic life, especially the reward structure of the social sciences, provides few incentives in this regard. Where the primary quest is to emulate the epistemologies of disciplines a perceived notch higher in academia's status hierarchy, rather than to address empirically and theoretically meaningful questions, and where method rides roughshod over significance, the aridity of technique naturally eclipses the value of substance. Rather than work that is intellectually powerful, much contemporary SIR scholarship offers findings that at best are commonplace, a good bit of which seems to be focused on demonstrating methodological mastery rather than illuminating major real-world problems. As scholars have come to tackle smaller, narrower, and sterile issues, practitioners have increasingly ignored them, and public foreign-policy intellectuals have lost standing in the university culture.

Accordingly, a major reason for the gap between scholarship and the policy process must be sought in the evolving cultures of academia and the policymaking community, rather than in the intellectual incompatibility of their respective enterprises.

Our second argument is that the notion of policy relevance should not be limited to knowledge of a directly instrumental sort, i.e. to that specifying a link between policy tools and desired outcomes, subject to certain (more or less fully elaborated) qualifying conditions. Useful knowledge has a greater span and can assume other forms. Specifically, it can help identify the context within which the instrumental relationships can be expected to operate, and it can help project the costs and consequences associated with the use of particular policy tools.

Contextual knowledge identifies the ceteris paribus conditions under which means lead to certain ends, and it specifies the circumstances that shape the availability or malleability of policy instruments, helping officials fully diagnose the challenges they confront. It is of little value, for example, to know that conventional deterrence can at times substitute for nuclear deterrence in controlling the outbreak of aggression, or that economic sanctions might change a target state's behavior, if those policy instruments are unavailable in practice (perhaps for political reasons), or could not work in a given context. At a time of pervasive international change, the right kind of contextual knowledge can help decisionmakers reevaluate whether old policy tools *are* still appropriate to the tasks at hand or whether new strategies must be devised.

Policymakers must also know what costs and consequences their actions might have beyond those directly intended. If the U.S. builds a limited missile shield to protect against threats or attacks from rogue states with modest ballistic-missile capabilities, how will that affect relations with Europe and China over the long term? If globalization continues at present rates for another generation or two, how much more day-to-day economic policy flexibility will U.S. leaders lose? These are issues that thoughtful policymakers and political leaders must understand, but will have a harder time grasping without policy-relevant SIR.

Our third major argument is that, whether instrumental, contextual, or consequential, the value of the professedly relevant knowledge depends on the quality of explanation it furnishes. Explanation of some positive statement (a conclusion) requires propositions about initial conditions (i.e., particular events, issues, or actors), *and* about generally applicable relationships (those that apply across various sets of initial conditions). While policymakers may provide much of the specific information required by explanation, scholars generally are better placed to furnish general propositions derived from, or embedded in, some theoretical structure. Thus, virtually any policy-relevant reasoning requires the kind of knowledge that SIR provides.

This is not to say that the fruits of SIR must always trump policymakers' "ordinary" knowledge, even when it comes to producing generalizations. For reasons discussed in chapter 2, some problems that interest government officials may have evoked little or no research from scholars. Aside from this, policymakers may be able to recognize patterns or diagnose situations that would be less intelligible to those lacking an applied background in foreign affairs. But the way in which officials obtain and use ordinary knowledge often leaves them prone to perceptual biases and inferential errors that distort what they see, how they react to it, and how they make decisions. Academics are by no means immune to such errors, but they are less apt to make them; and their professional peers can usually be counted on to notice them in the process of scholarly evaluation. It follows that policymaking should improve to the extent that officials become self-conscious about the content and process of their thinking—that is, insofar as their assumptions, their evidence, and their conclusions are subjected to rigorous examination and critique. Judicious use of SIR should help promote these goals.

Fourth, we explain that policy-relevant IR knowledge can reach officials by various paths, which are more numerous than is often assumed. For heuristic purposes, we assumed two ideal-typical models. In the demand-driven scenario, decisionmakers realize that they do not understand an issue on the policy agenda well enough to act effectively. They then request scholarly help: for example, from a university academic, a think tank, or from scholars serving in government positions. Consequently, useful knowledge that is not yet available becomes so following governmental demand. Alternatively, an analysis focused on the problem might originate from the scholarly community itself, independent of any explicit governmental commission, in response to a need to better understand an issue, and it might reach policymakers by various, often circuitous, paths.

While the demand-driven scenario provides direct access to policy-making, and generally involves responses to significant problems, the supply-driven model's virtue is that it expands scholarship's role beyond one that is merely reactive, to include shaping the policy agenda and anticipating problems. It can help to frame a problem as well as its solution, by encouraging new ways of thinking about existing issues. Moreover, scholars need not accept officials' values or their conception of ends-means relationships in order to make such a contribution. A key disadvantage with the supply-driven model is that the knowledge needed to inform policy may not exist; in the demand-driven scenario, by contrast, useful knowledge is explicitly brought forth.

In practice, elements of both models are often present. For example, an early wave of research—on, say, the interdemocratic peace—may stimulate official interest in associated scholarship. The academic reward structure notwithstanding, that interest may make the problem attractive to other scholars, who see its applicability to current policy issues as one reason to refine, critique, or replicate the early findings. Alternatively, at times when scholars are working on a problem for their own reasons, policymakers may seek additional or differently focused academic work within the same broad area. Senior decisionmakers may be more open to outside academic input at some times rather than others, and once a policy has been established, officials may be loath to reconsider it. But if an existing strategy is rendered obsolete by events, if senior officials disagree about some issue, or if political circumstances no longer favor a prior policy objective, scholars with something significant to say may be able to shape the terms of the policy debate.[1]

Significantly, relevant knowledge does not originate in a single institutional setting; rather, it is produced within four contexts of scholarly activity, distinguished largely by the extent to which they focus on generalizations or on concrete information. The four settings are those associated with General Theory (Group I), Empirically Focused Theoretical Analysis (Group II), Case-Specific Analysis (Group III), and Direct Policy Analysis and Advice (Group IV). Group I is furthest from concrete policy issues, Group IV is closest. There is thus a wide range of settings within which thinking on international relations is conducted, and members of the four groups interact more than is typically assumed. Their activities are supported by institutions and professional networks, including think tanks, foundations, and academic associations, that effectively create a transmission belt running from "pure" theory to "pure" policymaking and advice. In any case, relevant knowledge typically traces multiple, indirect, and sometimes discontinuous paths, and its impact on policy may have little to do with the purpose for which it was first produced. If policy-relevant IR knowledge exists, people who want to use it can do so.

The book's fifth major argument refutes a common misperception within academia—that relevant knowledge implies weak scholarship. This assertion cannot survive close scrutiny. As Abraham Kaplan pointed out, any theoretical argument concerning variables that *could* be policy-relevant *must* have real-world applications; otherwise, it becomes meaningless to claim that the argument explains much of anything.[2] If this is correct, IR theoretical knowledge must be at least potentially useful to foreign-policymakers, and the better the theory *qua theory*, the more useful it should be. After all, policymakers just as much as theorists need a sound and significant causal understanding of the world in order to do their jobs effectively. Sound theories, as we discussed in chapter 4, build on premises that are true, and omit no general proposition needed to address the phenomenon at hand. Valuable theories correctly explain a wide range of phenomena, and are significant in the sense of explaining important phenomena in ways that are not obvious. On its own terms, then, good theory provides a logically compelling account of a wide range of important phenomena in ways that add to our understanding of the real world. There is no reason why arguments that meet these criteria would *not* be more useful to foreign-policymakers than arguments that do not.

Consequently, it is wrong to assume that scholars would compromise their intellectual integrity by being useful. One can take cues from the world of practice without taking them from particular practitioners.[3] In any case, when scholars analyze whether, or when, a given policy would work, and with what direct and indirect effects, they can affect policy without necessarily accepting the particular ends-means connections that enjoy official favor at a given time.

From the perspective of SIR, a concern with policy relevance should help steer scholarship away from triviality, and keep the field's principal concepts tied to clear empirical referents. Until a few decades ago, when the incentive structure of modern university life made policy-relevant scholarship unfashionable, few would have argued that academics and practitioners do not have important common objectives. That commonality should be reexamined at a time when foreign-policy officials, navigating a sea of global uncertainty, need reliable analytic charts. We have found examples of valuable, *relevant* theoretical SIR to suggest that efforts to use it are worthwhile. Apart from what theories of the interdemocratic peace and of international institutions may contribute to policy within the subject matter they cover, they have broader uses as well. They demonstrate that scholarship can shed light on the range of the possible and on the consequences of various courses of action, and that it can do so with no costs to the quality of its work. Policy-relevant scholarship need be neither better nor worse than nonrelevant work (although it *may* be better); but it certainly stands to be more useful. Accordingly, we suggest some ways in which policymakers and IR theorists can benefit more from each others' insights and expertise.

Suggestions for Bridging the Gap

Realistically speaking there are substantial impediments to a broader use of relevant knowledge on the part of foreign policy makers. Government officials are far from convinced that scholarship might help them. Often they are too busy to do the priority official reading on their desks; the suggestion that they invest in what seems to be peripheral material, often written in arcane language, may be dismissed. Frequently, part of the problem is that the scholarship is not conclusive enough to be taken very seriously. Little social science is as authoritative as the best work in natural science: measurement is often too indirect, axiomatic postulates are rarely uncontested, and many substantive conclusions are submerged in caveats. On top of this, policymakers tend to frame questions differently than academics, they face unforgiving deadlines for answers, and typically they need crisper guidelines than scholars can provide.

For their part, many IR academics are quite comfortable with the gap. Some of their reasons are understandable, others are less defensible. On the one hand, scholars often are as happy to establish what we do not know as to push knowledge forward. Researchers cannot (at least should not) claim more authoritativeness than their research design or subject matter permits, and negative conclusions can more affirmatively be stated than affirmative conclusions. On the other hand, a purpose of scholarly research is to stimulate one's curiosity about a phenomenon. The result may be work that raises more questions than it answers. The fact that it is of little help to officials when quick action is needed need not be academia's main concern. All this is perfectly understandable and acceptable. Quite unjustified, however, is the fashionable conviction that relevant work reflects compromised academic aspirations. There also is little to support that all-too-common attitude among academics that they are more intelligent or thoughtful than government officials. It is easy to criticize official mistakes and misconceptions; it is more challenging to indicate how one would have acted differently under existing time pressures, political as well as international constraints, and informational constraints.

None of these obstacles to policy-relevant knowledge can be easily surmounted. Still, the gap is not yet a chasm. Some international relations scholars might reevaluate the benefits of producing useful knowledge—and some policymakers might then use more of it—if the communications barriers between the two groups were lowered and if the fruits of their interaction loomed larger. Practical suggestions for narrowing the gap should focus on these objectives.

One idea implied by our analysis is to build on the bridging role of Group III analysts: those who focus on specific IR cases, such as decisionmaking in particular crises, examples of multilateral bargaining, or instances of humanitarian intervention in civil conflicts. Scholars of this sort can play a pivotal part in connecting insights of Group I and Group II work to the concerns of policymakers. The link between Group II and Group III analysts is especially important in this regard. Group III work can benefit from Group II's efforts to provide empirical referents and findings that flesh out more abstract ideas. Correspondingly, Group II work may benefit from Group III's case-specific analyses, since these are often deeply grounded in practically useful examples. In sum, Group III scholars help transmit abstract yet potentially useful ideas and arguments to policymakers through in-depth empirical analyses that are often framed around theory-driven ideas. Because policymakers have neither the time nor expertise to probe the logical or evidentiary basis of theory-driven work, Group III analysts are especially valuable go-betweens for this purpose. And because many Group III analysts have strong ties to policy institutes, this bridging role makes them key suppliers of policy-relevant knowledge to interest groups, bureaucratic factions within government and IGOs, and other policy entrepreneurs—all of whom might wish to use or disseminate practical knowledge.

We suggested earlier that Group III analysts will probably play a larger role in providing and publicizing foreign-policy analysis as time goes on. In the United States, congressional interest in foreign policy is likely to remain low for the foreseeable future. Because their analysts typically have a good sense of the broader political context as well as their specific areas of expertise, international-affairs think tanks are well-positioned to shape the foreign-affairs agenda. At least some government officials recognize the value of generalizing about the effectiveness and appropriateness of various foreign-policy tools, although it is hard to judge how widespread this attitude is.[4] By synthesizing appropriate cases and general IR propositions in an accessible way, Group III analysts are well-suited to exploit this opportunity.

General IR propositions would "travel" better to policymakers if the contingent nature of causal claims were more explicitly specified. As discussed in chapter 3, many Group II arguments that are in fact highly conditional are presented by SIR literature in absolute terms; the contextual conditions that affect relationships among the variables are left unidentified. If these arguments were specified more carefully, it would be easier to connect empirically focused theoretical research (the product of Group II) to the in-depth analysis of real-world cases (the product of Group III). One way to incorporate ceteris paribus and contextual conditions more explicitly into the contingent generalizations that dominate Group II work is by analyzing typologies. A "type" is a group of cases—for example, wars produced by actors' misperceptions, or weapons-procurement decisions driven by similar sorts of domestic political pressures—in which the values of the variables are strongly associated. A typology, or set of such similarly grouped cases, rests on the assumption that the relevant variables occur together in fairly few combinations.[5] Typological analysis can help clarify the defining features of the research puzzles that dominate Group II work, both for those who focus on policy applications and those whose main interest is in solving the intellectual problems for their own sake. Typologies also provide a clear and accessible manner of communicating relational knowledge to those who are not scholars. This would not only help Group III analysts—and by extension, those policymakers who follow Group III work in their areas of interest— identify the Group II work they can use; it might also stimulate conversations about the dimensions and causal processes of international politics that transcend particular research puzzles.

Ultimately, however, the Group II–III connection can only be strengthened if policy-relevant SIR work becomes better appreciated within the academic community. A major and difficult task is to challenge an academic reward structure that penalizes relevance and celebrates technique. Left unchecked, such values make policy-*irrelevance* a self-fulfilling prophecy. Vicious circles get broken only when incentives outside the closed loop penetrate the processes inside it. In this regard, two developments may portend some change. Some of the constituencies behind public universities have come to demand that curricula reflect relevance. At their most thoughtful and compelling, such arguments insist that university courses acquaint students with the implications of what they are learning for their own lives, or for the society of which they are a part. While these demands are intermittent and often not well articulated, motivated university provosts, deans, and department chairs could incorporate relevance into the criteria by which hiring and promotion decisions are made. Insofar as doctoral programs in political science are attentive to the market for their product, such behavior on the part of university leaders could foster more respect (or at least tolerance) for IR research that suggests or demonstrates applications to real-world issues. Equally promising in this regard is a standard employed by the National Science Foundation in assessing project proposals for funding. The primary criterion is scientific merit, as judged by the panels of outside referees. But a project's potential applied consequences is also supposed to be considered (along with the qualifications of the researcher[s] and adequate support from available university facilities).

Professors might become more sympathetic to relevant knowledge in other ways as well. Editors at scholarly journals and university presses could ask authors to discuss what difference their findings and conclusions *might* make for policy issues. Any type of relevance would be appropriate in this regard—either heightened instrumental knowledge, contextual knowledge, or a better understanding of a policy's costs or other consequences. Obviously, not all scholarly output would have to be practically relevant, for reasons we have discussed. But if attentiveness to policy implications were an integral aspect of much published SIR, and if the cogency of such work were a measure by which scholarship was evaluated within academia, policy-relevance might become a criterion used in choosing their research problems. Further down the road, one can imagine scholarly debates and research agendas in international relations turning in part on the logical strength and evidentiary fit between the various arguments and their practical policy implications.

Even if relevant knowledge was provided, would it shape the calculations of policymakers? For this to happen, scholars should also reduce their jargon to the minimum needed to convey scientific information, elucidating substantive results as clearly as possible. Since policymakers can do their jobs, adequately in their view, without academic input, they tend to be impatient with the scholarly apparatus that accompanies scholarly conclusions. Even if they value the results, few are curious in any detail about how the conclusions were derived, and even fewer care what the knowledge implies for the scholarly field. Accordingly, scholars must learn to frame their work in ways that are meaningful both to their colleagues and to practitioners.

Taking such suggestions to heart would help revive the tradition of "public intellectuals" in this field. At their best, public intellectuals are people who speak astutely about public affairs *from a perspective honed by cogent theoretical analysis and a thoughtful immersion in substantive problems*. Neither by itself suffices to make an impact. Without a coherent theoretical foundation for their recommendations, outside analysts have little insight to offer practitioners beyond what they already know. Without carefully *connecting* their theoretical insights to important substantive problems over which decisionmakers have leverage, such intellectuals have nothing important to say about the real world. The title of "professor" by itself does not really validate such analyses, either outside the academy or within it; it is the ability to *connect* appropriate generalizations and initial conditions in a cogent way that matters.

Assume for the moment that scholars were to act on these suggestions and policy-relevant work became more prestigious and common within universities. Members of the policy community who want to use such research might still want some guidance in finding it. Two suggestions come to mind here. First, editors of policy journals might ask their authors to make explicit the intellectual basis of their recommendations, along with the most formidable opposing arguments. Bearing in mind that policy debates often do not turn on the logic of the arguments, this kind of presentation would at least summarize the analytic side of such debates from a practitioner's point of view. That summary could then be compared with the academic discussion on the comparable issues. If it turned out that academics were framing the issue in similar terms—differences in professional jargon aside—policymakers could see if the SIR discussion provided any new empirical generalizations or reasoning that might be of practical use. If the scholarly discussion was quite different, thoughtful practitioners might find new ideas, scenarios, or evidence to consider, even if this input was ultimately rejected.

For reasons discussed in chapter 1, no one has had very powerful incentives to build bridges across these literatures. Consequently, the discussion of globalization in *Foreign Policy* proceeds very separately from the one in *International Organization*, and discussions of weapons proliferation in *Sur-*

vival seldom refer to work on the same topic in *Security Studies*. Differences in jargon aside again, it is hard to imagine that the underlying analytic issues could be that different on the same subjects. The main difference should reside in the ratio of general statements to statements about initial conditions, and the degree to which each is discussed explicitly or in depth. If so, at least some readers of each type of journal would probably benefit from gaining the other kind of knowledge, if only to make their own arguments more effectively, and might do so more readily if that became more convenient. At the least, policy specialists would have an easier way to find relevant Group II (and, less often Group I) work on the issues they cared about, and journal editors might find the implicit exchange of views would broaden their readerships.

Our second suggestion is that more informal dialogue between theorists and practitioners be encouraged, especially in instances where the people on each side have interests in common. The most productive exchanges might take place between professors who had spent some time in government and government officials who had some academic training in social-scientific IR. The premise here is similar to that in the first suggestion. Stripped of the pressures of speaking formally to different audiences, the two groups might find that they thought more alike than differently, at least about diagnosing situations, speculating about causal relationships, and assessing prominent cases. Our hunch is that the major grant-making foundations interested in international affairs would welcome a proposal for this kind of interchange, perhaps structured around clusters of issues that might be expected to provoke reactions from both groups.

Two types of research projects might also help bridge the theory-practice gap. One would involve detailed case studies of past policy deliberations to determine what type of analysis was used (or might have been useful, if it had been available) at various points and whether good theory might have met the need for instrumental, contextual, or cost-related knowledge. For example, in diagnosing Mikhail Gorbachev's objectives and strategies in the mid-1980s, one could reconstruct how the United States tried to determine the range of possibilities for dealing with an unorthodox type of Soviet leader. What kinds of analogies and inferences did they use to make judgments? Did appropriate SIR knowledge exist at the time that might have sharpened their inferences or caused them to ask different questions? If so, would it have suggested other, less obvious policy options than the ones employed? More ambitiously, practitioners might be brought into a collaborative project with scholars to simulate various kinds of decision situations, and perhaps reconsider some actual decisions. Here, the proximate consumers of theory-driven policy recommendations would be asked explicitly what they need or would have needed analytically in order to make good decisions and how they would use that knowledge if it were available. The scholars might be asked to respond by critiquing their own product from this perspective, and then suggesting how good theoretical arguments might do better at satisfying these needs *without compromising intellectual quality*.

Final Thoughts

Representative democracies delegate the responsibility for formulating and conducting foreign policy to elected officials and their subordinates. Those officials typically know the issue-specific facts better than almost any outside observer—something Lyndon Johnson and Robert McNamara seldom hesitated to remind U.S. critics of the Vietnam War. We know better than our critics, they said, because we have the relevant data and they do not. Even so, the architects of that war did not understand the links between the sorts of aims and means involved, nor how to decide whether the war should have been fought and, if so, how the intervention might have produced the desired conclusion. That kind of knowledge is certainly not the exclusive property of scholars, but they are often better-suited to use and certainly to produce those generalizations than are policymakers.

It is not hard to think of prominent cases that *might* have worked out differently if political leaders and policymakers had possessed appropriate knowledge. The U.S. involvement in Vietnam, as is often noted, reflected flawed instrumental knowledge—bearing on the utility of force in the cultural and geopolitical context of Vietnam. It also reflected flawed contextual knowledge, involving, for example, the U.S. public's tolerance for a painful war of attrition. Similarly, as Bruce Jentleson argues, the U.S. policy to appease Saddam Hussein in the decade before he attempted to conquer Kuwait reflected a poor understanding of the conditions under which concessions can produce mutually satisfactory policy cooperation.[6]

Perhaps no conceivable scholarship would have affected official thinking in a way that would have prevented these failures. But this does not relieve either decisionmakers or scholars of their obligation to use and produce knowledge that can make a difference. The suggestions in this chapter might be seen as a way to produce the kind of theory-policy dialogue that makes such fiascoes less likely.

The Ivory Tower exists for a good reason: we expect university-based intellectuals to reflect on the world at some distance, and not simply to do the work of policy commentators or journalists at a slower pace. But in our view, the separation from the world of decisions and consequences has gone too far in international relations. It is odd to think that no practical implications should follow from a better understanding of the world. If scholars address important, real-world issues, they will more often than not improve their own work and have more to share with those who must act.

Notes

Chapter 1

1. Paul H. Nitze, *Tension Between Opposites: Reflections on the Practice and The- ory of Politics* (New York: Scribner's, 1993), p. 15.
2. Quoted in David D. Newsom, *The Public Dimension of Foreign Policy* (Bloom- ington: Indiana University Press, 1996), pp. 121, 138.
3. Christopher Hill, "Academic International Relations: The Siren Song of Policy Relevance," in Christopher Hill and Pamela Beshoff, eds. *Two Worlds of Inter- national Relations* (London: Routledge, 1994), pp. 16–17.
4. Robert Jervis, "Arms Control, Stability, and Causes of War," *Political Science Quarterly* 108(2) (Summer 1993): 242–243.
5. Newsom, *The Public Dimension of Foreign Policy*, p. 138.
6. John Vasquez, "World Politics Theory," in Mary Hawkesworth and Maurice Kogan, eds. *Encyclopedia of Government and Politics* 2 (New York: Routledge: 1992), p. 839.
7. This definition is adapted from the one used in James N. Rosenau, "Interna- tional Relations," in Joel Krieger, ed. *The Oxford Companion to the Politics of the World* (New York: Oxford University Press, 1993), p. 455.
8. For a good discussion of these issues, see Philip Zelikow, "Foreign Policy En- gineering," *International Security* 18(4) (Spring 1994): 155–171.
9. William Wallace, "Truth and Power, Monks and Technocrats: Theory and Prac- tice in International Relations," *Review of International Studies* 22 (1996): 301.
10. John Madge, *The Tools of Social Science* (Garden City, NY: Doubleday, 1965), p. 2.
11. Karl Deutsch, *The Analysis of International Relations* 3rd ed. (Englewood Cliffs, NJ: Prentice Hall, 1988), p. 3.

12. Kjell Goldmann, "International Relations: An Overview," in Robert E. Goodin and Hans-Dieter Klingemann, eds. *A New Handbook of Political Science* (Oxford: Oxford University Press, 1996), p. 410.

13. Peter Ordeshook, "Engineering or Science: What is the Study of Politics?," *Critical Review* 9(1–2) (Winter-Spring 1995): 180–181. See Joseph Ben-David, *The Scientist's Role in Society* (Chicago: The University of Chicago Press, 1971), pp. 150–151, for a discussion of how the field of statistics grew out of a need to relate statistical work done in applied fields with one another and with academic work in mathematics.

14. Mark V. Kauppi and Paul R. Viotti, *The Global Philosophers* (New York: Lexington Books, 1992), pp. 21–22. Although Postmodernists reject this objective, their work cannot be considered "traditional."

15. Goldmann, "International Relations: An Overview," p. 410.

16. Michael Banks, "The Evolution of International Relations Theory," in Michael Banks, ed. *Conflict in World Society: A New Perspective on International Relations* (New York: St. Martin's 1984), pp. 5–7.

17. Banks, "The Evolution of International Relations Theory," p. 5.

18. John A. Hobson, *Towards International Government* (London: Allen and Unwin, 1915), p. 8.

19. Banks, "The Evolution of International Relations Theory," pp. 7–8.

20. Robert S. Boynton, "The New Intellectuals," *The Atlantic Monthly* (March 1995), p. 53.

21. Martin Griffths, *Fifty Key Thinkers in International Relations* (London: Routledge, 1999), p. 36.

22. Jack Snyder, "Science and Sovietology," *World Politics* 40(2) (January 1988): 173.

23. Hedley Bull, "International Theory: The Case for a Classical Approach," *World Politics* 17(3) (April 1966): 366–376.

24. Philip Everts, "Academic Experts as Foreign Policy Advisers: The Functions of Government Advisory Councils in the Netherlands," in Michel Girard, Wolf-Dieter Eberwein, and Keith Webb, *Theory and Practice in Foreign Policy-Making* (London: Pinter, 1994), p. 68. For specific examples, see Gregg Herken, *Counsels of War* expanded edition (New York: Oxford University Press, 1985), pp. 205–210 and Fred Kaplan, *The Wizards of Armageddon* (New York: Touchstone, 1983), pp. 89–110, 117–124, 330–335. See also James Kurth, "Inside the Cave: The Banality of I.R. Studies," *The National Interest* No. 53 (Fall 1998), p. 34.

25. John G. Gunnell, *The Descent of Political Theory* (Chicago: The University of Chicago Press, 1993), p. 68.

26. Joseph Kruzel, "More a Chasm Than a Gap, But Do Scholars Want to Bridge It?," *Mershon International Studies Review* 38, Supplement 1 (April 1994), p. 179.

27. Gunnell, *The Descent of Political Theory*, p. 224.
28. David Easton, "Political Science," in David L. Sills, ed. *International Encyclopedia of the Social Sciences* 12 (New York: Macmillan, 1968), p. 296.
29. Easton, "Political Science," p. 297.
30. The quote is from J. David Singer, "Theorists and Empiricists: The Two-Culture Problem in International Politics," in James N. Rosenau, Vincent Davis, and Maurice A. East, eds. *The Analysis of International Politics* (New York: Free Press, 1972), p. 84.
31. Michel Girard, "Theory and Practice in Foreign Policy: Epistemological Problems and Political Realities," in Girard et al. *Theory and Practice in Foreign Policy-Making*, p. 5.
32. Warren O. Hagstrom, *The Scientific Community* (New York: Basic Books, 1965), pp. 33–35.
33. See Max Weber, "Politics as a Vocation," and Weber, "Science as a Vocation," in H. H. Gerth and C. Wright Mills, *From Max Weber: Essays in Sociology* (New York: Oxford University Press, pp. 77–128, 129–156; Hagstrom, *The Scientific Community*; Jerome R. Ravetz, *Scientific Knowledge and Its Social Problems* (Oxford: Clarendon Press, 1971); Joseph Ben-David, *The Scientist's Role in Society*; Joseph Ben-David, *Scientific Growth: Essays on the Social Organization and Ethos of Science* (Berkeley: University of California Press, 1991); Bernard Barber, *Social Studies of Science* (New Brunswick: Transaction Publishers, 1990); Robert K. Merton, *The Sociology of Science: Theoretical and Empirical Investigations* (Chicago: The University of Chicago Press, 1973); Michael Mulkay, *Science and the Sociology of Knowledge* (London: Allen and Unwin, 1979). For a critique of the political-science profession from this perspective, see David M. Ricci, *The Tragedy of Political Science* (New Haven: Yale University Press, 1984), pp. 209–248.
34. Ricci, *The Tragedy of Political Science*, p. 222. On the incentives for scientific originality, see Robert K. Merton, "Priorities in Scientific Discovery," in Merton, *The Sociology of Science*, pp. 293–296.
35. See Fenton Martion and Robert Goehlert, *Getting Published in Political Science Journals* (Washington, D.C.: The American Political Science Association, 1997).
36. See David Lalman and David Newman, "Alliance Formation and National Security," *International Interactions* 16(4) (1991): 251.
37. Max Weber, "Science as a Vocation," in Gerth and Mills, eds. *From Max Weber*, p. 143, emphasis in original.
38. Ben-David, "Science and the University System" in Ben-David, *Scientific Growth*, pp. 164–166; Ben-David, *The Scientist's Role in Society*, p. 156; Ravetz, *Scientific Knowledge and Its Social Problems*, p. 15.

39. Ordeshook, "Engineering or Science?," p. 178.
40. Michael M. Weinstein, "Economics Students Seek a Bit of Reality," *The New York Times* September 18, 1999, pp. A17, A19.
41. Ordeshook, "Engineering or Science?," pp. 181–182. See also Stanley Hoffmann, "An American Social Science: International Relations," *Daedalus* 106(3) (Summer 1977), p. 46.
42. Ben-David, *The Scientist's Role in Society*, p. 158.
43. Kurth, "Inside the Cave," p. 33. This problem seems especially pervasive in international relations where, as K. J. Holsti notes, research agendas appear, disappear, and reappear, often with a changed vocabulary. See K. J. Holsti, "Rooms and Views: Perspectives on the Study of International Relations," in Joseph Kruzel and James N. Rosenau, eds. *Journey Through World Politics* (Lexington, MA: Lexington Books, 1989), p. 35. One reason seems to be the prevalence in this field of large "isms" as the main theoretical frameworks— Realism, Liberalism, and Constructivism—all of which seem to draw inspiration from a few prominent cases or scenarios to the exclusion of others. When real-world events force a factor that had been ignored by the dominant "ism" onto people's attention, that framework suddenly comes into favor again. From the perspective of policy relevance, such cyclical rather than linear intellectual progress can only make IR theory seem particularly lacking in credibility and authoritativeness.
44. Wallace, "Truth and Power," p. 305.
45. Joseph S. Nye, Jr., "Studying World Politics," in Joseph Kruzel and James N. Rosenau, eds. *Journeys Through World Politics* (Lexington, MA: Lexington Books, 1989) p. 206.
46. See Edward D. Mansfield and Jack Snyder, "Democratization and the Danger of War," *International Security* 20(1) (Summer 1995): 5–38; Edward D. Mansfield and Jack Snyder, "Democratization and War," *Foreign Affairs* 74(3) (May/June 1995): 79–97.
47. Kruzel, "More a Chasm than a Gap," p. 180.
48. General John C. Galvin (Ret.), "Breaking Through and Being Heard," *Mershon International Studies Review* 38, Supplement 1 (April 1994): 173.
49. Alexander L. George, *Bridging the Gap: Theory and Practice in Foreign Policy* (Washington, D.C.: United States Institute of Peace, 1993), pp. 117–125. George also mentions "actor-specific behavioral models of adversaries" as a useful kind of knowledge, a point echoed by former NATO Commander Galvin (endnote 48). We do not discuss these in detail, as they do not constitute "theory" (general causal propositions) in the strict sense.
50. Kruzel, "More a Chasm than a Gap," p. 179.
51. Newsom, *The Public Dimension of Foreign Policy*, pp. 135–136.

52. For a fuller discussion, see Joseph Lepgold, "Is Anyone Listening? International Relation Theory and the Problem of Policy Relevance," *Political Science Quarterly* 113(1) (Spring 1998): 43–62.

53. See the remarks by Peter Katzenstein in Atul Kohli et al., "The Role of Theory in Comparative Politics: A Symposium," *World Politics* 48(1) (October 1995): 14–15.

54. Kruzel, "More a Chasm than a Gap," p. 180.

55. Norwood Russell Hanson, *Perception and Discovery* (San Francisco: Freeman, Cooper, and Company, 1969), pp. 149, 302–303; Robert Jervis, "Hypotheses on Misperception," *World Politics* 20(3) (April 1968): 455–457.

56. Alexander L. George, and Richard Smoke, *Deterrence in American Foreign Policy: Theory and Practice* (New York: Columbia University Press, 1974), pp. 536–547.

Chapter 2

1. This section draws upon Miroslav Nincic, "Policy Relevance and Theoretical Development: The Terms of the Tradeoff," in Miroslav Nincic and Joseph Lepgold, eds. *Being Useful: Policy Relevance and International Relations Theory* (Ann Arbor: University of Michigan Press, 2000), chapter 2.

2. One dictionary, in fact, defines "instrumental" in part as "helpful" or "useful." See *The Random House College Dictionary* rev. ed. (New York: Random House, 1988), p. 691. Most discussions of policy relevance in international relations similarly identify instrumental knowledge as the most practical kind of knowledge. See, for example, Oran R. Young, "The Perils of Odysseus: On Constructing Theories of International Relations," *World Politics* 24 (Supplement) (Spring 1972): 183.

3. Richard N. Haass, "Sanctioning Madness," *Foreign Affairs* 76(6) (November/ December 1997): 74.

4. Ibid.

5. Quoted in Haass, "Sanctioning Madness," p. 75.

6. The literature on this issue has become quite large. See, for example, Klaus Knorr, *The Power of Nations* (New York: Basic Books, 1975), chapter 6, pp. 134–165; David A. Baldwin, *Economic Statecraft* (Princeton: Princeton University Press, 1985), chapters 7–10, pp. 115–335; Robert A. Pape, "Why Economic Sanctions Do Not Work," *International Security* 22(2) (Fall 1997): 90–136; Gary Clyde Hufbauer and Jeffrey J. Schott, assisted by Kimberly Ann Elliott, *Economic Sanctions Reconsidered* (Washington, D.C.: Institute for International Economics); Kimberly Ann Elliott, "The Sanctions Glass: Half Full or Half Empty," *International Security* 23(1) (Summer 1998): 50–65; Robert A.

Pape, "Why Economic Sanctions *Still* Do Not Work," *International Security* 23(1) (Summer 1998): 66–77.

7. George E. Shambaugh IV, "Dominance, Dependence, and Political Power: Tethering Technology in the 1980s and Today," *International Studies Quarterly* 40(4) (December 1996): 559–588.

8. Edward N. Luttwak, "Toward Post-Heroic Warfare," *Foreign Affairs* 74(3) (May/June 1995): 109–122.

9. Edward D. Mansfield, "International Institutions and Economic Sanctions," *World Politics* 47(4) (July 1995): 588–598.

10. Andrew Bennett, Joseph Lepgold, and Danny Unger, "Burden-Sharing in the Persian Gulf War," *International Organization* 48(1) (Winter 1994): 39–75.

11. William C. Wohlforth, "The Stability of a Unipolar World," *International Security* 24(1) (Summer 1999): 14.

12. Christopher Layne, "The Unipolar Illusion: Why New Great Powers Will Arise," *International Security* 17(4) (Spring 1993): 5–51; Charles Krauthammer, "The Unipolar Moment," *Foreign Affairs* 70(1) (Winter 1990/91): 23–33.

13. Charles F. Doran, "Why Forecasts Fail," *International Studies Review* 1(2) (Summer 1999).

14. The quote is from Joseph Ben David, *Scientific Growth: Essays in the Social Organization and Ethos of Science* (Berkeley: University of California Press, 1991), p. 402.

15. Haass, "Sanctioning Madness," p. 81.

16. The quoted phrase is from Kaplan, *The Conduct of Inquiry*, p. 339. For a more detailed discussion, see Carl G. Hempel, *Philosophy of Natural Science* (Englewood Cliffs, NJ: Prentice-Hall, 1966), pp. 49–54.

17. Mario Bunge, *Finding Philosophy in the Social Sciences* (New Haven: Yale University Press, 1996), p. 124

18. Jon Elster, *Nuts and Bolts for the Social Sciences* (New York: Cambridge University Press, 1989), p. 18.

19. Philip E. Tetlock, "Psychological Advice on Foreign Policy: What Do We Have to Contribute?," in Neil J. Kressel, ed. *Political Psychology: Classic and Contemporary Readings* (New York: Paragon House, 1993), p. 327; James G. March, *A Primer on Decisionmaking* (New York: Free Press, 1994), p. 38.

20. Ernest Nagel, *The Structure of Science*, p. 555. See also Jack Snyder, "Science and Sovietology," *World Politics* 40(2) (January 1988): 174–175.

21. Paul H. Nitze, *Tension Between Opposites: Reflections on the Practice and Theory of Politics* (New York: Scribner's, 1993)

22. "Truth" itself is associated with more than one meaning. Here, the meaning referred to is that implied by the "correspondence theory" of truth which claims that a statement is true if and only if it corresponds to empirical reality. Other theories make different claims about truth. For example, the coherence theory contends that a statement is true if and only if it coheres with all true statements.

23. One of the best examinations of the nature of the scientific enterprise is Ernest Nagel's *The Structure of Science: Problems in the Logic of Scientific Explanation* (Indianapolis: Hacket, 1979). See chapter 13 for a discussion of the special case of the social sciences. See also, A. F. Chalmers, *What is This Thing Called Science?* (Indianapolis, Hacket, 1976).

24. For a further discussion of these issues, see Gary King, Robert O. Keohane, and Sidney Verba, *Designing Social Inquiry: Scientific Inference in Qualitative Research* (Princeton, NJ: Princeton University Press, 1994).

25. Discussions of cognitive dissonance are Leon Festinger, *A Theory of Cognitive Dissonance* (New York: Row, Peterson), 1957; and J. W. Brem and A. R. Cohen, *Explorations in Cognitive Dissonance* (New York: Wiley, 1962).

26. Ole R. Holsti, "The Belief System and National Images: A Case Study," in James N. Rosenau, *International Politics and Foreign Policy* (New York: The Free Press, 1969): 543–550.

27. For subsequent research that compares the thinking of Dulles to that of John F. Kennedy and Henry Kissinger, see Douglas Stuart and Harvey Starr, "Inherent Bad Faith Reconsidered: Dulles, Kennedy, and Kissinger," *Political Psychology* (Fall-Winter 1981–82): 1–33.

28. The classic work on attribution theory is Richard E. Nisbett and L. D. Ross, *Human Inference: Strategies and Shortcomings of Social Judgment* (Englewood Cliffs, NJ: Prentice Hall, 1983).

29. Deborah Welch Larson, *Origins of Containment: A Psychological Explanation* (Princeton, NJ: Princeton University Press, 1985).

30. See, for example, Robert Jervis, "The Drunkard's Search," in Shanto Iyengar and William J. McGuire eds. *Explorations in Political Psychology*, (Durham, NC: Duke University Press, 1993), pp. 338–360. Also Daniel Kahneman and Amos Tversky, "Prospect Theory: An Analysis of Decision Under Risk," *Econometrica* 47 (1979): 263–291.

31. See, in particular, Ernest P. May, *Lessons of the Past: The Use and Misuse of History in American Foreign Policy* (New York: Oxford University Press, 1973). Also David H. Fischer, *Historians' Fallacies: Toward a Logic of Historical Thought* (New York: Harper and Row, 1970). Chapter 9.

32. These heuristics are described in the following two pieces by Amos Tversky and Daniel Kahneman: "Availability: A Heuristic for Judging Frequency and Probability," *Cognitive Psychology* (5) 1973: 207–32, and "Judgments Of and By Representativeness," in Daniel Kahneman, Paul Slovic, and Amos Tversky eds., *Judgment Under Uncertainty: Heuristics and Biases* (New York: Cambridge University Press, 1982).

33. Alexander L. George, *Presidential Decisionmaking in Foreign Policy: The Effective Use of Information and Advice* (Boulder, CO: Westview Press, 1980), p. 61.

34. Henry A. Kissinger, *Diplomacy* (New York: Simon and Schuster, 1994), p. 717

35. Ibid p. 719.

36. George P. Shultz, *Turmoil and Triumph: My Years as Secretary of State* (New York: Scribner's, 1993), pp. 277–278.

37. Arthur A. Stein, "The Politics of Linkage," *World Politics* 33 (October 1980): 62–81.

38. For further developments of such thinking, see S. Lohman, "Linkage Politics," *Journal of Conflict Resolution* 41 (February 1977): 36–67.

39. Graham T. Allison, *Essence of Decision: Explaining the Cuban Missile Crisis,* (Boston: Little Brown, 1971), p. 176.

40. William Kaufmann, "Two American Ambassadors: Bullitt and Kennedy," in Gordon Craig and Felix Gilbert, eds., *The Diplomats* (Princeton: Princeton University Press, 1955), pp. 658–659.

41. Steve Smith, "Policy Preferences and Bureaucratic Position: The Case of the American Hostage Rescue Mission," in Eugene R. Wittkopf ed., *The Domestic Sources of American Foreign Policy*, 2nd. ed. (New York: St. Martins, 1994), p. 308.

42.. We are indebted to Emily Goldman for the Churchill and Weinberger examples.

43. Henry A. Kissinger, *Years of Upheaval* (Boston: Little, Brown, 1982), p. 445.

44. Charles E. Lindblom and David K. Cohen, *Usable Knowledge: Social Science and Social Problem Solving* (New Haven: Yale University Press, 1979), chapter 4.

45. Thorstein Veblen, *The Place of Science in Modern Civilization* (New York: Russell and Russell, 1961), p. 33.

46. See also, Eva Etzioni-Halevy, *The Knowledge Elite and the Failure of Prophecy* (London: George Allen and Unwin, 1985), Chapter 3.

47. See, for example, David M. Ricci, *The Tragedy of Political Science: Scholarship and Democracy*. (New Haven: Yale University Press, 1984), and Donald P. Green and Ian Shapiro, *Pathologies of Rational Choice Theory* (New Haven: Yale University Press, 1994).

48. Stephen M. Walt, "Rigor or Rigor Mortis? Rational Choice and Security Studies," *International Security* 23(4) (Spring 1999): 5–48.

49. Dale R. Herspring, "Practitioners and Political Scientists," *PS* September 1992, p. 159.

Chapter 3

1. For an exceptional example of relevant knowledge that is supply-driven and linked by a *singular* path to the decision-making process, see the discussion of the impact of Homer-Dixon's work, below.

2. Steven J. Brams and Alan D. Taylor, *Fair Division: From Cake-Cutting to Dispute Resolution* (New York: Routledge: 1990).

3. Steven J. Brams and Jeffrey M. Togman, "Camp David: Was the Agreement Fair?" *Conflict Management and Peace Science* 3 (1996): 99–112. An expanded

and updated version of this piece appears in Steven J. Brams and Alan D. Taylor, *The Win-Win Solution: Guaranteeing Fair Shares for Everybody* (New York: Norton, 1999).

4. Of course, the reason that organized interest do not press for a solution may be because they, like policymakers, do not see how it could be attained given the current state of knowledge.

5. See, for example, Bruce W. Jentleson, *Opportunities Missed, Opportunities Seized: Preventive Diplomacy in the Post–Cold War World* (Lanham, MD: Rowman and Littlefield, 1999).

6. See, for example, J. P. Hardt, "Soviet and East European Energy Supplies," in H. Franssen et al., *World Energy Supplies and International Security* (Cambridge, MA: Institute for Foreign Policy Analysis, 1983), and Carnegie Endowment for International Peace, *Challenges for US National Security: A Preliminary Report*, Part 2 (Washington DC: Carnegie Endowment for International Peace, 1981): 165–196.

7. For example, John Mueller, "A Quick Victory? It Better Be," *New York Times*, January 19, 1991, p. 31.

8. See especially Charles E. Lindblom, *The Intelligence of Democracy: Decision Making Through Mutual Adjustment* (New York: The Free Press, 1965), Erik Albaek, "Between Knowledge and Power: Utilization of Social Science in Public Policy Making," in *Policy Sciences* 28 (1995): 79–100; Douglas Torgerson, "Between Knowledge and Politics: Three Faces of Policy Analysis," *Policy Sciences* 19 (1986): 33–59.

9. Relevant scholars include Marshall Shulman, Adam Ulam, and Alex Inkeles.

10. Good histories of the development of U.S. nuclear doctrine are provided in Lawrence Freedman, *The Evolution of Nuclear Strategy* (New York: St. Martins, 1981), and Fred Kaplan, *The Wizards of Armageddon* (New York: Simon and Schuster, 1983).

11. For example, see Yehezkel Dhor, *Crazy States: A Counterconventional Strategic Problem* (Lexington, MA: D.C. Heath, 1971).

12. Samuel Huntington, *Political Order in Changing Societies* (New Haven: Yale University Press, 1972).

13. Bernard Brodie is an early example.

14. Lindblom, *Intelligence of Democracy*.

15. Erik Albaek, "Between Knowledge and Power: Utilization of Social Science in Public Policy Making," *Policy Sciences* 28 (1995): 85.

16. Michael D. Cohen, James G. March, and Johan P. Olsen, "A Garbage Can Model of Organizational Choice," *Administrative Science Quarterly*, (March 1972): 294–334.

17. Homer-Dixon's impact on official thinking in Washington DC is described in Ross Laver, "Looking for Trouble: Tad Homer-Dixon's Prophecies for a

Crowded Planet Have Created a Stir in Washington," *Macleans* (September 5, 1994): 18–22.

18. See, for example, Ashton B. Carter and David N. Schwartz eds, *Ballistic Missile Defense* (Washington DC: The Brookings Institution, 1986).

19. Carol Weiss, "Research for Policy's Sake: the Enlightenment Function of Social Research," in *Policy Analysis* 3 (4) (Fall 1977).

20. Of course, it is the scholar's responsibility to indicate to policymakers where the setting in which the knowledge is to be applied differs materially from that from which the knowledge was produced.

21. A partial exception is provided by political psychologists whose research is often of an experimental nature.

22. Charles E. Lindblom and David K. Cohen, *Usable Knowledge: Social Science and Social Problem Solving* (New Haven: Yale University Press, 1979), p. 76

23. This section draws on Joseph Lepgold, "Is Anyone Listening? International Relations Theory and the Problem of Policy Relevance," *Political Science Quarterly* 113(1) (Spring 1998): 48–60, and Lepgold, "Scholars and Statesmen: Framework for a Productive Dialogue," in Nincic and Lepgold, eds. *Being Useful*.

24. See also Ernest J. Wilson, "How Social Science Can Help Policymakers: The Relevance of Theory," in Nincic and Lepgold eds., *Being Useful*, pp. 109–128.

25. James N. Rosenau and Mary Durfee, *Thinking Theory Thoroughly* (Boulder, CO: Westview, 1995), p. 2.

26. For a somewhat different manner of establishing such taxonomies, see Wilson, "How Social Science Can Help Policymakers."

27. Norman Robert Campbell, *What is Science?* (New York: Dover, 1952), p. 79.

28. See, for example, Kenneth A. Oye, ed. *Cooperation Under Anarchy* (Princeton: Princeton University Press, 1986); Arthur A. Stein, *Why Nations Cooperate* (Ithaca: Cornell University press, 1990); Robert Jervis, "Realism, Game Theory, and Cooperation," *World Politics* 40(3) (April 1988): 317–349.

29. For representative statements of the Constructivist position, which argues that preferences result from the groups of which actors are a part, see Alexander Wendt, *Social Theory of International Politics* (Cambridge: Cambridge University Press, 1999), and Michael Barnett, "Institutions, Roles, and Disorder: The Case of the Arab States System," *International Studies Quarterly* 37(3): 271–296. For recent statements of the choice-theoretic position, which argues that preferences are largely exogenous to choice and interaction, see Bruce Bueno de Mesquita and David Lalman, *War and Reason* (New Haven: Yale University Press, 1992), and Robert Powell, *In The Shadow of Power: States and Strategies in International Politics* (Princeton: Princeton University Press, 1999).

30. See, for example, Alan C. Lamborn, *The Price of Power*, and Robert Putnam, "Diplomacy and Domestic Politics," *International Organization* 42(3) (Summer 1988): 427–460.

31. See the debate between Kenneth Waltz, *Theory of International Politics* (New York: McGraw-Hill, 1979), and Helen Milner, "The Assumption of Anarchy in International Relations Theory: A Critique," *Review of International Studies* 17 (1991): 67–85.

32. James N. Rosenau, "Before Cooperation: Hegemons, Regimes, and Habit-Driven Actors in World Politics," *International Organization* 40(4) (Autumn 1986): 852, 871.

33. Tetlock, "Psychological Advice on Foreign Policy," p. 322.

34. George *Bridging the Gap*, pp. 117–120.

35. George, *Bridging the Gap*, pp. 120–125.

36. Davis Bobrow, "The Relevance Potential of Different Products," *World Politics* 24, Supplement (Spring 1972), pp. 223.

37. Richard N. Haas, *Intervention* rev. ed. (Washington, D.C.: Brookings Institution, 1999).

38. Donald M. Snow and Eugene Brown, *Beyond the Water's Edge: An Introduction to U.S. Foreign policy* (New York: St. Martin's Press, 1997), pp. 239.

39. William Wallace, "Between Two Worlds: Think Tanks and Foreign Policy," in Christopher Hill and Pamela Beshoff, *Two Worlds of International Relations* (London: Routledge, 1994), pp. 146.

40. See George, *Bridging the Gap*, pp. 125–131, for some good examples of this type of knowledge.

41. Bobrow, "The Relevance Potential of Different Products," p. 221.

42. Bobrow, "The Relevance Potential of Different Products," p. 223; Young, "The Perils of Odysseus," p. 200.

43. Bobrow, "The Relevance Potential of Different Products," p. 223.

44. This section draws on Lepgold, "Is Anyone Listening?," and Lepgold, "Scholars and Statesmen."

45. See, for example, Stephen M. Walt, "Rigor or Rigor Mortis: Rational Choice and Security Studies," *International Security* 23(4) (Spring 1999): 5–48, and Donald P. Green and Ian Shapiro, *Pathologies of Rational Choice Theory* (New Haven: Yale University Press, 1994).

46. Bruce Bueno de Mesquita, "The Benefits of a Social-Science Approach to Studying International Affairs," in Ngaire Woods, ed. *Explaining International Relations Since 1945* (Oxford, UK: Oxford University Press, 1996), p. 67.

47. Bruce Bueno de Mesquita, David Newman, and Alvin Rabushka, *Forecasting Political Events* (New Haven: Yale University Press, 1985), p. 7.

48. Daniel W. Drezner, "Conflict Expectations and the Paradox of Economic Coercion," *International Studies Quarterly* 42(4) (December 1998): 709–731.

49. Mark H. Moore, "Social Science and Policy Analysis," in Daniel Callahan and Bruce Jennings, eds. *Ethics, the Social Sciences, and Policy Analysis* (New York: Plenum Press, 1983), p. 290.

50. Young, "The Perils of Odysseus," pp. 200–201.

51. Steven Erlanger, "Policy Centers Rethink Their Images," *New York Times* July 20, 1997, p. A10.

52. George, *Bridging the Gap*, p. 4, and chapter 1, note 2, pp. 147–148.

53. Erlanger, "Policy Centers Rethink Their Images."

54. Robert Jervis, "Models and Cases in the Study of International Conflict," in Robert L. Rothstein, ed. *The Evolution of Theory in International Relations* (Columbia: University of South Carolina Press, 1991), pp. 64, 67.

55. Dean G. Pruitt, "Stability and Sudden Change in Interpersonal and International Affairs," *Journal of Conflict Resolution* 13(1) (March 1969): 35.

56. Arthur Stinchcombe, *Constructing Social Theories* (Chicago: University of Chicago Press, 1968), pp. 44, 47.

57. Christopher H. Achen and Duncan Snidal, "Rational Deterrence Theory and Comparative Case Studies," *World Politics* 16(2) (January 1989).

58. John C. McKinney, *Constructive Typology and Social Theory* (New York: Appleton-Century Crofts, 1966), p. 36; Paul Diesing, *Patterns of Discovery in the Social Sciences* (Chicago: Aldine Atherton, 1971), p. 189.

59. "Introduction," in Carol H. Weiss ed., *Using Social Research in Public Policy Making* (Lexington, MA: D.C. Heath, 1977), p. 18.

Chapter 4

1. For a critique of this position, see Michael Walzer, *Interpretation and Social Criticism*. (Cambridge: Harvard University Press, 1987), especially chapter 2.

2. Michael Root, *Philosophy of Social Science The Methods, Ideals, and Politics of Social Inquiry* (Oxford: Blackwell, 1993), Especially chapter 1.

3. For a different view, see Peter deLeon, *Advice and Consent: The Development of the Policy Sciences* (New York: Russel Sage, 1988).

4. Root, *Philosophy of Social Science*, p. 16.

5. George Herbert Meade, "Scientific Method and the Moral Sciences," *Selected Writings* (Chicago: University of Chicago Press, 1964).

6. John F. A. Taylor, *The Public Commission of the University* (New York: New York University Press, 1981), Chapter 6.

7. Alexander George and Richard Smoke, "Theory for Policy in International Relations," in *Policy Sciences* (December 1973): 388.

8. For an examination of the concept of national interest, see Miroslav Nincic, "The National Interest and Its Interpretation," *Review of Politics* (January 1999): 29–55.

9. George and Smoke, *Deterrence in American Foreign Policy*, p. 619.
10. Joseph Ben David, "Innovations and their Recognition in Social Science," *History of Political Economy* 7(4) (1975): 434–455.
11. Scott Greer, *The Logic of Social Inquiry* (Chicago: Aldine, 1969).
12. Except, of course, where importance refers to the actual or assumed ethical or social implications of discoveries in the natural sciences.
13. Knowledge designed as an end in itself is variously referred to as "basic," "pure," or "disinterested" knowledge. Here, we will use the third term.
14. A good and somewhat related conception is provided by Abraham Kaplan, who defines theory as "more than a synopsis of the moves that have been played on the game of nature; it also sets forth some idea of the rules of the game by which the moves become intelligible." Abraham Kaplan, (San Francisco: Chandler, 1964), p. 302.
15. For discussions of the components of good theory, see Ernest Nagel, *The Structure of Science: Problems in the Logic of Scientific Explanation* (New York: Harcourt, Brace and World, 1961), chapters 5 and 6; Johan Galtung, *Theory and Methods of Social Research* (New York: Columbia University Press, 1967), chapter 6; Karl Popper, *The Logic of Scientific Discovery* (New York: Harper, 1968), chapter 3.
16. For a discussion of the relation between explanation and prediction see Abraham Kaplan, *The Conduct of Inquiry*, chapter 40. Also, Michael Nicholson, *The Scientific Analysis of Social Behavior* (London: Pinter, 1983), chapter 9.
17. For a good discussion, see Nazli Choucri and Thomas Robinson eds., *Forecasting in International Relations: Theory, Methods, Problems* (San Francisco: W.H. Freeman, 1965), part IV.
18. As Stephen Toulmin point out: "Scientists are interested in 'forecasting techniques' only incidentally, and any more satisfactory sense of prediction takes for granted the idea of explanation, rather than defining it." *Foresight and Understanding: An Enquiry into the Aims of Science* (New York: Harper and Row, 1961), p. 99. See also, Kenneth N. Waltz, "Evaluating Theories," *American Political Science Review* (December 1997): 913–917).
19. Realism in this sense has nothing to do with political realism (*realpolitik*).
20. The distinction is discussed in A. F. Chalmers, *What Is This Thing Called Science?* (Stratford: Open University Press, 1978), chapter 13, and Ernst Nagel, *The Structure of Science: Problems in the Logic of Scientific Explanation* (New York: Harcourt Brace, 1961), pp. 129–152. For a particularly well-argued statement of the realist position, see Richard W. Miller, *Fact and Method: Explanation, Confirmation and Reality in the Natural and Social Sciences* (Princeton, NJ: Princeton University Press, 1987), Chapters 8–11.
21. See Richard L. Kikham, *Theories of Truth A Critical Introduction:* (Cambridge: MIT Press, 1992), and Laurence Bonjour, *The Structure of Empirical Knowledge* (Cambridge: Harvard University Press, 1985).

22. See, for example, William H. Brenner, Logic and Philosophy (Notre Dame: University of Notre Dame Press, 1993), chapter 4, and Milton Hobbs, *The Objectives of Political Science* (New York: University Press of America, 1993), chapter 1.

23. In Milton Friedman ed., *Essays in Positive Economics* (Chicago: University of Chicao Press, 1953), pp. 3–43.

24. Imre Lakatos, "The Methodology of Scientific Research programs," in Imre Lakatos and A. Musgrave, *Criticism and the Growth of Knowledge* (Cambridge: Cambridge University Press, 1970)

25. Vladimir I. Lenin, *Imperialism: The Highest Stage of Capitalism* (New York: International Publishers, 1939). First published in 1917.

26. Kenneth N. Waltz, *Theory of International Politics* (Reading, MA: Addison-Wesley, 1979).

27. Hans J. Morgenthau, *Politics Among Nations: The Struggle for Power and Peace* (New York: Knopf, 1948).

28. Milton Hobbs, *The Objectives of Political Science* (New York: University Press of America, 1993), pp. 10–13.

29. For example, the concept of "transaction costs" as the basis for the establishment of *economic* organizations has been extensively studied by professional economists. When the same notion was uncritically imported into political science in an attempt to account for the creation of *military* alliances, the significance of the venture was undermined by the fact that it could not be demonstrated that transaction costs had similar meaning to those involved in establishing in military organizations. In other words, the concept was now bereft of real empirical meaning. See Katja Weber, "Hierarchy Amidst Anarchy: A Transaction Cost Approach to International Security Cooperation," *International Studies Quarterly* (June 1997): 321–340.

30. John Henry Cardinal Newman, *The Idea of a University* (New York: Longmans, Green, 1947 [1852]), p. 101. For a provocative discussion of this issue, see Bertrand Russell, "Useless Knowledge," in Bertrand Russell ed., *In Praise of Idleness and Other Essays* (London: Allen and Unwin, 1935), pp. 9–29.

31. This is discussed in Nicholson *The Scientific Analysis of Social Behavior*, pp. 95–100.

32. Philip H. Melanson, *Political Science and Political Knowledge* (Washington DC: Public Affairs Press, 1975), p. 130.

33. For a discussion of this concern and an examination of its foundations, see Nico Stehr, *Practical Knowledge: Applying the Social Sciences* (Newbury Park, CA: Sagee, 1992), pp. 147–149.

34. A discussion of some of the empirical issue involved in the debate on the Democratic Peace can be found in Michael E. Brown et al., eds., *Debating the Democratic Peace* (Cambridge: MIT Press, 1996).

35. David Morris, *Measuring the Condition of the World's Poor: The Physical Quality of Life Index* (New York: Pergamon, 1979).

36. Richard Miller defines a "bias toward the superficial" characteristic of much deductive work in the social sciences. This bias is reflected in "an unjustified preference for theories denying the operation of causal factors which are relatively hard to observe . . . [arising from] at least three aspects of deductivism: the rejection of the hedges and defense on which deeper theories usually depend; the neglect of causal depth in assessing explanations; and the neglect of the actual context of scientific development in the choice among hypotheses." *Fact and Method*, p. 262.

37. Morgenthau, *Politics Among Nations*, p. 39.

38. Waltz, *Theory of International Politics*, 1979, especially chapter 6.

39. Waltz's major contribution to policy-relevant thinking is found in his work on nuclear proliferation. Kenneth N. Waltz and Scott Sagan, *The Spread of Nuclear Weapons: A Debate* (New York: Norton, 1995).

40. David M. Ricci, *The Tragedy of Political Science: Politics, Scholarship and Democracy* (New Haven: Yale University Press, 1984)

41. Abraham Flexner, "The Usefulness of Useless Knowledge," *Harper's Magazine* 179 (1939): 535.

42. Hill, "Academic International Relations," pp. 7–9.

43. For some recent discussion in the area of political philosophy, see Jeremy Waldron "What Plato Would Allow," in Ian Shapiro and Judith Wagner DeCew eds., *Theory and Practice* (New York: New York University Press, 1996), pp. 138–177, and, Jeffrey C. Isaac, "The Strange Silence of Political Theory," *Political Theory* (November 1995): 636–688.

44. Kaplan, *The Conduct of Inquiry*, p. 399

45. As in note 31, above.

46. In this regard, it is worth noting that the professional journal that has, in recent years, provided the best *theoretical* articles in the area of international relations, *International Security*, is also a journal that has produced some of the best work on matters of applied foreign policy.

Chapter 5

1. Bruce Russett, *Grasping the Democratic Peace: Principles for a Post-Cold War World* (Princeton: Princeton University Press, 1993), p. 1.

2. Hans J. Morgenthau, *Politics Among Nations: The Struggle for Power and Peace* (New York: Knopf, 1948)

3. Ibid., p. 37.

4.   Mercier de la Reviere, "L'Order Naturel et Essentiel des Systemes Politiques," in Edgar Depitre ed., *Collection des Economistes et des Reformateurs Sociaux de la France* (Paris, 1910), pp. 242–252).

5.   See Geoffrey Blainey, *The Causes of War*, 3rd ed. (New York: The Free Press, 1988). Especially chapter 6.

6.   See, for example, the discussion of Kant, below. Of course, a federation would represent the ultimate achievement of the institutional approach to world politics discussed in chapter 6.

7.   Condorcet, Marquis de, *Oeuvres*, Volume 9.(Paris: Firmin Didot Freres, 1847), p. 41.

8.   Ibid.

9.   Most democracies now have that requirement. In the United States, despite the constitutional requirement that wars be declared by Congress, the war-making prerogatives of the executive continue to be fiercely defended by U.S. presidents, a matter at the heart of the executive-legislative struggle over war powers.

10. Condorcet, *Oeuvres*, pp. 45–46.

11. Immanuel Kant, *To Perpetual Peace: A Philosophical Sketch* (Indianapolis: Hacket. 1983 [1795]). Translated by Ted Humphrey.

12. The other principles are an international federation of states (broadly consistent with the retention of national sovereignty) and the guarantee of international hospitality, so that the citizens of one nation would not be ill-treated in other countries.

13. Kant, *To Perpetual Peace*, p. 113.

14. An interesting possibility is that democracies need stronger (or at least different) reasons for fighting than non-democracies do. In turn, this could imply that, once they mobilize to fight, democracies may be more uncompromising with regard to the terms by which they cease hostilities.

15. Felix Gilbert, *To the Farewell Address: Ideas of Early American Foreign Policy.* (Princeton: Princeton University Press, 1961).

16. Quoted in Thomas J. Knock, *To End All wars: Woodrow Wilson and the Quest for a New World Order* (New York: Oxford University Press, 1992), p. 6.

17. Ibid., p. 121.

18. It must be observed that some of these studies focused on international conflict more generally, some forms of which fall short of war.

19. Michael Haas, "Societal Approaches to the Study of War," *Journal of Peace Research* 2(4) (1965): 304–323.

20. See, for example, Maurice East and Philip M. Gregg, "Factors Influencing Cooperation and Conflict in the International System," *International Studies Quarterly* (September 1967): 244–269; Stephen A. Salmore and Charles F.

Hermann. "The Effect of Size, Development, and Accountability on Foreign Policy," *Peace Science Society Papers* 14 (1969): 16–30; Dina Zinnes and Jonathan Wilkenfeld. "An Analysis of Foreign Conflict Behavior of Nations," in Wolfram F. Hanreider ed., *Comparative Foreign Policy* (New York: McKay, 1971), pp. 200–216.

21. Rudolph J. Rummel, *Understanding Conflict and War: Volume 4* (New York: Sage, 1979), p. 292.

22. Stephen Chan, "Mirror, Mirror on the Wall . . . Are the Freer Countries More Pacific?" *Journal of Conflict Resolution* 28 (December 1984): 617–648.

23. Zeev Maoz and Nasrine Abdolali, "Regime Types and International Conflict, 1817–1976," *Journal of Conflict Resolution* (March 1989): 3–35.

24. Zeev Maoz and Bruce M. Russett, "Alliance, Contiguity, Wealth, and Political Stability: Is the Lack of Conflict Among Democracies a Statistical Artifact?" *International Interactions* 17(3) (1992): 245–267.

25. Jack S. Levy, "Domestic Politics and War," *Journal of Interdisciplinary History* 18 (Spring 1988): 653–677.

26. Russett, *Grasping the Democratic Peace*, pp. 31–38.

27. Michael W. Doyle, "Kant, Liberal Legacies, and Foreign Affairs," in Michael E. Brown, Sean M. Lynn-Jones, and Steven Miller, *Debating the Democratic Peace* (Cambridge: The MIT Press, 1996).

28. Anthony Lake, "From Containment to Enlargement," Address delivered at the School of Advanced International Study, Johns Hopkins University. September 21, 1993.

29. Bill Clinton, "Address by the President to the 48th Session of the United Nations General Assembly." The White House. Office of the Press Secretary. September 27, 1993.

30. White House, *A National Strategy for Engagement and Enlargement*. February 1996, p. 7 (our emphasis).

31. Ibid.

32. Strobe Talbott, "Remarks Before the Carnegie Endowment for International Peace," March 1, 1996.

33. White House, *A National Security Strategy for a New Century*. February 1997, and White House. *A National Security Strategy for a New Century*. October 1998.

34. Joseph Bouchard, "National Security Strategy and U.S. Foreign Policy," Talk given at the Institute on Government Affairs, University of California, Davis. February 11, 1999.

35. David E. Spiro, "The Democratic Peace: And Yet It Squirms," *International Security* (Spring 1995): 177–180.

36. Ted Robert Gurr, Keith Jaggers, and Will H. Moore, *Polity II Codebook* (Boulder, CO: Department of Political Science, University of Colorado, 1989).

37. Raymond D. Gastil, "The Comparative Survey of Freedom: Experiences and Suggestions," *Studies in Comparative International Development* 25 (Spring 1990): 25–50.
38. Alex Inkeles, "Introduction: On Measuring Democracy," *Studies in Comparative International Development* 25 (Spring 1990): 3–6.
39. Erich Weede, "Some Simple Calculations on Democracy and War Involvement," *Journal of Peace Research* 29 (November 1992): 649–664.
40. However, Weede's study covers a considerably shorter period (1962–1980) than most others within this area.
41. James Lee Ray, *Democracy and International Conflict* (Columbia, SC: University of South Carolina Press, 1995).
42. Stuart A. Bremer. "Dangerous Dyads: Conditions Affecting the Likelihood of Interstate War, 1816–1965," *Journal of Conflict Resolution.* 36 (June 1992): 309–341.
43. Arvid Raknerud and Havard Hegre, "The Hazard of War: Reassessing the Evidence for the Democratic Peace," *Journal of Peace Research.* 34 (4) (1997): 385–404.
44. Max Singer and Aaron Wildavsky, *The Real World Order.* (Chatham, NJ: Chatham House, 1993), p. 194.
45. Strobe Talbott, "Democracy and the National Interest," Remarks to the Denver Summit of the Eight Initiative on Democracy and Human Rights. October 1, 1997
46. Lewis A. Coser. *The Functions of Social Conflict.* (Glencoe, IL: The Free Press, 1956).
47. John R. Oneal and Bruce M. Russett. "The Classical Liberals Were Right: Democracy, Interdependence, and Conflict, 1950–1985," *International Studies Quarterly* 41(2) (1997): 267–294.
48. In this regard, it is worth noting the finding by Beck and Tucker (1998) that the democratic peace appears to be a recent (post–World War I) phenomenon. In other words, it is only evident during a period that includes the Cold War.
49. Oneal and Russett, "The Classical Liberals Were Right." See also by the same authors, "The Kantian Peace: The Pacific Benefits of Democracy, Interdependence, and International Organizations, 1885–1992," *World Politics* 52(1) (October 1999): 1–37.
50. Blainey, *The Causes of War*, chapter 5.
51. Zeev Maoz and Bruce M. Russett, "Alliance, Contiguity, Wealth, and Political Stability: Is the Lack of Conflict Among Democracies a Statistical Artifact?" *International Interactions.* 17(3) (1992): 245–267.
52. See, for example, Ted R. Gurr, "Persistence and Change in Political Systems: 1800–1971," *American Political Science Review* 48 (December 1974): 1482–1504.

53. Samuel P. Huntington, "Democracy's Third Wave," *Journal of Democracy*. 2 (Spring 1991): 12–34.

54. For example, Robert A. Dahl. *Polyarchy: Participation and Opposition* (New Haven: Yale University Press, 1971); Samuel Huntington. "Will Countries Become More Democratic?" *Political science Quarterly* 99(2) 1984): 193–218; Seymor Martin Lipset. *Political man: The Social Bases of Politics* 2d edition (Baltimore: Johns Hopkins University Press), 1981); Alex Hadenius. *Democracy and Development* (New York: Cambridge University Press, 1992).

55. See James S. Coleman, "Conclusion," in Gabriel Almond and James S. Coleman, *The Politics of the Developing Areas* (Princeton, NJ: Princeton University Press, 1960), and Bruce M. Russett, "Inequality and Instability: The Relation of Land Tenure to Politics," *World Politics* 16 (1964): 442–54.

56. Robert A. Dahl, *Polyarchy*, p. 55

57. Richard Packenham, *Liberal America and the Third World* (Princeton, NJ: Princeton University Press, 1973).

58. Adam Przeworksi and Fernando Limongi, "Modernization: Theory and Facts," *World Politics* 49 (January 1997): 155–183.

59. Hadenius, *Democracy and Development*, p. 84.

60. Przeworksi and Limongi, "Modernization," p. 159.

61. Ibid., pp. 161–167.

62. Barrington Moore Jr., *Social Origins of Dictatorship and Democracy* (Boston: Beacon Press, 1966), p. 418.

63. Hadenius, *Democracy and Development*, p. 91.

64. Samuel Huntington, "Will Countries Become More Democratic?" *Political Science Quarterly* 99 (2) (1984): 207–209.

65. Samuel Huntington, *Political Order in Changing Societies* (New Haven: Yale University Press, 1968), p. 398.

66. H. H. Gerth and C. Wright Mills, eds., *From Max Weber: Essays in Sociology* (New York: Oxford University Press, 1946).

67. Hadenius, *Democracy and Development*, pp. 134–136.

68. See, for example, Michiel de Vrics, "Democracy and the Neutrality of Public Bureaucracy," in Haile K. Asmeron and Elisa P. Reis, *Democratization and the Bureaucratic Neutrality* (New York: St. Martin's, 1996): 107–126. Also, Malcolm Wallis, *Bureaucracy: Its Role in Third World Development* (London: Macmillan, 1989).

69. See Constantine P. Danopoulos, *From Military to Civilian Rule* (New York: Routledge, 1992), and Talukder Maniruzzaman, *Military Withdrawal from Politics: A Comparative Study* (Cambridge, MA: Ballinger, 1987).

70. Guillermo O'Donnell, Philippe C. Schmitter, and Laurence Whitehead. *Transitions from Authoritarian Rule: Prospects for Democracy* (Baltimore: Johns Hopkins University Press, 1968) 4: 3–5.

71. Larry Diamond, Juan J. Linz, and Seymour Martin Lipset eds. *Democracy in Developing Countries* (Baltimore: Johns Hopkins University Press, 1981).

72. See, for example, Stephan Haggard and Robert R. Kaufman eds. *The Politics of Economic Adjustment: International Constraints, Distributive Conflicts, and the State* (Princeton: Princeton University Press, 1992).

73. For example, Devesh Kapur, "The IMF: A Cure or a Curse," *Foreign Policy* (Summer 1998): 114–131.

74. A partial exception is Thomas Carothers, *Aiding Democracy Abroad: The Learning Curve*. (Washington, DC: Carnegie Endowment for International Peace, 1999).

75. Quoted in Jane Perlez, "Albright Debates Rights and Trade With Chinese," *New York Times*. March 2, 1999.

76. See Edward D. Mansfield and Jack Snyder, "Democratization and War," *Foreign Affairs* 74(3) (1995): 79–97, and, by the same authors, "Democratization and the Danger of War," *International Security* 20 (Summer 1995): 5–38.

77. "Democratization and the Danger of War," p. 5.

78. Ibid p. 12.

79. Ibid p. 38.

80. Michael D. Ward and Kristian S. Gleditsch. "Democratizing for Peace," *American Political Science Review* 92 (March): 51–61.

81. See also, Kristian S. Gleditsch and Michael D. Ward, "War and Peace in Space and Time: The Role of Democratization," *International Studies Quarterly* 44(1) (March 2000):1–30.

82. Oneal and Russett, "The Classical Liberals Were Right."

83. Ibid., p. 287.

Chapter 6

1. Robert O. Keohane, "International Institutions: Can Interdependence Work?," *Foreign Policy* no. 110 (Spring 1998): 83.

2. Barbara Crossette, "Americans of Two Minds on Sanctions, A Poll Finds," *The New York Times* April 23, 2000, p. A10; Joseph Kahn, "Seattle Protestors are Back, With a New Target," *The New York Times* April 9, 2000, p. A4.

3. Ronald B. Mitchell, "Regime Design Matters: Intentional Oil Pollution and Treaty Compliance," *International Organization* 48(3) (Summer 1994): 431.

4. For these definitions, see Robert O. Keohane and Joseph S. Nye, "Two Cheers for Multilateralism," in *Power and Interdependence* 2nd ed. (Glenview, IL: Scott, Foresman, 1989, p. 271, and Mark W. Zacher, "International Organizations," in Joel Krieger, ed. *The Oxford Companion to the Politics of the World* (New York: Oxford University Press, 1993), p. 451. Broadly defined, international institutions also comprise international nongovernmental organizations (NGOs) and enduring, if nonformal, patterns of trans-state relationships. But

national officials are less able to directly manipulate NGOs than interstate institutions, so knowledge about NGOs would tend to be less useful to them instrumentally. We thus exclude non-state international institutions from detailed consideration in this chapter. NGOs may, however, be a key part of the context in which international policy is made, a point discussed in section III.

5. Zacher, "International Organizations," p. 451.
6. Inis L. Claude, Jr., *Swords Into Plowshares: The Problems and Progress of International Organization* 4th ed. (New York: Random House, 1971), p. 35.
7. Robert O. Keohane and Craig Murphy, "International Institutions," in Mary Hawkesworth and Maurice Kogan, eds. *Encyclopedia of Government and Politics*, II (New York: Routledge, 1992), p. 872.
8. Keohane, "International Institutions," p. 84.
9. Keohane and Murphy, "International Institutions," p. 878.
10. M. S. Anderson, *The Rise of Modern Diplomacy, 1450–1919* (London: Longman, 1993), pp. 211–221.
11. Craig N. Murphy, *International Organization and Industrial Change* (Oxford: Oxford University Press, p. 16.
12. Ian Clark, *The Hierachy of States* (Cambridge: Cambridge University Press, 1989), pp. 51–54.
13. Anderson, *The Rise of Modern Diplomacy*, pp. 233, 227.
14. Kenneth Thompson, *Political Realism and the Crisis of World Politics* (Princeton: Princeton University Press, 1960), p. 28, quoted in Clark, *The Hierarchy of States*, p. 58.
15. Barry Buzan, "Peace, Power, and Security: Contending Concepts in the Study of International Relations," *Journal of Peace Research* 21(2) (1984): 113.
16. Keohane and Murphy, "International Institutions," p. 878.
17. There was also a French Functionalist tradition, represented during the 19th century by Saint-Simon and August Comte. Because its intellectual and political roots were idiosyncratic to French conditions, it resonated less widely than the British tradition. See F. Parkinson, *The Philosophy of International Relations* (Beverly Hills, CA: Sage Publications, 1977), pp. 101–106.
18. Parkinson, *The Philosophy of International Relations*, p. 100. For an interpretation of the post-World War II economic regimes from this perspective, see John Gerard Ruggie, "International Regimes, Transactions, and Change: Embedded Liberalism in the Postwar Economic Order," *International Organization* 26(2) (Spring 1982): 379–415.
19. David Mitrany, *A Working Peace System* (Chicago: Quadrangle Books, 1966), p. 70.
20. William C. Olson and A. J. R. Groom, *International Relations Then and Now* (London: HarperCollins, 1991), p. 191.
21. Claude, *Swords Into Plowshares*, p. 382.

22. Mitrany, *A Working Peace System*, p. 63.

23. Ernst B. Haas, *Beyond the Nation-State* (Stanford: Stanford University Press, 1964), pp. 47–50.

24. Robert O. Keohane, *After Hegemony* (Princeton: Princeton University Press, 1984), pp. 85–88. In this argument, international institutions are seen as an efficient response to a form of market failure. In international politics, this type of situation is evident when policymakers avoid agreements with other states they might otherwise prefer because participation involves high uncertainties about others' future behavior. The reasoning in this argument is guardedly optimistic, even though it rejects the assumption, held by Orthodox Functionalists, that cooperation on socioeconomic issues is virtually costless and risk-free. Like other arguments within the broad Liberal tradition, it assumes that unrealized possibilities for cooperation are likely to exist. But it carries a key caveat: it applies only when actors' objectives are compatible enough for them to prefer joint action in the first place.

25. Keohane, *After Hegemony*, pp. 88–100; Keohane, "International Institutions," p. 86; Stephen D. Krasner, "Structural Causes and Regime Consequences: Regimes as Intervening Variables," *International Organization* 36(2) (Spring 1982): 191–192.

26. For an example of Liberal approach that tries to explain interests, see Andrew Moravcsik, "Taking Preferences Seriously: A Liberal Theory of International Politics," *International Organization* 51(4) (Autumn 1997): 513–553.

27. Clark, *The Hierarchy of States*, pp. 68–73; Hans J. Morgenthau, *Politics Among Nations* 5th ed. (New York: Knopf, 1978), p. 299.

28. Keohane, "International Institutions," pp. 87–88.

29. Kenneth N. Waltz, *Theory of International Politics* (New York: McGraw-Hill, 1979), p. 105. For a more extended version of this argument, see Joseph M. Grieco, "Anarchy and the Limits of Cooperation: A Critique of the Newest Liberal Institutionalism," *International Organization* 42(3) (Summer 1988): 485–507.

30. John J. Mearsheimer, "The False Promise of International Institutions," *International Security* 19(3) (Winter 1994–95): 47.

31. Stephen D. Krasner, "State Power and the Structure of International Trade," *World Politics* 28(3) (April 1976): 317–347; Robert Gilpin, *War and Change in World Politics* (Cambridge: Cambridge University Press, 1981).

32. Joseph M. Grieco, "Realism and Regionalism: American Power and German and Japanese Institutional Strategies During and After the Cold War," in Ethan B. Kapstein and Michael Mastanduno, eds. *Unipolar Politics: Realism and State Strategies After the Cold War* (New York: Columbia University Press, 1999), pp. 338–340.

33. Keohane, *After Hegemony*, chapters 3 and 9.

34. Martha Finnemore, *National Interests in International Society* (Ithaca, New York: Cornell University Press, 1996), pp. 2, 128.

35. Finnemore, *National Interests in International Society*, pp. 144–147; Alan C. Lamborn, "Theory and the Politics in World Politics," *International Studies Quarterly* 41(2) (June 1997): 193–194.

36. Friedrich Kratochwil and John Gerard Ruggie, "International Organization: A State of the Art on an Art of the State," in Frierich Kratochwil and Edward D. Mansfield, eds. *International Organization: A Reader* (New York: Harper-Collins, 1994), p. 11; Friedrich Kratochwil, "The Force of Prescriptions," *International Organization* 38(4) (Autumn 1984): 705; Nicholas Greenwood Onuf, *World of Our Making* (Columbia, SC: University of South Carolina Press, 1989), p. 145. As U.S. representatives to the UN noted in the 1970s and 1980s, a failure to respond to the prevailing rhetoric in institutional forums can, by default, legitimize it more broadly in world politics. See Keohane and Nye, "Two Cheers for Multilateralism,"p. 269.

37. Finnemore, *National Interests in International Society*, chapters 2–4.

38. An exception is Keohane and Nye, "Two Cheers for Multilateralism."

39. Kenneth W. Abbott and Duncan Snidal, "Why States Act Through Formal International Organizations," *Journal of Conflict Resolution* 42(1) (February 1998): 15.

40. Janice Gross Stein, "Detection and Defection: Security 'Regimes" and the Management of International Conflict," *International Journal* 40(4) (Autumn 1985): 615–620.

41. Peter van Ham, *Managing Non-Proliferation Regimes in the 1990s: Power, Politics, and Policies* (New York: Council on Foreign Relations Press, 1994), pp. 41–42.

42. Ibid., p. 34.

43. Ibid.. p. 35.

44. Ibid.. p. 42.

45. Keohane, *After Hegemony*, pp. 92–96

46. Ibid., pp. 103–106.

47. Keohane and Nye, "Two Cheers for Multilateralism," p. 272.

48. Oran Young, "The Effectiveness of International Institutions: Hard Cases and Critical Variables," in James N. Rosenau and Ernst-Otto Czempiel, *Governance Without Government: Order and Change in World Politics* (Cambridge: Cambridge University Press, 1992), pp. 177–178.

49. Mitchell, "Regime Design Matters," pp. 430–458.

50. Mancur Olson, *The Logic of Collective Action* (Cambridge: Harvard University Press, 1971), pp. 53–65; Robert Axelrod and Robert O. Keohane, "Achieving Cooperation Under Anarchy: Strategies and Institutions," in Kenneth A. Oye, ed. *Cooperation Under Anarchy* (Princeton: Princeton University Press, 1986), pp. 234–238.

51. The basic distinction noted here is between what Arthur Stein calls a dilemma of common aversions and a dilemma of common interests. See Arthur A. Stein, *Why Nations Cooperate* (Ithaca: Cornell University Press, 1990), pp. 32–44. See also James D. Fearon, "Bargaining, Enforcement, and International Cooperation," *International Organization* 52(2) (Spring 1998): 274–275, and Keohane and Nye, "Two Cheers for Multilateralism," pp. 273–274.

52. Fearon, "Bargaining, Enforcement, and International Cooperation," p. 279.

53. While Neoliberal Institutionalists belong in this broad group, a wide range of other scholars has contributed to this discussion. The school that has focused on these issues is sometimes referred to as the "New Institutionalism." See, for example, Douglass C. North, *Institutions, Institutional Change, and Economic Performance* (Cambridge: Cambridge University Press, 1990) and Karol Soltan, Eric M. Uslaner, and Virginia Haufler, eds. *Institutions and Social Order* (Ann Arbor: University of Michigan Press, 1998). For international relations applications, see James D. Morrow, "Modeling the Forms of International Cooperation: Distribution versus Information," *International Organization* 48(3) (Summer 1994), and Fearon, "Bargaining, Enforcement, and International Cooperation," as well as the citations therein.

54. Keohane, *After Hegemony*, pp. 89–92; Robert O. Keohane, "The Demand for International Regimes," in Robert O. Keohane, *International Institutions and State Power: Essays in International Relations Theory* (Boulder, CO: Westview Press, 1989), pp. 111–113.

55. Fearon, "Bargaining, Enforcement, and International Cooperation," p. 298.

56. Keohane and Nye, *Power and Interdependence*, pp. 64–65, 87–90.

57. Keohane, "The Demand for International Regimes," pp. 112–113; Keohane and Nye, "Two Cheers for Multilateralism," pp. 272.

58. Keohane, *After Hegemony*, p. 91.

59. In many cases, observed compliance with international accords may result from an absence of any deep commitments. See George W. Downs, David M. Rocke, and Peter N. Barsoom, "Is the Good News About Compliance Good News About Cooperation,"? *International Organization* 50(3) (Summer 1996): 382–397.

60. Keohane and Nye, "Two Cheers for Multilateralism," p. 275.

61. Joseph Kahn, "From Minks to Mules, U.S. Issues China Trade Details," *The New York Times* March 15, 2000, p. A10.

62. James K. Sebenius, "Designing Negotiations Toward a New Regime: The Case of Global Warming," *International Security* 15(4) (Spring 1991). We are not suggesting here that Sebenius is a Neoliberal, but simply that his assumptions and conclusions are consistent with that school.

63. Stephen D. Krasner, "Global Communications and National Power: Life on the Pareto Frontier," *World Politics* 43(3) (April 1991): 342–360.

64. Among others on these points, see Buzan, "Peace, Power, and Security"; Helen Milner, "The Assumption of Anarchy in International Relations: A Critique," *Review of International Studies* 17 (1991): 68–81; Robert O. Keohane, "Institutional Theory and the Realist Challenge After the Cold War," in David A. Baldwin, ed. *Neorealism and Neoliberalism: The Contemporary Debate* (New York: Columbia University Press, 1993), pp. 274–283.

65. Robert Powell, "Anarchy in International Relations Theory: The Neorealist-Neoliberal Debate," *International Organization* 48(2) (Spring 1994).

66. Lamborn, "Theory and the Politics in World Politics," pp. 191–194.

67. Keohane, "Institutional Theory and the Realist Challenge After the Cold War," p. 276.

68. George Yeo, "China in the WTO? A Leap Forward," *Washington Post* February 29, 2000, p. A 19.

69. Edward C. Luck, *Mixed Messages: American Politics and International Organization, 1919–1999* (Washington, D.C.: Brookings Institution Press, 1999), p. 45.

70. Keohane, *After Hegemony*, pp. 100–103; Robert B. McCalla, "NATO's Persistence After the Cold War," *International Organization* 50(3) (Summer 1996): 461–469.

71. G. John Ikenberry, "Institutions, Strategic Restraint, and the Persistence of American Postwar Order," *International Organization* 23(3) (Winter 1998/99).

72. Luck, *Mixed Messages*, pp. 2, 4–5; Barbara Crossette and Eric Schmitt, "U.N. Ambassadors in Helms Land: Smiles On, Gloves Off," *The New York Times* March 31, 2000, p. A8.

73. James Traub, "Holbrooke's Campaign," *The New York Times Magazine* March 26, 2000, p. 42.

74. James Traub, "Holbrooke's Campaign," p. 43.

75. For further discussion of these issues, see Charles A. Kupchan, "After Pax Americana: Benign Power, Regional Integration, and the Sources of a Stable Multipolarity," *International Security* 23(2) (Fall 1998), and Joseph Lepgold, NATO's Post-Cold War Collective Action Problem," *International Security* 23(1) (Summer 1998).

76. For this point and the next, see Steven Weber, "Institutions and Change," in Michael W. Doyle and G. John Ikenberry, eds. *New Thinking in International Relations Theory* (Boulder, CO: Westview, 1997), pp. 243–244.

77. Emanuel Adler, "Seeds of Peaceful Change: The OSCE's Security Community-Building Model," in Emanuel Adler and Michael Barnett, eds. *Security Communities* (Cambridge: Cambridge University Press, 1998), pp. 119–123.

78. Peter M. Haas, "Epistemic Communities and International Policy Coordination," in Peter M. Haas, ed. *Knowledge, Power, and International Policy Coor-*

dination (Columbia, South Carolina: University of South Carolina Press, 1997, pp. 1–7; Emanuel Adler and Peter M. Haas, "Conclusion: Epistemic Communities, World Order, and the Creation of a Reflective Research Program," in Haas, ed. *Knowledge, Power, and International Policy Coordination*, pp. 372–385. For a related though somewhat broader discussion, see Ernst B. Haas, *When Knowledge Is Power: Three Models of Change in International Organizations* (Berkeley: University of California Press, 1990), pp. 20–49.

79. See essays by Emanuel Adler, Peter M. Haas, and Ethan B. Kapstein, all in Haas, ed. *Knowledge, Power, and International Policy Coordination*.

80. Haas, *When Knowledge Is Power*, p. 12; Finnemore, *National Interests in International Society*, pp. 28–29.

81. Abbott and Snidal, "Why States Act Through Formal International Organizations," pp. 24–26.

82. Stephen Haggard, "Structuralism and Its Critics," in Emanuel Adler and Beverly Crawford, *Progress in Postwar International Relations* (New York: Columbia University Press, 1991), p. 415.

83. On this point, see Zacher, "International Organizations," p. 452.

84. Luck, *Mixed Messages*, p. 45.

85. Claude, *Swords Into Plowshares*, p. 39.

86. Keohane, *After Hegemony*, p. 89.

87. Immanuel Kant, "Second Supplement: Secret Article for Perpetual Peace," in *Perpetual Peace* (New York: The Liberal Arts Press, 1957), p. 33.

88. George W. Ball, "Introduction," in Douglas Brinkley and Clifford Hackett, eds. *Jean Monnet: The Path to European Unity* (London: Macmillan, 1991), p. xiii. Monnet said as much in his memoirs, arguing that "[I]f the victors and vanquished agreed to exercise joint sovereignty over part of their joint resources . . . a solid link would be forged between them, the way would be wide open for further collective action, and a great example would be given to the other nations of Europe." See Jean Monnet, *Memoirs* (Garden City, NY: Doubleday, 1978), p. 293.

89. See Van Ham, *Managing Non-Proliferation Regimes in the 1990s*, chapter 3, pp. 33–50; Glenn E. Schweitzer, "A Multilateral Approach to Curbing Proliferation of Weapons Know-How."

Chapter 7

1. Alexander L. George, "Some Guides to Bridging the Gap," *Mershon International Studies Review* 38, Supplement 1 (April 1994), p. 172.

2. Abraham Kaplan, *The Conduct of Inquiry* (New York: Chandler, 1964), pp. 295–296.

3.   Christopher Hill, "Academic International Relations: The Siren Song of Policy Relevance," in Christopher Hill and Pamela Beshoff, *Two Worlds of International Relations* (London: Routledge: 1994), p. 17.
4.   George, "Some Guides to Bridging the Gap," p. 172.
5.   Arthur Stinchcombe, *Constructing Social Theories* (Chicago: University of Chicago Press, 1968), pp. 44, 47.
6.   Bruce W. Jentleson, *With Friends Like These: Reagan, Bush, and Saddam* (New York: Norton, 1984).

Index